MODERN HUMANITIES RESEARCH ASSOCIATION

TUDOR & STUART TRANSLATIONS

VOLUME 5

General Editors
ANDREW HADFIELD
NEIL RHODES

HUMPHREY LLWYD

THE BREVIARY OF BRITAIN

with selections from

The History of Cambria

HUMPHREY LLWYD

THE BREVIARY OF BRITAIN

with selections from

The History of Cambria

Edited by

Philip Schwyzer

MODERN HUMANITIES RESEARCH ASSOCIATION
2011

Published by

The Modern Humanities Research Association,
1 Carlton House Terrace
London SW1Y 5AF

© The Modern Humanities Research Association, 2011

Philip Schwyzer has asserted his right under the Copyright, Designs and Patents Act 1988 to be identified as the author of this work.

Parts of this work may be reproduced as permitted under legal provisions for fair dealing (or fair use) for the purposes of research, private study, criticism, or review, or when a relevant collective licensing agreement is in place. All other reproduction requires the written permission of the copyright holder who may be contacted at rights@mhra.org.uk.

First published 2011

ISBN 978-0-947623-93-7

Copies may be ordered from www.tudor.mhra.org.uk

MHRA TUDOR AND STUART TRANSLATIONS

GENERAL EDITORS

Andrew Hadfield (University of Sussex)
Neil Rhodes (University of St Andrews)

ASSOCIATE EDITORS

Guyda Armstrong (University of Manchester)
Fred Schurink (University of Northumbria)
Louise Wilson (University of St Andrews)

ADVISORY BOARD

Warren Boutcher (Queen Mary, University of London); Colin Burrow (All Souls College, Oxford); A. E. B. Coldiron (Florida State University); José María Pérez Fernández (University of Granada); Robert S. Miola (Loyola College, Maryland); Alessandra Petrina (University of Padua); Anne Lake Prescott (Barnard College, Columbia University); Quentin Skinner (Queen Mary, London); Alan Stewart (Columbia University).

For details of published and forthcoming volumes please visit our website:

http://www.tudor.mhra.org.uk

TABLE OF CONTENTS

General Editors' Foreword viii

Preface ix

Introduction 1

THE BREVIARY OF BRITAIN 37

Glossary of Welsh words...................... 143

THE HISTORY OF CAMBRIA 145

Glossary.. 181

List of Authors...................................... 183

Bibliography... 191

Index: *The Breviary of Britain* 197

Index: *The History of Cambria*............. 207

GENERAL EDITORS' FOREWORD

The aim of the *MHRA Tudor & Stuart Translations* is to create a representative library of works translated into English during the early modern period for the use of scholars, students and the wider public. The series will include both substantial single works and selections of texts from major authors, with the emphasis being on the works that were most familiar to early modern readers. The texts themselves will be newly edited with substantial introductions, notes, and glossaries, and will be published both in print and online.

The series aims to restore to view a major part of English Renaissance literature which has become relatively inaccessible and to present these texts as literary works in their own right. For that reason it will follow the same principle of modernisation adopted by other scholarly editions of canonical literature from the period. The series will have a similar scope to that of the original *Tudor Translations* published early in the last century, and while the great majority of the works presented will be from the sixteenth century, like the original series it will not be rigidly bound by the end-date of 1603. There will, however, be a very different range of texts with new and substantial scholarly apparatus.

The *MHRA Tudor & Stuart Translations* will extend our understanding of the English Renaissance through its representation of the process of cultural transmission from the classical to the early modern world and the process of cultural exchange within the early modern world.

Andrew Hadfield
Neil Rhodes

PREFACE

I am grateful to the General Editors for giving this edition a home in *MHRA Tudor & Stuart Translations*, and to Louise Wilson for her exemplary support and guidance at every stage of the process. I owe a special debt of thanks to my colleague Edward Paleit for his good counsel on various aspects of translation. Naomi Howell has saved me from a hundred errors, and from a few moments of despair.

Thomas Twyne, in his Preface to *The Breviary of Britain*, writes fearfully of the 'reprehension I have incurred in the Englishing of names [...] some English, some Scottish, but especially Welsh or British.' I am conscious that my efforts at modernizing the multilingual text have placed me in similar danger – and I can only crave from the reader a greater patience and charity than I have sometimes felt for Twyne.

One aspect of this edition requires particular explanation. In place of a single general index, this book has two, based on the original indices (or 'tables') of *The Breviary of Britain*, and *The History of Cambria*. This format has been adopted because these indices, especially that of the *Breviary*, are documents of considerable interest and value in themselves, pursuing and in many cases clarifying the scholarly and ideological agendas of the texts. Thus, the *Breviary*'s entry for Boadicea tells the reader not only on which pages her name can be found, but also that she was 'a valiant queen'; the entry for the Greek geographer Ptolemy indicates both those pages upon which he is 'reproved' and those where he is 'excused'. It is hoped that the intrinsic interest of these indices will compensate for the occasional inconvenience of having to look up the same name in two places. Both indices are keyed to the Introduction.

The texts also have a considerable number of marginal notes. These are indicated in the footnotes to this edition by the abbreviation '**Marg.**'

INTRODUCTION

In August 1568, the Welsh scholar Humphrey Llwyd of Denbigh lay dying. Writing for the last time to his friend Abraham Ortelius in Antwerp, he reported that 'a very perilous fever [...] hath so torn this poor body of mine these ten continual days that I [have been] brought into despair of my life' (p. 50). Along with the letter Llwyd enclosed a pair of maps, one of Wales and one of England and Wales, destined for inclusion in Ortelius's atlas. Llwyd further enclosed 'certain fragments written with mine own hand which [...] (if God had spared me life) you should have received in better order, and in all respects perfect' (p. 50). These 'fragments' belonged to an unfinished topographical description of Britain, more than half of which was devoted to the history and description of Wales. The Latin text was published at Cologne in 1572, under the title *Commentarioli Britannicae descriptionis fragmentum*. Only a year later it appeared in the English translation of Thomas Twyne under the title *The Breviary of Britain*.

Parcelling out the island of Britain from his deathbed, Llwyd was perhaps conscious of how his letter to Ortelius echoed another last bequest, made some twenty-seven centuries before. Near the dawn of the eleventh century BC, Brutus, great-grandson of Aeneas and first king of the island of Britain, had made a similar division of the kingdom, in this case among his three sons. To his eldest, Locrine, he bequeathed the fertile region east of the river Severn and south of the Humber; the portion west of the Severn he gave to his second son, Camber, and the northern remnant to the youngest, Albanactus. This is the story as it appears in Geoffrey of Monmouth's *Historia regum Britanniae* (c. 1136), and from this story Humphrey Llwyd derived the vision of Britain that runs throughout his work. Just as Geoffrey's history, for all its absurdities, helped shape medieval identities in a profound way, so Llwyd's textual and cartographical labours had an impact on the development of national consciousness in more than one early modern British nation.

Humphrey Llwyd was among the most gifted and provocative scholars of his generation. Born in Denbigh in 1527, he was educated at Brasenose College, Oxford, and entered the service of Henry FitzAlan, the nineteenth Earl of Arundel. Under Arundel's patronage he served as Member of Parliament for East Grinstead,

Sussex, in 1559. By 1563 he seems to have returned to his native Denbigh, and as MP for Denbigh was instrumental in the passage of legislation for the translation of the Bible and Book of Common Prayer into the Welsh language. William Salesbury, who took on the task of translation, hailed Llwyd in a letter to Matthew Parker as 'the most famous *antiquarius* of all our country. [...] This gentleman after John Leland and John Bale, of all that I know in this isle, is most universally seen in histories and most singularly skilled in rare subtleties'.[1] Llwyd was also the subject of eulogies from Gruffudd Hiraethog of Llangollen, the leading Welsh poet of his generation, who praised him as a pearl in the House of Parliament ('Perl mewn Ty Parlment yw hwn').[2] His growing prominence in Welsh scholarly and literary circles did not weaken his adherence to Arundel. *The Breviary of Britain* refers to a sojourn in Shropshire, looking after the Earl's estates, which led to his discovery of the Iron Age hill-fort of Caer Caradoc (p. 82). In 1566-67 he joined Arundel on a tour of Italy. It was on his way home from this journey that, passing through Antwerp, he was introduced (by Richard Gough of Denbigh) to the pre-eminent cartographer Abraham Ortelius. The encounter with Ortelius seems to have brought a new focus to his already advanced studies in British and Welsh history, topography, and place names.

Although Llwyd survived scarcely more than a year following his return to Britain, he was able to provide Ortelius with a wealth of material. A polished disquisition on the antiquities of the island of Anglesey, *De Mona druidum insula [...] epistola*, saw print in Ortelius's great atlas, *Theatrum orbis terrarum* (1570). The maps of Wales and of England with Wales (Figure 1) which he enclosed with his final letter would appear in an *Additamentum* or supplement to the atlas published in 1573. The same year saw the republication of the short treatise on Anglesey in one volume with the late Welsh scholar Sir John Prise's *Historiae Brytannicae defensio* (1573) and, crucially, the appearance of Twyne's translation of the *Fragmentum*, *The Breviary of Britain*. Five years after his death, Llwyd, who had published nothing in his lifetime,

---

[1] Quoted in G. Penrhyn Jones, 'Humphrey Lhuyd (1527-1568): A Sixteenth Century Welsh Physician', *Proceedings of the Royal Society of Medicine*, 49 (1956), 521-28 (p. 524).
[2] D. J. Bowen, 'Gruffudd Hiraethog ac Argyfwng Cerdd Dafod', *Llen Cymru*, 2 (1952-53), 147-60 (p. 154).

Figure 1. Humphrey Llwyd's map of England and Wales, 'Angliae Regni florentissimi nova descriptio,' from Abraham Ortelius, *Additamentum Theatri orbis terrarum* (Antwerp, 1573). By permission of Llyfrgell Genedlaethol Cymru / The National Library of Wales.

was recognized on both sides of the English Channel (or, as he preferred to term it, the British Ocean) as the leading authority on the antiquity and geography of Britain. Although this status would not last – his achievement would be all but eclipsed in 1586, with the appearance of the first edition of Camden's *Britannia* – Llwyd's work left a lasting mark on the literatures of both England and Wales. It is unlikely that Camden's great work would have taken quite the same form – or even borne the same title – without the prior example and influence of the *Breviary*.

As a central figure in the Tudor discovery of Britain, and in the origins of later British imperial ideology, Humphrey Llwyd's achievement merits wider recognition today. His relative obscurity in the history of Tudor scholarship and antiquarianism owes something to the difficulty involved in pinning down his allegiances, both national and international. His birth, *c.* 1527, made him an exact contemporary of men like Ralph Holinshed and

John Stow, though the extent of his links with such London-based English chroniclers is not easy to gauge. He was an active and well-respected participant in Welsh scholarly and literary networks; yet although he made some translations into Welsh[3] and worked for the translation of the Bible into his native tongue, he wrote more often in Latin or in English, addressing himself to a wider British and international audience. It is perhaps fair to say that he was more often in the position of speaking for the people of Wales than to them. Llwyd described himself as a 'Cambro-Briton', an intriguing phrase apparently of his own coining, which at once preserves the familiar identification of the Welsh as Britons, whilst implicitly expanding the category of Britishness to include other inhabitants of the island (Anglo-Britons and Scoto-Britons). At once a Welsh patriot, a British nationalist, and a cosmopolitan participant in international humanist networks, he refused to draw distinctions between any of these roles. Wales was for him not a certain corner of Britain but its origin and essence. Britain, in turn, was part of the larger Europe shaped and described by the ancients.

Significantly, Llwyd traced the origins of his investigations into British history and topography to his patriotic desire to confute an Italian and a Scot:

> When I chanced of late years to come to the sight of Polydorus Vergilius the Italian and Hector Boethius the Scot, their British histories – whereof the first mainfully sought not only to obscure the glory of the British name, but also to defame the Britons themselves with slanderous lies; the other, while he goeth about to raise his Scots out of darkness and obscurity, whatever he findeth that the Romans or Britons have done worthy commendation in this island, all that he attributeth unto his Scots, like a foolish writer. (p. 56)

Polydore Vergil (*c*. 1470-1555) was the author of the *Anglica Historia* (1534), a work which had provoked outrage among a certain class of British patriots for its pronounced scepticism as to the existence of both Brutus and King Arthur, and the aspersions it appeared to cast upon the valour of the ancient Britons. Polydore

---

[3] Llwyd apparently translated works on genealogy and heraldry into Welsh for Gruffudd Hiraethog and his circle.

derided Geoffrey of Monmouth as an impudent liar, quoting with approval the early medieval Welsh monk Gildas's denunciation of the Britons as 'neither [...] stout in battle, nor faithful in peace'.[4] By the time Llwyd wrote, the *Anglica Historia* had already been subjected to a string of patriotic counter-attacks from English and Welsh writers including John Leland, Arthur Kelton, and Sir John Prise. Llwyd's second adversary, Hector Boece (1465-1536), the Principal of King's College, Aberdeen, was the author of the *Scotorum Historia* (1527), a work which outlined a legendary history of ancient Scotland no less glorious than – and quite incompatible with – Geoffrey's history of ancient Britain. Particularly galling for Llwyd was Boece's appropriation for the Scottish nation of certain ancient British heroes, such as Caratacus, who had so ably resisted the Roman onslaught.

In the *Breviary*, Llwyd refers to a work he has in preparation defending Brutus and the Galfridian tradition: 'I purpose to confirm (by bringing forth many weighty reasons, and authorities, which I have ready in store for a British History) both his coming and also to establish the credit of the British History' (p. 58). Yet the *Breviary* itself is only intermittently concerned with upholding the credit of Geoffrey of Monmouth. It is rather a patient if incomplete survey of the topography and antiquities of England, Scotland, and Wales (treated in that order), rooted in contemporary learning and classical erudition far more than in medieval tradition. There is much more of Tacitus than Geoffrey in these pages. Although Llwyd never misses an opportunity to correct Polydore or Boece in their errors regarding British antiquity and topography – and these passages of invective undoubtedly lend pleasure and variation to what is sometimes dry material – his real difference is not over facts but over focus. Boece had written a Scottish history, Polydore an English one. From Llwyd's perspective, such histories could only be partial, chauvinistic, and myopic. In eschewing national history in order to focus on the multinational space of the island of Britain, Llwyd prefigures the scholarly trends of the late twentieth and early twenty-first centuries. His work provides the

---

[4] Polydore Vergil, *Polydore Vergil's English History: From an Early Translation*, ed. by Henry Ellis (London: Camden Society, 1846), p. 29.

earliest precedent for the 'New Subject' of 'British History' for which J. G. A. Pocock pleaded as recently as 1974.[5]

Llwyd's multinational focus does not prevent his book from betraying a strong national bias. Whereas the survey of Wales unfolds over almost seventy pages, Scotland is dispatched in fewer than thirty, the majority of which are devoted to confuting Boece's claim that the Scots and Picts had occupied the land before the coming of the Romans. Although this drastic imbalance might have been diminished in the finished version of the *Fragmentum*, there is no doubting Llwyd's Welsh patriotism or his specific contempt for Scottish antiquity. Yet it would be a mistake to see him solely as a Welsh or Cambro-British chauvinist. For all its biases, the *Breviary* conveys a far from simplistic understanding of archipelagic relations. This is apparent in Llwyd's (correct) demonstration that the Siluri mentioned by Roman writers dwelt in South Wales, not in Scotland as both Polydore and Boece had claimed on the basis of a reference in Pliny:

> although that Plinius writeth that out of the region of the Siluri over into Ireland was but a very short cut, we must thus take it, that at his time Britain was not sufficiently known, nor the people of Albania long after that subdued. Whereby when certain of the Romans (as Englishmen use nowadays) had passed over into Ireland out of South Wales, others (which never saw Britain) supposed it to be a very short cut. (p. 128)

This subtle passage maps out a range of archipelagic vectors from a privileged Welsh vantage point. There is an intriguing implicit link between the English and the Romans, conquering peoples who use the ports of Pembrokeshire in South Wales as points of departure for Ireland because they have limited knowledge of or access to the whole island of Britain. The remoteness of Scotland is underscored, both in its having been unknown to the Romans, and more so in the apparent inability of Scottish writers to imagine what Britain might look like from an angle other than their own. England, Scotland, and Ireland appear here as three sides of a British triangle which has Wales at its

---

[5] J. G. A. Pocock, 'British History: A Plea for a New Subject', *Journal of Modern History*, 47 (1975), 601–24.

centre, permitting the Welsh an unparalleled panoptic perspective on the whole archipelago.

Llwyd's version of the story of Macbeth, which involves the origins of the Stuarts, likewise marries an overt Welsh patriotism to a sense of the dynastic and political interrelation of several nations. The Scottish account held that Fleance, son of Banquo, 'after that King Macabaeus had slain his father, by flight escaped into Wales' (p. 83); there he impregnated the daughter of King Trahernus with a son, Walter, who would return to Scotland as founder of the Stuart line. Llwyd suggests that this Walter was in fact a Welsh prince who fled to Scotland to escape a murderous Welsh tyrant. Hence the ruling Scottish dynasty is entirely Welsh in origin:

> And this can be no great fraud or disgracing to the name of the Stuarts, that they are descended from the blood of the most noble and antique British kings, from which also most honourable family the same Owen Tudor, grandfather to King Henry the Seventh of that name, king of England, lineally descended by the father's side [...] (p. 83)

Alongside the Welsh chauvinism, the passage conveys a rare grasp of the interconnectedness of British nations and national histories. The histories of England, Scotland, and Ireland cannot be understood without reference to Wales, nor, indeed, without reference to each of the others.

In the later Middle Ages and into the early sixteenth century, it was common for chroniclers to state that with the coming of the Saxons, the name of the island as a whole had changed from Britain to England. No less than 'Albion', the word 'Britain' conjured a mixture of quaint historical associations; it denoted a place and a way of being that belonged firmly to the past. The 1540s had seen a short-lived movement to resurrect a contemporary British identity, with John Leland employing the term as a name for Henry VIII's empire, and English propagandists wooing the Scots with the promise of unity and equality under the common name of Britons. Yet no writer of the sixteenth century is more responsible than Llwyd for the revival of 'Britain' as the natural and inevitable term for the island in the present day. We can detect Llwyd's influence in Ortelius's map of the Atlantic Archipelago, labeled 'Angliae, Scotiae et Hiberniae, sive Britannicar insularum descriptio'. This is among the first early modern references to the 'British Isles', a term used anciently by Pliny but rarely in the medieval period or earlier in the sixteenth century. The phrase 'British Isles' is also found in John Dee's *General and Rare Memorials* (1577), as is 'British Empire' – a phrase which Dee had almost certainly first encountered in the pages of *The Breviary of Britain*.[6] Through Dee and Ortelius, and subsequently through the poetry of Edmund Spenser and Michael Drayton, Llwyd's vision of an actually existing Britain was disseminated to English and international audiences, contributing to the development of British imperial ideology.

Early Reception and Translation

Admiration for Llwyd's work on the continent was not unmixed, in spite of Ortelius's loyal support. On 28 January 1574, the French diplomat and humanist scholar Hubert Languet wrote to his protégé, the young Philip Sidney, with a blunt assessment of the *Fragmentum*:[7]

> As my ill luck would have it, I chanced the other day upon two most charming writers, one of whom describes France, the other, England. The former is Robert Coenalis, Bishop of Avranches, a very silly and ignorant person. The other would think himself greatly affronted if I called him English, since he repeatedly proclaims himself a Cambrian, not an Englishman. His name is Humphrey Lhuid, and if he is not learned, he is a man of extensive reading, but now and then forms his judgements in such a way that he seems totally destitute of common sense. He scourges the unfortunate Hector Boetius and Polydore Virgil so cruelly that even if they have grievously erred, the punishment seems greater than the fault. It is well for you that your ancestors drew their blood from France: for he

---

[6] John Dee, *General and Rare Memorials pertayning to the perfect arte of navigation* (London: John Day, 1577); for 'British Isles,' see p. 65; for 'British Empire,' p. 3 and passim. See Bruce Ward Henry, 'John Dee, Humphrey Llwyd, and the Name "British Empire"', *Huntington Library Quarterly*, 35 (1971-72), pp. 189-90.

[7] Languet's letter and Sidney's reply are quoted from Steuart A. Pears, *The Correspondence of Sir Philip Sidney and Hubert Languet* (London: Pickering, 1845), pp. 31-36.

says the Saxons, from whom the English are descended, were nothing but pirates and robbers.

You know that the German writers have plundered us poor Gauls of the empire which they declare we never possessed. They say that the expedition of Godfrey of Bouillon to Jerusalem was theirs: and that the Greek and Latin writers, early and late, are talking nonsense when they say that the Gauls made so many irruptions into Italy, burned Rome, penetrated into Greece and even into Asia, since these all were undoubtedly Germans. But the good Welshman is so far from being touched with these our misfortunes, that he adds insult to them; some of the Germans had left us the incendiary Brennus, in consideration of his sacrilege and horrible death; but he takes him away from us and makes him a Welshman.

And now hear the man's wretched fate, or rather the vengeance of the Gods; for I conclude that Vulcan, grateful for his wife's detection, desired to make some return to Apollo, who was still angry with Brennus and all his admirers for the sacrilege perpetrated at Delphi. I had gone on half asleep reading my good Welshman till very late at night; and somehow or other it fell out that the flame of my lamp caught the book, and before I could put the fire out, it was well-nigh burnt up, for it was not bound. I was distressed at first, but when I recovered myself I began to laugh, and reflected that it was a good thing for me, as it deprived me of the occasion of wasting my time on such follies. I was on the point of sending you the scorched remains of my poor Cambrian, that you might desire your Griffin, his countryman, to perform his obsequies, while you offered a laugh to appease the ghost. But I beseech you tell Griffin to write him an epitaph in Welsh and send it to me.

Fixing on the story of Brennus, Languet identifies what is perhaps the weakest link in Llwyd's work. It was Geoffrey of Monmouth who first identified the Celtic chieftain Brennus, whose sack of Delphi in 279 BC was supposed to have provoked a devastating earthquake, as a Briton – and, moreover, as the same person who had led the Gauls in their sack of Rome more than a century earlier. Both chronologically and ethnographically, the claim was ludicrous, as Polydore Vergil had duly observed. Yet Brennus the Briton was a keystone of at least one version of national identity in the Tudor century, as had become clear in the

1530s in the negotiations over Henry VIII's divorce from Catherine of Aragon. As the Duke of Norfolk had boasted to the ambassador of the Holy Roman Empire, King Henry 'had a right of empire in his kingdom, and recognized no superior. There had been an Englishman who had conquered Rome, to wit Brennus'.[8] In seeking to demonstrate 'that Brennus was a perfect Briton', Llwyd was bolstering a central plank of English as well as Welsh identity.

Reaching Sidney in Padua, Languet's letter put the young Englishman in a distinctly awkward position. Sidney recognized that Languet was not simply sharing a joke, but challenging him to disassociate himself from this sort of outmoded jingoistic absurdity. On an intellectual level, Sidney quite probably shared the French scholar's convictions as to the absurdity of the Brennus tradition. Yet in spite of this, and much as he wished to retain Languet's respect and admiration, he found himself unable to participate in an unequivocal rejection of Llwyd and Brennus, as his anxiously playful reply of 11 February makes clear:

> Verily our poor Cambro-Briton, who has drawn on himself the wrath of Apollo and Vulcan for the fault of Brennus, has met with handsome treatment at your hands; and yet I think I observe a slight failing of your usual benevolence. For, as if you thought his crime not fully atoned for in the fire, you proceed to rob him of that which he is proud to claim as his own by right of inheritance. As to his assertion that the Saxons were pirates and thieves, see you to that: I am strong in the consciousness of my French blood, and grant it with all my heart. My regard for you, however, urges me to bid you reflect, and it is a serious matter, that our unknown saint, whoever he may be, who is of the same country and quality, may be ill pleased that you should raise such a laugh at his cousin after the flesh: and so perchance in his anger may wield against you his hieroglyphical monad, like Jove's lightning.[9] Such is the wrath of heavenly spirits.
>
> Griffin had a good deal to say in memory of Master Lhuid, and made him a sort of funeral oration, while I appeased his

---

[8] Quoted in Richard Koebner, '"The Imperial Crown of this Realm': Henry VIII, Constantine the Great, and Polydore Vergil', *Bulletin of the Institute of Historical Research*, 26 (1953), 29-52 (p. 40).

[9] The reference is to John Dee's *Monas Hieroglyphica* (Antwerp: William Sylvius, 1564), about which Sidney and Languet had apparently shared a joke in the past.

ghost with a hearty laugh. Among other things, in order to efface the brand of folly which you had stamped on the worthy Lhuid, he says that as far as regards Brennus he is quite right, and proves it from the name, for in their language, the ancient Briton, Brennus means king, and was as much in vogue with them as Pharaoh or Ptolemy with the Egyptians, Arsaces among the kings of Parthia, and Hubert among hunters. And from this argument, not so strong as it might be, he concludes that this most notable robber was a countryman of his own. And let me entreat you grant him so much. But enough of jesting [...]

In spite of his repeated insistence that he can hardly contain his laughter, Sidney's unease and his determination to win the point about Brennus are almost painfully apparent. As Katherine Duncan-Jones observes, 'Languet seems to have been unimaginative about how deeply even the most sophisticated Elizabethans were attached to Tudor claims for the Celtic roots of British culture'.[10] Languet in his reply was gracious enough to concede the point – also inviting Sidney to adopt any other great robbers from antiquity into his nation.

If, as the Sidney-Languet exchange suggests, the impact of the *Fragmentum* on the continent was limited at best, it swiftly won an enthusiastic audience in Britain, and in England as much as in Wales.[11] Within a year of its initial publication the book had been translated by Twyne and printed at London by Richard Johns, with commendatory verses supplied by a range of English scholars including Edward Grant, the highly regarded headmaster of Westminster School. Twyne dedicated the translation to Edward de Vere, Earl of Oxford. (In light of the subsequent rivalry between Oxford and Philip Sidney, it is tempting if probably anachronistic to regard the dedication as a rebuke to the latter, who had been less than honest or whole-hearted in his defence of Llwyd.)

Thomas Twyne was in many ways the ideal translator of Llwyd's book. He was the son of John Twyne, the Canterbury

---

[10] Katherine Duncan-Jones, *Sir Philip Sidney: Courtier Poet* (London: Hamish Hamilton, 1991), pp. 72-73.
[11] Enthusiasm for Llwyd's endeavours was less pronounced in Scotland, to say the least, given Llwyd's implicit advocacy for a united Britain ruled from the south. George Buchanan derided the 'hodge-podge trash of Llwyd, raked by him out of the dunghill'; see *Buchanan's History of Scotland* (London: J. Bettenham, 1733), p. 6.

schoolmaster and antiquary (d. 1581); in 1590, Thomas oversaw the publication of his father's *De rebus Albionicis, Britannicis, atque Anglis Commentariorum libri duo*, a treatise on ancient Britain composed before 1550. Twyne's other works in the field of translation show an interest in related themes; in 1573, he completed and published the translation of the *Aeneid* begun in the 1550s by the Welsh MP Thomas Phaer. He was also an admirer of John Dee, sharing with him an interest in astrology as well as in Welsh and British affairs.

For all this, his translation is at points unexpectedly clumsy. His difficulties in dealing with Llwyd's Welsh are not surprising (the challenges involved in modernizing the Welsh of the *Breviary* will be discussed later in this introduction). Yet even his handling of Latin is not always assured. Certain passages, such as the final pages of the description of England, are particularly crowded with minor errors, suggesting he was working at speed. Twyne's rendering of passages from late antique panegyrists such as Claudian and Ammianus Marcellinus can verge on incoherence. He habitually translates the common word *vallum* as 'valley', where the meaning is rather 'rampart' or 'wall'. Misconstruing Llwyd's reference to a Greek author 'maioris nominis' (of greater name), he creates a new classical authority named Maior, and then inserts him into the list of authors cited. Sadly, among the most garbled passages in the book is that describing how King Duncan's son Fleance, fleeing the tyranny of Macbeth, came to North Wales and impregnated the daughter of a Welsh prince, thus fathering the Stuart dynasty.

Where Twyne's prose springs suddenly to life is in the denunciation of knavish and foolish authors, Polydore and Boece of course being chief among them. Here he has no difficulty in grasping what is at stake or conveying the urgency and sting of the invective:

> [O]ut of this place of Dion it is gathered how much a man without shame that Polydorus Vergilius is, who doubteth not to affirm that Claudius Caesar vanquished the Britons without any battle [...] But an infamous baggage groom, full fraught with envy and hatred, what dareth he not do or say? I omit his schoolmaster Boethius who, besides these lies, speaketh of a mighty war which Claudius made upon the people of the

Orcades, affirming the same to be true, too too impudently. (p. 71)

Elsewhere we find Polydorus denounced for his 'gnarring and doggish mouth' (p. 138), and Boethius given the lie: 'O impudent face, whereabout did Tacitus speak thus of the Brigantes?' (p. 78).

Such passages made a strong impression on early readers of the *Breviary*, if we may judge by the commendatory verses, which repeatedly refer to the author's confutation of the meddlers and sceptics. It is reasonable to suppose that English readers would have seized upon these moments of invective, not only for their liveliness and readability, but because they permitted a sense of common grievance with Llwyd the Cambro-Briton, and common cause in standing against foreign (Italian and Scottish) interpreters.

The charged nature of the national questions raised by Llwyd's project is indicated in Twyne's opening epistle to the reader. Twyne avers that he has produced his translation: 'for the English reader's sake, which understandeth not the Latin tongue. To whom I thought it as much appertaining to know the state and description of his own country as to the learned, be he Englishman or stranger' (p. 43). Here the English reader might reasonably retort, in a paraphrase of Shakespeare's MacMorris, 'what is my "own country"?'. The awkward national question is raised again, albeit with great delicacy, in the dedication to the Earl of Oxford, where Twyne expresses the hope that:

> in consideration that being as yet but in your flower and tender age, and generally hoped and accounted of in time to become the chiefest stay of this your commonwealth and country, you would receive into your self-tuition the written name and description of that Britain which, as it is in part your native soil, so your duty biddeth you to defend and maintain it. (p. 40)

The slightly tortured phrasing leaves it unclear whether De Vere is native to only part of British soil (i.e. England), or whether Britain is only part of the soil to which De Vere is native (in that part of his ancestry, like Sidney's, is French).

Other contributors to the front matter of the *Breviary* were less reticent than Twyne in laying claim to a British identity. Verses by 'A Friend' convey a clear understanding of Britain both as a term for the island as a whole ('The British soil, with all therein that lies,

/ The surging seas which compass it about'), and as a nation which can serve as the object of loyalty and patriotism:

> Thy country, Llwyd, is bounden much to thee,
> Which mak'st it unto us not only known,
> But unto such as in far countries be,
> Whereby thy fame the greater way is flown,
> And eke thy countries praise the more is grown.
> So by one deed two noble things are chanced:
> Britain, and Llwyd, to heaven are advanced. (pp. 44-45)

Conversely, Edward Grant, a confirmed British nationalist who also contributed verses to Prise's *Historia Brytannicae Defensio* (1573), stops short of identifying 'Britain' with a united island. His verses prefacing the Breviary are vehemently anti-Scottish, whilst coining the word 'Britanists' to encompass, apparently, British patriots amongst both the English and the Welsh (both of whom are identified in the poem with 'Brute his brood').

At least some early readers of the *Breviary* shared Twyne and Grant's conviction that the contents of the book concerned them as lovers of their country. Receiving a copy of the translation from Hugh Broughton, Gabriel Harvey inscribed upon the title-page 'Tractatus, cuique Anglo necessarius; non ignoranti, rudique suae patriae' (A treatise necessary for every Englishman who would not be uncultivated and ignorant of his country).[12] Following the Epistle to the Reader, Harvey notes 'Nihil turpius quam domi esse peregrinum: nihil magis pudendum, quam ignarum esse suae Patriae' (Nothing fouler than to be an exile from one's home; no greater shame than to be ignorant of one's country). At the conclusion of the book there is a note in English: 'Mr Floyd, a rare antiquary, and this tract replenished with many notable antiquities; some memorials of singular use, as well in action as in discourse.' Harvey avoids commenting directly on the quality of Twyne's translations, which left some learned readers less than satisfied. The reader of the copy now known as Oxford Douce L. 533 appears to have had the *Fragmentum* open alongside the *Breviary*, crossing out some of Twyne's less felicitous phrases (including the

---

[12] G. C. Moore, *Gabriel Harvey's Marginalia* (Stratford-upon-Avon: Shakespeare Head Press, 1913), p. 164. Further quotations are from this edition and page.

reference to the Greek author Maior) and suggesting better alternatives in the margin.

Since 1573, *The Breviary of Britain* has been reprinted only once. In 1729, it appeared in one volume with John Lewis of Llynwene's *History of Great Britain*. Lewis (d. 1615/16) had been another ardent defender of Geoffrey of Monmouth and, in the early years of the reign of King James, an advocate of the political unification of Britain. The texts had been prepared for publication by the Welsh antiquary Hugh Thomas who, however, died nine years before they saw print. The appearance of *The Breviary* apparently sparked sufficient interest in Llwyd's work to prompt a reprinting of the original Latin text under the title of *Humfredi Llwyd, armigeri, Britannicæ descriptionis commentariolum* (1731). Neither the Latin text nor Twyne's translation has appeared in a new edition since the first half of the eighteenth century.

From *Breviary of Britain* to *History of Cambria*

Whilst Philip Sidney hedged his bets over the value of Llwyd's scholarship, his father would take a more decided view. In his long service as Lord President of the Council in the Marches of Wales (1560-86), Sir Henry Sidney developed a keen interest in Welsh history and antiquities.[13] It is at least possible that Sir Henry and Humphrey Llwyd had been personally acquainted; although the Lord President was largely absent from Wales and the Marches in the 1560s, serving simultaneously as Lord Deputy of Ireland, he returned for a brief period of residence at Ludlow in 1567-68, and may have met Llwyd in the months before his death. Whether he first encountered Llwyd in person or in the pages of the *Breviary* (or the *Fragmentum*), Sir Henry can only have been intrigued by Llwyd's views on the geographical extent of Wales, and even more so by intriguing references to another work of the same author's, certain 'histories written in the British tongue, which of late, so far as I suppose, were by me first translated into English' (p. 56).

Llwyd's major unpublished work, the *Cronica Walliae*, was a translation of the medieval Welsh chronicle *Brut y Tywysogion* (the

---

[13] On Sidney's tenure as Lord President, see Penry Williams, *The Council in the Marches of Wales under Elizabeth I* (Cardiff: University of Wales Press, 1958), esp. pp. 250-75.

Brut of the Princes), covering the history of Wales from the seventh century to the 1270s, when the last independent Welsh principality succumbed to England's Edward I. Llwyd's decision to translate this history into English reflected his belief that the history of Wales was, in a fundamental sense, the history of Britain, and hence of interest and consequence to all inhabitants of the island:

> I was the first that took the province in hand to put these things into the English tongue. For that I would not have the inhabitants of this isle ignorant of the histories and chronicles of the same, wherein I am sure to offend many because I have opened their ignorance and blindness thereby, and to please all good men and honest natures that be desirous to know and understand all such things as passed betwixt the inhabitants of this land from the first inhabiting thereof to this day.[14]

Llwyd's book may well have opened Henry Sidney's eyes to his ignorance and blindness, but he determined to prove his own good and honest nature by ensuring its dissemination to a wider public.

By the early 1580s, Henry Sidney had succeeded in tracing not only a copy of the *Cronica Walliae*, but a body of related texts dealing with the history of medieval Wales, creating something of a national archive at Ludlow. The Lord President was then in a position to make arrangements for the text's completion and publication. He entrusted the task to his chaplain at Ludlow, David Powel, a distinguished clergyman and Doctor of Theology hailing from Denbighshire. In *The History of Cambria,* published in 1584, Powel reports that Sidney had Llwyd's text 'lying by him a great while, and being desirous to have the same set out in print, sent for me in September last, requesting me to peruse and correct it in such sort as it might be committed to the press' (p. 148).

Given the significant differences between the *Cronica* and the *History* in terms of content, scope, and sources employed, it must be considered doubtful whether Powel would have been able to achieve revisions of this nature and bring the work to print in a matter of months. It may be that he was attempting to disguise the degree of his own involvement in the final text by suggesting that

---

[14] Humphrey Llwyd, *Cronica Walliae*, ed. by Ieuan M. Williams (Cardiff: University of Wales Press, 2002), p. 82.

he had only been allowed time for relatively minor alterations. By his own report, the manuscript with which Sidney provided him was unpolished, 'having yet many imperfections, not only in the phrase, but also in the matter and substance of the history'. This manuscript is not known to survive. Late in the process of revision, however, Powel 'received another larger copy of the same translation, being better corrected, at the hands of Robert Glover Somerset Herald'. This second copy has been identified as Bodleian Library, Ashmole MS 847. It is a copy made by Glover of Cotton Caligula MS Avi, a manuscript belonging to John Dee, whose interest in Llwyd's work has been noted above; Glover's transcription includes Dee's quite extensive notes and insertions.

The version of *Brut y Tywysogion* from which Llwyd made his translation presents something of a puzzle. Llwyd never specifies the title of 'the Welsh book' or 'British book' he translates, and likewise refers to the author only as 'the Welsh chronicler' or 'my Welsh author'. If Llwyd was indeed working, as he claimed, from a single source, then it can only have been a version of the *Brut* that has not survived, since a number of key passages find no parallel in the extant texts. It seems probable, however, that his translation incorporates material from a range of sources, and perhaps also from oral tradition. Powel's revision brought Llwyd's *Cronica* more closely into accord with the *Brut*, of which he possessed or had access to 'two ancient copies' (p. 150). At the same time, Powel also appended much material of his own, marking these insertions with an initial asterisk and a smaller typeface. For his additions to Llwyd's text, Powel drew on a wide range of medieval and early modern English and Welsh authors, of whom almost thirty are named in the preface.

Powel dedicated *The History of Cambria* to Sir Philip Sidney, whilst filling that dedication with praise for his father, the Lord President:

> Your father, with his great expenses and labour, having procured and gotten to his hands the histories of Wales and Ireland (which countries for many years with great love and commendation he governed) committed unto me this of Wales to be set forth in print, with direction to proceed therein, and necessary books for the doing thereof [...] I have done mine endeavour, and now do present the same unto your worship, as

by good reason due to the son and heir of him that was the procurer and bringer of it to light [...]¹⁵

Both in the dedication to Sir Philip and in the main body of the text, Powel stresses the disinterestedness of Sir Henry's care for Wales and Ireland, as witnessed above all in his keenness to acquire manuscripts, rather than estates. His 'disposition is rather to seek after the antiquities and the weal public of those countries which he governeth, than to obtain lands and revenues within the same, for I know not one foot of land that he hath either in Wales or Ireland' (p. 148). That Sir Henry's interest in Celtic antiquities is a mark of disinterested benevolence is, for Powel, self-evident. It does not seem to cross the translator's mind that the publication of a text such as *The History of Cambria* might be connected with the more pragmatic agendas of English rule in Wales and the Marches.

Although Powel does not specify to what extent the Lord President's 'direction to proceed' involved direct instructions regarding content, the differences between Llwyd's *Cronica* and Powel's *History* offer some indication of Sidney's motives and priorities in pursuing publication of the latter text. Both translations, to be sure, acknowledge the same general intention of making the history of medieval Wales available to an English audience. But whereas Llwyd depicts the aim of his work as the instruction of an ignorant English audience in the history of the British nation, Powel, writing for a powerful English patron, is a good deal more diplomatic. The English, he suggests, have been misled by biased medieval chroniclers (always an easy target in the post-Reformation era):

> such writers as in their books do enforce everything that is done by the Welshmen to their discredit, leaving out all the causes and circumstances of the same; which do most commonly not only elevate or dissemble all the injuries and wrongs offered and done to the Welshmen, but also conceal or deface all the acts worthy of commendation achieved by them. Search the common chronicles touching the Welshmen, and commonly thou shalt find that the King sendeth some nobleman or other with an army to Wales, to withstand the rebellious attempts, the

---

¹⁵ David Powel, *Historie of Cambria* (London: Henry Denham and Ralph Newbury, 1584), sig. ¶3ᵛ (passage not included in this edition).

proud stomachs, the presumptuous pride, stir, trouble and rebellion of the fierce, unquiet, craking, fickle and inconstant Welshmen, and no open fact laid down to charge them withal, why war should be levied against them, nor yet they swerving abroad out of their own country to trouble other men. (pp. 148-49)

The professed aim of the *History* is thus to teach the English greater respect for the Welsh, and specifically to demonstrate that, where they are well-governed, the Welsh are a peaceable and law-abiding people. This is both less and more than Llwyd's aim, which was to teach the English something about themselves.

In a passage of notable political subtlety and tact, Powel manages to suggest that the union of Wales with England has been a blessing for Wales in that it has delivered Wales not only from internal divisions, but also from the arbitrary exercise of English power, by placing the whole country under the jurisdiction of the Council in the Marches:

> there was never anything so beneficial to the common people of Wales as the uniting of that country to the crown and kingdom of England, whereby not only the malady and hurt of the dissension that often happened between the princes of the country, while they ruled, is now taken away, but also an uniformity of government established, whereby all controversies are examined, heard, and decided within the country. So that now the country of Wales (I dare boldly affirm it) is in as good order for quietness and obedience as any country in Europe. For if the rulers and teachers be good and do their duties, the people are willing to learn, ready to obey, and loath to offend or displease. (p. 152)

It can be no accident that Powel's comments on the governability of Wales in a comparative European context very precisely echo the Lord President's own remarks on the subject in a letter written to Francis Walsingham on St David's Day in the previous year: 'A happy place of government it is, for a better people to govern or better subjects to their sovereign, Europe holdeth not.'[16]

---

[16] PRO SP12, 159/1, Letter from Sidney to Walsingham, 1 March 1583, quoted in Williams, *Council in the Marches*, pp. 259-60.

The joint insistence of Sidney and Powel that the Welsh responded well to good government involved something more than a merely rhetorical or diplomatic compliment to the governed. Rather, it reflects on Sidney's increasingly embattled position on the Council in the latter years of his presidency. Partly due to his frequent absences from the territory, Sidney was fond of insisting that Wales was easy to govern if governed easily. Not all members of the Council agreed. Dr David Lewis, associated with a faction opposed to Sidney's policy of relative lenience, lamented the consequences of the Lord President's overgentleness: 'My country is so far out of order at this time as doth require severe remedy, and in every commonwealth severity used with indifferency of justice to all men is more commended than lenity.'[17]

It is tempting to perceive here a variation on the plot of Shakespeare's *Measure for Measure*, with Sidney intentionally leaving a body of Angelo-like figures in charge of enforcing discipline in Wales during his own absence in Ireland, so as to avoid personal association with draconian measures. Yet it is clear that, by the end of the 1570s, Sidney's dominance over the increasingly factionalized council had been much eroded. The publication of *The History of Cambria* gave the Lord President a means of countering his critics by demonstrating the historical efficacy of lenience, and, more to the point, the disastrous consequences of punitive and inconsistent rule.

The History of Cambria was no less serviceable on a second front. In addition to countering his rivals on the Council, Sidney was required to cope throughout his term of office with the vociferous demands of English cities and counties that they should be exempted altogether from the Council's jurisdiction. He can only have been painfully aware that, under his Lord Presidency, the jurisdiction of the Council in the Marches had notably diminished. The city of Bristol had won exemption from its authority in 1562, shortly after Sidney's appointment, and the county of Cheshire had followed in 1569. Worcestershire, too, had sought exemption in 1574, but without success. It is thus apparent that at the very time that Henry Sidney was seeking out old Welsh histories, he was also seeking for a means of demonstrating the integral and historically justified nature of the Council's jurisdiction. He found the answers

---

[17] PRO SP12, 107/4, Letter from Lewis to Walsingham, 3 January 1576, quoted in Williams, *Council in the Marches*, p. 259.

he needed in Llwyd's *Breviary* and in the 'Description of Wales' prefixed to the *Cronica Walliae*. In both these works – as in the maps he drafted for Ortelius's Atlas – Llwyd stuck adamantly to his position that the true boundary of Wales was the river Severn.

Llwyd's map of Wales depicted the Principality divided into its three traditional regions, Gwynedd, Deheubarth, and Powys, with the eastern bounds of Powys extending to the Severn (Figure 2). Wales is made to extend as far as Worcester and Tewkesbury, at some points more than doubling in width.

Figure 2. Humphrey Llwyd, 'Cambriae Typus', from Ortelius, *Additamentum Theatri orbis terrarum* (Antwerp, 1573). By permission of Llyfrgell Genedlaethol Cymru / The National Library of Wales.

The principles behind this apparently audacious cartographical land-grab are set forth very clearly in *The Breviary of Britain*:

> let us now proceed to Wales, the third part of Britain. The same is divided from Lloegr, that is England, by the rivers Severn and Dee, and on every other side is environed by the Vergivian, or Irish Ocean. And it was called Cambria, as our chronicles do

report, of Camber, the third son of Brutus, like as Lloegr of Locrinus, and Albania of Albanactus, his other sons also. This same only, with Cornwall, a most ancient country of Britons, enjoyeth as yet the old inhabitants. The Welshmen use the British tongue, and are the very true Britons by birth. And although some do write that Wales doth not stretch forth on this side the River Vaga, or Wye, this can be no fraud to us. For we have taken in hand to describe Cambria and not Wallia, 'Wales' as it is now called by a new name, and unacquainted to the Welshmen. In North Wales, the Welshmen keep their old bounds. But in South Wales the Englishmen are come over Severn, and have possessed all the land between it and Wye. So that all Herefordshire, and the Forest of Dean, and Gloucestershire, and a great part of Worcestershire, and Shropshire on this side Severn are inhabited by Englishmen at this day. (p. 98)

Herefordshire, with the larger parts of Worcestershire, Shropshire, and Gloucestershire, lay within the limits of Llwyd's Cambria. The four English counties over which the Council was battling to maintain a grip were, according to this view, not English at all.

In spite of Powel's insistence that Henry Sidney's disposition was 'to seek after [...] antiquities', Sidney seems to have done little more in this regard than pursue the publication of the *History* itself. Other projects of pressing interest to Welsh humanists of the era – the codification of Welsh grammar, the translation of the Bible into Welsh – do not seem to have stirred the Lord President's interest to the same extent.[18] Yet Sidney's limited foray into the field of Welsh antiquities had long-lasting effects. It is legitimate to speculate that the *History of Cambria* helped shape the political future, providing an historical underpinning for the Council's jurisdiction in the Marches and thereby contributing to its successful preservation; although the inhabitants of the English marcher counties became increasingly vociferous in their demands

---

[18] Access to Sidney's Ludlow library probably did assist Powel when, in 1585, he came to publish Ponticus Virunnius's *Britannicae historiae libri sex* (a brief digest of Geoffrey of Monmouth's *Historia regum Britanniae*) and Gerald of Wales's *Itinerarium Cambriae* and *Cambriae descriptio*. Ever-politic, Powel printed only the first book of Gerald's *Cambriae descriptio*, not the second, which includes both advice to the English on how to complete the conquest of Wales, and advice to the Welsh on how to resist.

for release, between 1569 and 1641, when the Council itself was dissolved by Parliament, no further counties were successful in their quest for exemption from the Council's authority. The impact of the book on Welsh historical consciousness was even more far-reaching. Powel's book in original or revised form remained the standard history of medieval Wales for several centuries. William Wynne's revision and augmentation of Powel's text, printed under the title of *The History of Wales* in 1697, was reprinted in 1702, 1774, 1812, and 1832; the original text of 1584 was itself reprinted in 1811. Only by John Edward Lloyd's *A History of Wales from the Earliest Times to the Edwardian Conquest* (1911) was the authority of Llwyd and Powel definitively superseded. There is no modern edition of *The History of Cambria*, although an edition of Llwyd's *Cronica Walliae*, edited by Ieuan M. Williams, was published by University of Wales Press in 2002.

The History of Cambria is a substantial work of over 400 pages, more than three times the length of *The Breviary of Britain*. The five extracts included in this edition amount to no more than a tenth of the original. The extracts have been chosen for their intrinsic interest and historical influence, as well as with an eye to distribution throughout the period covered. The first contains the Epistle to the Reader and the second the commencement of the history, recounting the exile and abdication of Cadwaladr, the last King of the Britons, in the seventh century. The third extract tells of the discovery of the New World by Madoc, a Welsh prince of the twelfth century; Madoc's supposed voyage, for which no earlier source is known than Llwyd's *Cronica*, was swiftly seized upon by John Dee amongst others to advance English claims in the Americas, and would inspire poets from Robert Southey to Paul Muldoon. The fourth extract, dealing with events of the 1190s, highlights the theme that internecine conflict sapped the ability of the Welsh to withstand the Normans; this section concludes with a remarkable diatribe against the Roman Catholic clergy attributed to the legendary bard Taliesin. The final selection covers the reign of Llywelyn ap Gruffudd of Gwynedd, whose defeat and death in 1282 marked the effective end of Welsh independence: 'And so the King passed through all Wales, and brought all the country in subjection to the crown of England to this day' (p. 179). Although the conclusion of this selection lies near the end of the *History*, it is not in fact the conclusion of the book, for Powel appends some twenty-five pages devoted to 'The Princes of Wales of the Blood Royal of England', from Edward II to Elizabeth.

Literary Reception and Influence: Drayton and Spenser

The influence of Llwyd's scholarship and his British vision can be traced in the politics of the ensuing era, in the chronicle and antiquarian tradition, and in the literatures of England and Wales. Llwyd's work had a definite impact on the first edition of Holinshed's *Chronicles* (1577), where quite extensive use is made of the *Breviary* as well as of the treatise on Anglesey. It is possible that Holinshed also had access to *Cronica Walliae* in manuscript, a work which might well have furnished him with the basis for a history of Wales to sit alongside those of England, Scotland, and Ireland. The reuse of woodcuts from the first edition of Holinshed in *The History of Cambria* strongly suggests that Powel's book was intended to serve as a supplement to, or part of, the *Chronicles* – the missing piece of the archipelagic jigsaw. *The History of Cambria* is in turn cited frequently in the second edition of Holinshed (1587).

The *Chronicles* naturally cite Llwyd as an authority on Welsh antiquity and topography, but not only in that context. *The History of Scotland* follows him in refuting Boece's claim that the Siluri, a people mentioned by Tacitus, had been inhabitants of Scotland.[19] Appropriately enough, the *Chronicles* cite Llwyd with particular frequency on the subject of ancient relations between the different nations of Britain. Both the *History of England* and the *History of Ireland* cite him as a source for the Pictish invasions of Scotland, resisted by the British King Marius or Meurig, whom Llwyd identifies with Arviragus. William Harrison, who contributed *The Description of Britain* to Holinshed's *Chronicles*, cites Llwyd on several occasions, usually with reference to Wales but also on the antiquities of St Albans, where he refers to him blandly as 'Humphrey Llwyd our countryman'.[20] Taking it as his brief to record the essential truths of British geography rather than ever-

---

[19] Raphael Holinshed, et al., *The First and Second Volumes of Chronicles* (London: Henry Denham, 1587), vol. 5, p. 49.
[20] Holinshed, et. al., *First and Second Volumes of Chronicles*, vol. 1, p. 192.

shifting political realities, Harrison follows Llwyd in insisting that the Severn marked the boundary between England and Wales.

Probably no aspect of Llwyd's work had a more profound impact on the English imagination, and on English literature, than his arguments regarding the status of the Severn. For more than half a century following the initial publication of the *Breviary* and the map of Wales, references to the Severn as border abound in poetry and prose. Thomas Churchyard's *The Worthines of Wales* (1587) includes the entire west bank within its survey of the principality, with more attention paid to the author's native Shrewsbury than to any part of Wales as commonly defined. Christopher Ocland wrote of 'Wales on part of Albion land, which doth on Severn bound, / (Severn a mighty flood, which twixt the borders, sliding flows)'.[21] In the next century, John Stradling's adoration of Charles I emanated 'from Sabrine's farthest shore, / (The semicircling bound of that dominion, / Where hardy Britons your great name adore)', and William Slatyer in his *Palae-Albion* gave praise to 'The sandy stream that Sea-like flows, / And Wales, and England's parting shows'.[22] Such references are particularly prominent in the early years of the reign of James I, regarded by some as a second Brutus destined to repair the division of the island made by the first. Anthony Munday's civic pageant *The Triumphs of Re-United Britannia* (1605) is one of several works in which the Severn is made to celebrate its demise as a border. As late as 1634, Milton's *Masque Performed at Ludlow Castle*, an entertainment for the Lord President of the Council, gives the Severn a special and indeed salvific significance in the form of the nymph Sabrina.[23]

The significance of the Severn as border in Michael Drayton's *Poly-Olbion* (1612) demands special consideration. The front matter of the long chorographical survey of England and Wales includes a special message 'To My Friends the Cambro-Britons', in which Drayton describes himself as:

---

[21] Christopher Ocland, *The Valiant Actes and Victorious Battailes of the English Nation*, trans. by John Sharrock (London: Robert Waldegrave, 1585), n.p.

[22] John Stradling, *Divine Poemes* (London: William Stansby, 1625), sig. A3ʳ; William Slatyer, *The History of Great Britain* [*Palae-Albion*] (London: William Stansby, 1621), p. 93

[23] Philip Schwyzer, 'Purity and Danger on the West Bank of the Severn: The Cultural Geography of *A Masque Presented at Ludlow Castle, 1634*', *Representations*, 60 (1997), 22-48.

[s]triving, as my much loved (the learned) Humfrey Floyd, in his description of Cambria to Abraham Ortelius, to uphold her ancient bounds, Severn and Dee, and therefore have included the parts of those three English Shires of Gloster, Worster, and Sallop, that lie on the west of Severn, within their ancient mother Wales: In which if I have not done her right, the want is in my ability, not in my love.[24]

The Severn plays multiple roles in *Poly-Olbion*; as the border between England and Wales, she is queen of western Britain, reigning over her tributaries of both nations and resolving their factional disputes. This she does by prophesying that soon the island will be truly united, and her own role as border finished forever: 'Why strive ye then for that, in little time that shall / (As you are all made one) be one unto you all' (5.77-8). Yet later in the poem the river laments the theft of her west bank by the English, and she cheers the oppressed Cambrians by reminding them of their high and ancient lineage: 'My Wales, then hold thine own, and let the Britons stand / Upon their right, to be the noblest of the Land' (8.375-6). Such partisanship is hardly in keeping with her previous desire '[t]hat she would not be found t'incline to either side' (4.40), but is reminiscent of Llwyd's own struggles to balance his Welsh patriotism with a broader British nationalism.

Although the first instalment of Drayton's chorographical survey of Britain (or, in the final event, of England and Wales) did not appear until 1612, Drayton had been working on the poem since the mid-1590s. At the time of the project's conception, only two published works, *The Breviary of Britain* and William Camden's *Britannia*, could have served as an inspiration and model for Drayton's poetic survey. Although *Britannia* was by far the more learned and detailed study, there is some reason to suppose that the *Breviary* lies nearer the heart and origin of Drayton's vision. Much like the *Breviary*, *Poly-Olbion* devotes a disproportionate amount of space to the survey of Wales, which is the subject of a full third of the Songs in the original edition.

---

[24] Michael Drayton, *Poly-Olbion*, in *The Works of Michael Drayton*, ed. by J. W. Hebel, 4 vols (Oxford: Shakespeare Head Press, 1961), IV, p. 12. Further references to the poem, with Song and line numbers, are given after quotations in the text.

Drayton follows Llwyd (and differs markedly from Camden, as well as from his own scholarly annotator, John Selden) in upholding the Brutus tradition and related legends of ancient Britain. Finally, a striking feature of the poem that seems to point to an early encounter with the *Breviary* is the airborne progress of Drayton's Muse. The first Song describes the Muse as 'hovering while she hung / Upon the Celtic wastes', and the imagined perspective of aerial survey is sustained at least intermittently throughout the poem. The seed of this perspective may well lie in the commendatory poem of 'A Friend' prefixed to the *Breviary*, where Llwyd is imagined viewing Britain from above:

> Juno to skies plucked him to view the land,
> Else surely could he not have done so well,
> That thus so right of everything doth tell,
> As though he stood aloft and down did look,
> And what he saw wrote straight into his book. (p. 44)

Certain passages in the poem indicate that Drayton must have had the *Breviary* and *Britannia* open side by side. Hovering over the north-eastern corner of Wales in the Tenth Song, Drayton relies on Camden for the pleasing etymology of Tegeingl as 'Fair England' (as opposed to Llwyd's 'Englishmen's Tegenia'), and for the ensuing description of Winifred's famous Well (to which Llwyd devotes only two rather stand-offish sentences). Yet in the midst of this passage Drayton finds room to praise another marvellous spring:

> That naturally remote, sixe British miles from Sea,
> And rising on the Firme, yet in the naturall day
> Twice falling, twice doth fill, in most admired wise.
> When Cynthia from the East unto the South doth rise,
> That mighty Neptune flowes, then strangly ebs thy Well:
> And when againe he sinks, as strangely shee doth swell [...]
> (5.133-38)

There is no equivalent to this passage in Camden; its source lies rather in the following observation in the *Breviary*:

> In Tegenia is a well of a marvellous nature which, being six miles from the sea, in the parish of Cilcain, ebbeth and floweth

twice in one day. Yet have I marked this of late, when the moon ascendeth from the east horizon to the south (at what time all seas do flow), that then the water of this well diminisheth and ebbeth. (p. 116)

Drayton has prettified the passage with mythological names and eliminated the first-person perspective and tone of scientific observation of the *Breviary*. Yet some vestige of Llwyd's inquisitive gaze survives in the description of the spring filling and falling 'in most admired wise'.

In the Songs devoted to Wales, Drayton made close and extensive use of the *History of Cambria* as well as of the *Breviary*. In Song Nine, where proud Mount Snowdon sings some 200 lines in praise of the medieval princes of Wales, Drayton follows Powel's text very closely indeed (with, needless to say, quite heroic condensation). His way of working may be seen in his adaptation of the remarkable passage in the *History* dealing with the supposed discovery of the New World by Madoc ap Owain Gwynedd:

Madoc, another of Owain Gwynedd his sons, left the land in contention betwixt his brethren, and prepared certain ships with men and munition, and sought adventures by seas, sailing west and leaving the coast of Ireland so far north that he came to a land unknown where he saw many strange things. This land must needs be some part of that country of which the Spaniards affirm themselves to be the first finders sith Hanno's time; for by reason and order of cosmography this land to the which Madoc came must needs be some part of Nova Hispania or Florida. Whereupon it is manifest that that country was long before by Britons discovered, afore either Columbus or Americus Vespucius led any Spaniards thither. (p. 157)

Drayton's version is as follows:

As Madock his brave sonne, may come the rest among;
Who, like the God-like race from which his Grandsires sprong,
Whilst heere his Brothers tyr'd in sad domestick strife,
On their unnaturall breasts bent eithers murtherous knife;
This brave adventurous Youth, in hote pursute of fame,
With such as his great spirit did with high deeds inflame,
Put forth his well-rigg'd Fleet to seeke him forraine ground,

And sayled West so long, untill that world he found
To Christians then unknowne (save this adventrous crue)
Long ere Columbus liv'd, or it Vesputius knew;
And put the now-nam'd Welsh on India's parched face,
Unto the endlesse praise of Brutes renowned race,
Ere the Iberian Powers had toucht her long-sought Bay,
Or any eare had heard the sound of Florida.

(9.307-20)

Second only to Drayton among major English poets to profit from Llwyd and Powel's instruction was Edmund Spenser. In her study of the sources of the British chronicle material in *The Faerie Queene*, Carrie Harper identified *The Breviary of Britain* among the books Spenser used for Merlin's prophecy in Book 3, Canto 3.[25] Although it has since been argued that *The History of Cambria* could have been the sole source for the material in question, it remains plausible that Spenser knew and used the *Breviary*, to which he may have been introduced by his friend Gabriel Harvey.[26] There can in any case be no doubt of Spenser's debt to Powel in Merlin's foretelling of the trials and sufferings of the Britons from the age of Arthur to the Tudor era. Spenser was admittedly less careful (or more creative) than Drayton in his use of the *History*. Where the source states that Cadwaladr, last King of Britain, spent eight years in Rome, Spenser transfers these years to Brittany. When Merlin prophesies that 'Rhodoricke, whose surname shalbe Great. / Shall of him selfe a braue ensample shew, / That Saxon kings his friendship shall intreat', Spenser conflates Rhodri Mawr (d. 878) with Rhodri Molwynog (d. 754).[27]

The influence of Llwyd and Powel on Spenser's work almost certainly extends beyond those passages with an explicit Welsh focus. Like many of his contemporaries, Spenser looked to the history of Anglo-Welsh relations for a model of how the English

---

[25] Carrie A. Harper, *Sources of the British Chronicle History in Spenser's Faerie Queene* (Philadelphia: J. C. Winston, 1910), pp. 157-58.
[26] Rudolf B. Gottfried, 'Spenser and *The Historie of Cambria*', *Modern Language Notes*, 72 (1957), 9-13. Spenser also seems to have consulted Prise's *Historiae Brytannicae Defensio*, making acquaintance with the *Breviary* still more probable; see Philip Schwyzer, *Literature, Nationalism and Memory in Early Modern England and Wales* (Cambridge: Cambridge University Press, 2004), pp. 41-43.
[27] Edmund Spenser, *The Faerie Queene*, ed. by A. C. Hamilton, 2nd edn (London: Longman, 2006), 3.3.45.

should deal in Ireland. Christopher Highley has drawn attention to the contemporary resonances of the insistence in the *History* that too much oppression can bestialize a civil people.[28] As Powel remarks forcefully near the conclusion of the book, with reference to the Penal Laws of Henry IV, 'let any indifferent man therefore judge and consider whether this extremity of law, where justice itself is mere injury and cruelty, be not a cause and matter sufficient to withdraw any people from civility to barbarism.'[29] Whilst Spenser did not prove a consistent advocate of gentleness with the Irish, this theme in the *History* resonates with the *Faerie Queene*'s abiding fascination with degeneration and metamorphosis. More conciliatory Spenser found Llwyd's emphasis on a British imperium. As David Armitage has argued:

> Spenser adopted the conception of the British Empire found in the works of Humphrey Llwyd and John Dee, to show that the Protestant New English settlers were reviving the "British" dominion in Ireland which had originally been established by King Arthur.[30]

Through his influence on Dee and Spenser, Llwyd thus emerges as a seminal figure in the ideological origins of the *Britannicum imperium* or, in Twyne's translation, 'the British Empire' (p. 138).

---

[28] Christopher Highley, *Shakespeare, Spenser, and the Crisis in Ireland* (Cambridge: Cambridge University Press, 1997), pp. 73-74.
[29] Powel, *Historie of Cambria*, p. 388.
[30] David Armitage, *The Ideological Origins of the British Empire* (Cambridge: Cambridge University Press, 2000), p. 52.

Note on Welsh Words and Place Names

The *Commentarioli Britannicae descriptionis fragmentum* presented some unique problems to its Tudor translator, challenges which in a different way also confront the modern editor. Although written in Latin, the text is deeply and intimately bound up with the Welsh language which, as the tongue of the ancient Britons, Llwyd takes to be the root source of the majority of place names in England and Scotland as well as Wales. Throughout the text, Llwyd glosses the modern names of cities, counties, rivers and regions with what he takes to be their original Welsh versions. He is often correct in his deductions, though at times, as in his derivation of Ely from 'Ynys Helig', or the Isle of Willows (rather than the English 'Isle of Eels'), his etymological theories have found few followers.

The Welsh words and phrases encountered in the pages of the *Breviary* are typically several steps removed from the Welsh commonly spoken and written by Llwyd's contemporaries. To begin with, like some other Welsh intellectuals of his day, Llwyd took a mildly eccentric approach to Welsh orthography, preferring 'dh' and 'lh' to the more common 'dd' and 'll'. As he explains in his introductory comments on the propriety of the Welsh tongue this is the practice 'amongst the learned' (p. 49). It has not remained so. In addition to employing his distinctive spellings, Llwyd commonly Latinizes the names of Welsh places and persons. Thus, he habitually refers to North Wales as Guynedhia, rather than either the standard Welsh Gwynedd or the Latin Venedotia.

As no manuscript of Llwyd's work survives, it is impossible to say how faithfully the text printed in Cologne reproduces the Welsh of the original; it is unlikely that anyone employed in the shop of the printer Johann Birckman had expertise in Welsh. Nor, by his own admission, did Thomas Twyne. For help with the Welsh passages, Twyne drew on the assistance of a learned Welsh speaker, the civil lawyer Thomas Yale (d. 1577). Twyne hoped that he had profited from Yale's guidance so much that 'I have deserved less blame in that than in any other one part of my translation' (p. 41). Be that as it may, many of the Welsh words and place names in the *Breviary* – having migrated in and out of Latin as well as bearing the mark of Llwyd's peculiar orthography – would have proven barely recognizable to a contemporary Welsh speaker or reader. At times the text lapses into absurdity. When Llwyd quotes, as an example of the historical use of the term Prydain, the bardic phrase 'pen post Prydain' (the chief pillar of Britain), the phrase appears in the *Fragmentum* as 'payn post Prydain', and in the *Breviary* as 'paun post Prydain', which would in fact mean 'the peacock-pillar of Britain'. There are also points where Twyne's difficulties with Latin lead to redoubled difficulties with Welsh. Mistranslating Llwyd's 'Vallum Severi' as Severus's Valley rather than Severus's Wall, he is forced to assume that *gwal* in the equivalent Welsh phrase 'gwal severus' also means valley rather than wall. Twyne then inserts the word *gwal*, defined as valley, into the mini-dictionary of Welsh words that concludes the work. One can imagine the difficulties that might have been encountered by an English visitor to Wales attempting to make use of Twyne's phrasebook, in which walls become valleys, beavers become otters, and Brittany is a beach.

In this edition, the Welsh words and phrases are presented, in so far as is possible, in their modern Welsh forms. This includes the regularization of 'lh' and 'dh' as 'll' and 'dd'. Although the sometimes splendid weirdness of the *Breviary*'s Welsh is thereby sacrificed, the modernization of place names in particular has been deemed essential, allowing the reader to follow the peregrinations of the text on a modern map.

FURTHER READING

There is as yet no definitive study of Humphrey Llwyd's life and works. Beyond the entry in the *Oxford Dictionary of National Bibliography*, further information may be found in R. Geraint Gruffydd, 'Humphrey Llwyd of Denbigh: Some Documents and a Catalogue', *Transactions of the Denbighshire Historical Society*, 17 (1968), 54-107. There is also a useful biography in G. Penrhyn Jones, 'Humphrey Lhuyd (1527-1568): A Sixteenth Century Welsh Physician', *Proceedings of the Royal Society of Medicine*, 49 (1956), 521–528. (The long-held belief that Llwyd was a physician and a translator of medical treatises is now considered doubtful). Llwyd's achievements as a cartographer are explored in F. J. North, *Humphrey Lhuyd's Maps of England and of Wales* (Cardiff: National Museum of Wales, 1937); and Philip Schwyzer, 'A Map of Greater Cambria', *Literature, Mapping and the Politics of Space in Early Modern Britain*, ed. by Andrew Gordon and Bernhard Klein (Cambridge: Cambridge University Press, 2001), pp. 35-44.

Llwyd's *Cronica Walliae*, the chief source for Powel's *History of Cambria*, can be read in the modern edition of Ieuan M. Williams (Cardiff: University of Wales Press, 2002). A version of Llwyd's ultimate source, the medieval chronicle *Brut y Tywysogion,* can be read in the translation of Thomas Jones (Cardiff: University of Wales Press, 1952).

On the broader cultural context of post-Reformation Welsh scholarship, see Glanmor Williams, *Wales and the Reformation* (Cardiff: University of Wales Press, 1997); R. G. Gruffydd, 'The Renaissance and Welsh Literature', in *The Celts and the Renaissance: Tradition and Innovation*, ed. by Glanmor Williams and Robert Owen Jones (Cardiff: University of Wales Press, 1990), pp. 17-39; and Ceri Davies, *Latin Writers of the Renaissance* (Cardiff: University of Wales Press, 1981). Andrew Hadfield situates Llwyd's work within the wider context of Elizabethan historical scholarship: 'Skeptical History and the Myth of the Historical Revolution', *Renaissance and Reformation / Renaissance et Réforme*, 29 (2005), 25-44.

Studies of the literary influence of the *Breviary* and the *History* have concentrated chiefly on the works of Michael Drayton and Edmund Spenser. On the sources of the Welsh material in Drayton's *Poly-Olbion*, see John E. Curran, 'The History Never Written: Bards, Druids, and the Problem of Antiquarianism in

Poly-Olbion', *Renaissance Quarterly*, 51 (1998), 498-526; William H. Moore, 'Sources of Drayton's Conception of Poly-Olbion', *Studies in Philology*, 65 (1968), 783-803; I. Gourvitch, 'The Welsh Element in *Poly-Olbion*: Drayton's Sources', *Review of English Studies*, 4 (1928), 69-77; Robert Cawley, 'Drayton's Use of Welsh History', *Studies in Philology*, 22 (1925), 234-55. On the use of the *History of Cambria* in Merlin's prophecy in *The Faerie Queene*, see Rudolf B. Gottfried, 'Spenser and *The Historie of Cambria*', *Modern Language Notes*, 72 (1957), 9-13; and Carrie A. Harper, *Sources of the British Chronicle History in Spenser's Faerie Queene* (Philadelphia: J. C. Winston, 1910). A route between Humphrey Llwyd and John Milton is charted in Philip Schwyzer, 'Purity and Danger on the West Bank of the Severn: The Cultural Geography of *A Masque Presented at Ludlow Castle, 1634*', *Representations*, 60 (1997), 22-48. Whether or not Shakespeare was familiar with Llwyd's work remains difficult to determine, but several of the essays in *Shakespeare and Wales: From the Marches to the Assembly*, ed. by Willy Maley and Philip Schwyzer (Farnham: Ashgate, 2010) are suggestive.

The influence of Llwyd and Powel's work extended beyond the literary sphere. Llwyd's seminal role in the construction of a British imperial ideology is discussed in David Armitage, *The Ideological Origins of the British Empire* (Cambridge: Cambridge University Press, 2000). See also Bruce Ward Henry, 'John Dee, Humphrey Llwyd, and the Name "British Empire"', *Huntington Library Quarterly*, 35 (1971-72), 189-90; and Philip Schwyzer, *Literature, Nationalism and Memory in Early Modern England and Wales* (Cambridge: Cambridge University Press, 2004). The legend of Madoc, the medieval Welsh discoverer of America introduced to the world by Humphrey Llwyd, is explored in fascinating detail in Gwyn A. Williams, *Madoc: The Making of a Myth* (Oxford: Oxford University Press, 1987). On the relevance of *The History of Cambria* to contemporary debates over Anglo-Irish relations, see Christopher Highley, *Shakespeare, Spenser, and the Crisis in Ireland* (Cambridge: Cambridge University Press, 1997).

ABBREVIATIONS

L. Humphrey Llwyd, *Commentarioli Britannicae descriptionis fragmentum* (Cologne: Johann Birckman, 1572)

T. Humphrey Llwyd, *The Breviary of Britain*, trans. by Thomas Twyne (London: Richard Johns, 1573)

W. Welsh

THE BREVIARY OF BRITAIN

THE BREVIARY OF BRITAIN

As this most noble and renowned island was of ancient time divided into three kingdoms, England, Scotland, and Wales; containing a learned discourse of the variable state, and alteration thereof, under divers as well natural as foreign princes and conquerors, together with the geographical description of the same, such as neither by elder nor later writers the like hath been set forth before. Written in Latin by Humphrey Llwyd of Denbigh, a Cambro-Briton, and lately Englished by Thomas Twyne, Gentleman.

To the Right Honourable Edward De Vere,[31] Lord Bulbeck, Earl of Oxford, Lord Great Chamberlain of England, Thomas Twyne wisheth long life, perfect health, increase of honour, and endless felicity.

Nobility is a precious gift, which so glittereth in the eyes of all men that there is no one corporal thing in this world whereof we make a greater account, for so is it esteemed of all, desired of all, and reverenced of all. Virtue, sayeth Tully,[32] and before him Plato, if it might be seen with our bodily eyes, doubtless it would procure marvellous love and good liking unto itself, the show thereof would appear so fair and amiable. The uniting of which two most noble graces with all other furniture° of Nature and Fortune within your person, Right Honourable and my very good Lord, hath so bent my judgement and brought me into such liking and admiration thereof that I have rested no small time, not only not satisfied in being one of the admirators, but also desirous to be one of the participators of those Your Honour's most laudable dispositions, whereunto I do now humbly submit myself. And in token of my dutiful meaning herein, am so hardy as to present your honour with this simple travail, which I so term in respect of my pains in translating the same (howbeit I am persuaded that it cost Master Llwyd, who first and not long since wrote the same in Latin, no small labour and industry in the gathering and penning); regarding

---

[31] Edward De Vere] The 17th Earl of Oxford (1550-1604) was a noted patron and the subject of a great many dedications.
[32] Tully] Marcus Tullius Cicero

your honour to be amongst the rest a very fit patron for it, in consideration that being as yet but in your flower and tender age, and generally hoped and accounted of in time to become the chiefest stay of this your commonwealth and country, you would receive into your self-tuition the written name and description of that Britain which, as it is in part your native soil, so your duty biddeth you to defend and maintain it.[33]

Hereon, when Your Honour shall be at leisure to look, bestowing such regard as you are accustomed to do on books of geography, histories, and other good learning (wherein I am privy your honour taketh singular delight), I doubt not but you shall have cause to judge your time very well applied. And so much the rather for that, in the study of geography, it is expedient first to know exactly the situation of our own home where we abide, before that we shall be able to judge how other countries do lie unto us, which are far distant from us. Besides that it were a foul shame to be inquisitive of the state of foreign lands and to be ignorant of our own (as Your Honour, being already perfectly instructed, is not now to learn at my hand). But for my part, it shall be sufficient that Your Honour would deign to accept this small present, or rather therein my hearty good will, which, being no other wise able to gratify the same, shall never cease to pray to God that he would always direct you in the commendable race of virtue and learning which you have begun, augment your honour with many degrees, and in the end reward you with immortal felicity.

Your Honour's most humble at commandment, Thomas Twyne.

---

[33] in part your native soil] Ambiguous, probably meaning that de Vere is native to one part of Britain (England), but also perhaps glancing at de Vere's Norman French ancestry.

The Preface of the Translator's to the Reader.

When I first took in hand this book, gentle reader, and was determined to translate it into English, I considered the great judgement and learning of the author, and mine own simplicity and unskilfulness, by conference whereof I was eftsoons° driven from my determination. For I perceived how dangerous a thing it was for me who, God knoweth, am but a simple antiquary,[34] and but slenderly practised in the antiquities of this island, to give forth my absolute sentence in such matters as are in controversy, not only amongst the most approved and best learned ancient writers in this behalf, but also between such as have been very well seen therein in our time, whereof some be dead and some be yet living – which I saw that of necessity I must do. As for this one example, among many: although it be not yet fully agreed upon what town in England the ancient name of Calleva doth signify, and the place thereof be also as uncertain, as upon which side of the Thames it should lie, yet following mine author so near as I may, I am enforced to determine some way, I am sure not without misliking of many.[35]

The like reprehension I have incurred in the Englishing of names of divers° places mo,° some English, some Scottish, but especially Welsh or British. In so much that I was determined to have set them down as I had found them in Master Llwyd's Latin book, which he, for that he wrote in Latin, had so nigh as he could made them all Latin words in sound and termination.[36] But being therein much lightened, especially by the help of the right worshipful Master Doctor Yale of London,[37] I trust I have deserved less blame in that than in any other one part of my translation; howbeit, for my little skill in that tongue, I am the more (I hope) to be borne withal. And whereas the author in the Latin copy, reciting the peculiar letters and the pronunciation of them with the propriety of the British tongue, instead of a double letter as *Dd*, or a letter with an aspiration as *Ll*, would for brevity sake have them written

---

[34] a simple antiquary] A novice in antiquarian studies.
[35] See below, pp. 65-66. The location of Roman Calleva, now firmly identified with Silchester in Hampshire, would remain a matter of dispute among antiquaries for another two hundred years.
[36] On the Englishing of Welsh names, see Introduction, pp. 31-32.
[37] Doctor Yale of London] Probably Thomas Yale (d. 1577), a prominent civil lawyer originally from Denbigh.

with the same letter and a prick under the foot:[38] for want of the like letters we have throughout the whole work expressed the same
90 to that very effect in the double letter, or with aspiration, from place to place, where he hath used the same under-pricked letter. So that hereby, saving for his conceit of writing, there is no error committed at all. And herein I thought it needful to admonish thee.

Moreover, if there shall haply appear any fault by us now committed, either in misnaming any person, town, or other thing, wrong placing of words, evil allegation of writers, altering of the author's meaning by false pointing, one word put for another, or such like, the truth whereof I could not exactly try out by diligent animadversion° or due conference in so short time, I most heartily
100 crave pardon, and must needs impute the most part thereof unto the falseness and disorder of the Latin copy, printed at Cologne. Whose errata are more then I have commonly seen in a book of no greater quantity, and yet if the printer would have noted all he should have noted twice so many as he did – besides that there are many *errata in erratis*.[39]

But perhaps some will marvel, what is my reason that I have termed this work in English *The Breviary of Britain*, since it is not entitled so in Latin? To them I answer that, if they deem of the Latin title aright, they shall perceive that I have not strayed one jot
110 from the author's meaning. For, where he calleth this book *Commentarioli Britannicae descriptionis fragmentum*, that is to say a fragment of a little treatise or discourse of the description of Britain, weigh and judge indifferently (good reader) how much I have gone beside the purpose.[40]

And here peradventure it may be looked for (according unto the custom of some translators) I should fine and pick my pen[41] to set forth the commendation of mine author (as, in very deed, some of them had need to do). But I fear me much, lest in mine over-rash attempt in taking so worthy a writer in hand, not being furnished

---

[38] In his discussion of Welsh spelling and pronunciation, Llwyd suggests that *Dd* and *Ll* may be written, for brevity, with a 'puncto supposito,' as Ḍ and Ḷ.

[39] *errata in erratis*] 'errors in the list of errors'.

[40] Twyne skirts over the religious implications of the English title, which might be read to imply that the Matter of Britain had the status of holy doctrine. Yet other authors had used 'breviary' in the titles of secular works, e.g. Andrew Boorde, *The Breviary of Health* (London: William Middleton, 1547).

[41] fine and pick my pen] That is, prepare his writing implements for a passage of ornate prose.

with any greater skill and learning in this his kind than I am known to be, I have deserved just blame, and Master Llwyd, if he were living, would have desired me of less acquaintance. Whose passing earnest travail in attaining skill and knowledge hath deservedly purchased unto him immortal fame, and so much the rather for that he hath therein endeavoured himself to do his country good, whereunto all men are naturally bound; and not only contented to take the pains for his own knowledge sake, but willing to pleasure other thereby, hath communicated the same unto the world.

Which commendable example of his, I trust shall be a provocation unto some other in this realm that have travailed long time, and taken much pains in the searching out of antiquities and ancient monuments of Britain, not without their great charges (whose singular learning, without suspicion of partiality, I may not commend), to attempt the like, unless that they be hindered by such who, willing to do nothing themselves, of duty ought to be furtherers and helpers to others.[42] And for my part, I have taken the pains with hazard of mine estimation for the English reader's sake, which understandeth not the Latin tongue. To whom I thought it as much appertaining to know the state and description of his own country as to the learned, be he Englishman or stranger. Only for recompense, gentle reader, let me have thy good word and lawful favour, and I ask no more. Farewell heartily, and enjoy it.

---

[42] Foremost among the 'others' preparing works on Britain and its antiquities in the 1560s was William Lambarde, whose *Alphabetical Description of the Chief Places in England and Wales* would remain unpublished until 1730; in the next generation, William Camden's *Britannia* (1586) would win immediate recognition as the definitive work in the field.

A Friend, in Praise of the Author.

The British soil, with all therein that lies,
The surging seas which compass it about,
In what estate of heat, or cold of skies
150   It stands, with many things of other rout,°
Llwyd in this book hath put them out of doubt:
Which, though in view it be of body small,
In brief discourse it doth comprise them all.

Ptolem[43] his pen it seems he had in hand;
Sometimes in seas with Neptune[44] he did dwell;
Juno[45] to skies plucked him to view the land,
Else surely could he not have done so well,
That thus so right of everything doth tell,
160   As though he stood aloft and down did look,[46]
And what he saw wrote straight into his book.

Each hill, each dale, each water worth the name,
With forests wide, and many a standing wood,
Each city, town, each castle great of fame,[47]
Each king and prince sprung forth of noble blood –
Were bad his reign, or were it just and good –
So much as skilled him for to touch therein,
To tell the truth he forced not a pin.[48]
170

Thy country, Llwyd, is bounden much to thee,
Which mak'st it unto us not only known,
But unto such as in far countries be,

---

[43] Ptolem] Claudius Ptolemaeus, or Ptolemy.
[44] Neptune] Roman god of the seas.
[45] Juno] Wife of Jupiter, Queen of the Gods.
[46] As though he stood aloft and down did look] The image prefigures and perhaps inspires Drayton's conceit of an airborne Muse in *Poly-Olbion*.
[47] The catalogue of topographical phenomena recalls John Leland's boast: 'there is almost neither cape, nor bay, haven, creek or pier, river or confluence of rivers, breaches, washes, lakes, meres, fenny waters, mountains, valleys, moors, heaths, forests, woods, cities, burgs, castles, principal manor places, monasteries, and colleges, but I have seen them'; *Laboryouse Serche of Johan Leland* (London: S. Mierdman, 1549), sig. D4^v.
[48] he forced not a pin] Proverbial? To force a pin might suggest gathering an excessive amount of material together by forcing a single pin through the folds.

Whereby thy fame the greater way is flown,
And eke° thy countries praise the more is grown.
So by one deed two noble things are chanced:
Britain, and Llwyd, to heaven are advanced.

In Latin thou, the learned sort to please,
180 In single pain a double skill didst show.
In English Twyne hath turned, for greater ease
To those, the Roman tongue that do not know.
The work is one, though tongues be twain I trow.
The Latin thou, the English Twyne did twist,
The learned laud you both, dispraise who list.
 Finis.

Thomae Brounei, Praebendarii Westm., in *Commentariolos*
190 *Britannicae descriptionis* Humfredi Lhuyd Denbyghiensis, Cambri Britanni.[49]

 Flumine Lhuyde fluis, laxis effusus habenis,
 Dulcis, & irrigno flumine Lhuyde fluis,
 Nereides, viridesque Deae, pater Inachus aiunt,
 Parnassi ex ipso vertice Lhuyde venis.
 In mare dulcisono Lhuydus fluit amne Britannum:
 Clamant Cluydae flumina, Lhuydus adest.
 Et novus ille, novis auxit faelicius undis
200 Fontes, Annales, inclite Brute tuos.
 Nomina vera docet Regionis, fluminis, urbis,
 Et cuiusque loci quae sit origo, docet.
 Ut vere scripsit: sic vero interprete gaudet,
 Sed Lhuydus Latii fluminis amne fluit.
 Anglus hic interpres, Romanum iam facit Anglum.
 Scripsit uterque bene: laus sit utrique sua.[50]

---

[49] Thomae Brounei [...] Cambri Britanni] 'Thomas Browne, prebendary of Westminster, on the *Breviary of Britain* by Humphrey Llwyd of Denbigh, Cambro-Briton.'
[50] The verses pun laboriously on Llwyd's name, which Browne supposes to be pronounced like the Latin *fluit* (flows).

['You flow with a flowing, Llwyd, poured forth after the
    loosening of your reins,
210 Sweetly and with a well-watered flowing, Llwyd, you flow,'
Say the Nereids, and the green goddesses and father Inachus,
'From the very summit of Parnassus, Llwyd, you come.'
Into the British sea Llwyd flows, with a sweet-sounding stream.
The streams of Clwyd shout out 'Llwyd is here!'
And this new Llwyd has more fruitfully than new waters
    augmented
Your sources, the chronicles, renowned Brutus.
He teaches the region's true names, and the river's and city's,
And teaches what the beginning of each place is.
220 As he has written truly, so he rejoices in a true translator,
But Llwyd flows with a Latin river's torrent.
Now this English translator makes the Roman English.
Each has written well: let each have his praise.]

Edward Grant,[51] Schoolmaster of Westminster, in commendation of this treatise of Brittany, penned in Latin by Humphrey Llwyd and translated into English by Thomas Twyne.

230 If for to write of Brutus' brood[52] each Briton's brain be bound,
For zeal he owes to country soil, and eke his native ground:
Then Wales may boast, and justly joy, that such a Briton bred
Which hath with serious search of brain and toiling travel spread
Throughout the coasts of Brittany,[53] and foreign countries strange,
The lively fame of Brutus' name, that through the world doth
    range;
That long lay hid in dungeons dark, obscured by tract of time,
And almost smouldered with the smoke of ignorance's crime,
But now revived and polished by Llwyd his busy brain,
240 And brought to light and former frame by his exhausted pain.
Whose diligence and judgement great I can but muse to see,
That with such skill doth paint the praise of Brute and Brittany,
That with such love to country's soil doth bring again to light

---

[51] Edward Grant] (d. 1601), headmaster of Westminster School, succeeded in that post by William Camden.
[52] Brutus' brood] The descendants of Brutus or, by association, Britons generally.
[53] Brittany] Great Britain

The shining shape, and stately stamp° of that was darkened quite.
By whose endeavour Polydore⁵⁴ must now surcease to prate,
To forge, to lie, and to defame King Brutus' worthy state.
By whose great pains, proud Hector⁵⁵ must now leave off to babble,
250   Such vaunts as of his Scottish soil, Scot, he whilom seemed to fable.
By Llwyd their brags be beaten down, their forging lies be spied,
And Britain needs must challenge fame that erst° it was denied.
Llwyd findeth forth her former fame, and antique° names doth tell:
And doth refute their forged lies that did of rancour smell.
Brute's worthy race is blazèd here by trump of flickering fame,
And Llwyd it is, a flowing flood, that hath revived the same;
Who, though interred now in earth, yet shall he never die,
But live amongst his Britanists,⁵⁶ by this his *Brittany*;
Whose thread of life would God the Fates had yet not sought to spoil:
260   Then had we had a larger scope of Brutus' sacred soil.
Go little volume, go thy ways, by Llwyd in Latin penned,
And new attired in English weed, by Twyne that thee doth send
To Brute his brood, a labour sure that well deserveth praise:
Go show thy self to Britanists, whose glory thou dost raise.
    Finis.

Lodowick Lloyd,⁵⁷ in Praise of the Author.
270

Go on, be bold, thou little book, sound forth thy author's fame,
Advance the travail tried of him that christened first thy name;
Thy state exiled, thy age unknown, thy line that long was lost
Is now returned, and known again in ancient Britain's coast.
From Scythia shore, from Phrygia fields, where long thyself have lain,
From raging rocks and crazed crags thou art come home again.⁵⁸

---

⁵⁴ Polydore] Polydore Vergil
⁵⁵ Hector] Hector Boece
⁵⁶ Britanists] Possibly Britons generally, but more specifically British nationalists and upholders of the Brutus tradition.
⁵⁷ Lodowick Lloyd] (d. 1607), Welsh courtier and author of works including *The Pilgrimage of Princes* (1573).

>
> Thy patron grand, and ancient sire, Aeneas Trojan stout
> Did never toil on land and seas, as thou hast ranged about;
> From mountains high, where to thyself alone wast wont to talk,
> Llwyd taught thy steps to tread in court, with princes wise to walk.
> If then Solinus[59] merit fame, that Caesar's stirp° have penned:
> The same ought Llwyd of right to claim that Brutus' line defend.
> If Curtius[60] be advanced on high, Alexander's fame to feed,
> Then well ought Llwyd commended be to honour Hector's seed.
> What praise had Livy then in Rome, or Herodot in Greece,[61]
> That praise ought never Humphrey Llwyd in native soil to leese.°
> Who, being alive, could Argus[62] make with sugared talk to sleep:
> And now, being dead, might Argus make with hundred eyes to weep.
> Who, though his corpse is clothed in clay, in mouldered dust to lie,
> In spite of Parcas[63] yet his fame doth scale the empire sky.
> And though that age outliveth youth, yet death doth age exile:
> Though fame surviveth death again, yet time doth fame defile.
> So youth to age, and age to death, and death to fame in field,
> And fame to time, and time to God, this Llwyd knew well to yield.
> Sith° then he found Misenus' trump[64] to sound again the fame
> That once was won, and then was lost, extol each one his name.
> And give him then his due desert, enrol his noble mind,
> That first have taught his countrymen their country state to find.
>   Finis.

---

[58] The opening lines prefigure the prophecy of Merlin in Spenser's *Faerie Queene* (Book 3, canto 3), recounting the sufferings of the Britons and their eventual restoration to the throne through the Tudor bloodline. Here that dynastic restoration is conflated with the restoration of Welsh historical traditions in the *Breviary*. The references to Phrygia and Scythia recall the Britons' Trojan origins and their supposed links to ancient Scythia through the Cimmerians or Cimbri (see below, pp. 99-100).

[59] Solinus] Gaius Julius Solinus, Roman writer of the third century AD, author of *Polyhistor*.

[60] Curtius] Quintus Curtius Rufus, Roman historian of the first century AD, author of *Historiae Alexandri Magni*.

[61] Livy [...] Herodot] Titus Livius and Herodotus, historians of Rome and Greece, respectively.

[62] Argus] In Greek mythology, a hundred-eyed giant who was lulled to sleep with words and then murdered by the god Hermes.

[63] Parcas] The Fates

[64] Misenus' trump] Hector's trumpeter, who figures in Virgil's *Aeneid*.

Laurence Twyne, to his Brother Thomas Twyne, in Praise of his Translation.

All that which learned Llwyd of late in Latin did indite,°
Of Britons' race, their ancient state, their guise, and country's rite,°
310 Lo, now in English tongue, by true report and cunning's skill,
Twyne hath set forth, th'unlearned sort their pleasure to fulfil;
Wherein who list to look with heed straight Britain's state shall know,
And wherewithal this noble land in ancient time did flow.
Llwyd's pains was much, in Latin style which wrote the same before:
But brother, sure in my conceit thou thanks deservest more
Of Britons, and of British soil, which mak'st them understand,
A thing more meet (methinks) for them than for a foreign land.
320 Wherein, as thou by toil hast won the spurs and praises got,
So reap deserved thanks of those for whom thou brak'st the knot.
    Finis.

John Twyne, to the Readers of his Brother's Translation.

As they of all most praise deserve that first with pen did show
To us the sacred laws of God, whereby his will we know,
So, many thanks are due to those that beat their busy brain
330 To let us learn our earthly state in which we here remain.
Amongst the rest that ever wrote none hath of us deserved
Like praise to Llwyd who, lo, his toil hath here to us preferred.
Wherein thou may'st the whole estate of this our native land,
What so is worthy to be known, by reading understand.
And 'cause the author wrote the same in tongue enstranged° to some,
Twyne hath it taught the English phrase in which it erst was dumb.
Accept it well, and when thou read'st, if ought thereby thou gain:
For recompense yield thy good will to him that took the pain.
340   Finis.

The epistle of the author to the most adorned, and best deserving to be reverenced of all that love the knowledge of the mathematics, Abraham Ortelius of Antwerp.[65]

Dearly beloved Ortelius, that day wherein I was constrained to depart from London I received your description of Asia,[66] and before I came home to my house I fell into a very perilous fever, which hath so torn this poor body of mine these ten continual days that I was brought into despair of my life. But my hope, Jesus Christ, is laid up in my bosom. Howbeit, neither the daily shaking of the continual fever, with a double tertian, neither the looking for present death, neither the vehement headache without intermission, could put the remembrance of my Ortelius out of my troubled brain. Wherefore, I send unto you my Wales,[67] not beautifully set forth in all points, yet truly depainted,° so be that certain notes be observed, which I gathered even when I was ready to die.

You shall also receive the description of England, set forth as well with the ancient names as those which are now used, and another England also drawn forth perfectly enough. Besides, certain fragments written with mine own hand which, notwithstanding that they be written forth in a rude hand, and seem to be imperfect, yet doubt not they be well grounded by proofs and authorities of ancient writers; which also (if God had spared me life) you should have received in better order, and in all respects perfect. Take, therefore, this last remembrance of thy Humphrey, and forever *adieu*, my dear friend Ortelius.

From Denbigh in Gwynedd, or North Wales, the 30th of August, 1568.

Yours both living and dying, Humphrey Llwyd.

---

[65] The Flemish geographer Abraham Ortelius (1527-1598), compiler of the *Theatrum Orbis Terrarum* (1570).
[66] Ortelius had produced a wall-map of Asia in 1567.
[67] Llwyd's maps, one of Wales and one of England and Wales, would be printed in a supplement to Ortelius's atlas published in 1573.

The Breviary of Britain

For so much as in my last letters which I wrote unto you, right learned sir, in the which I promised within few days after to send you the geographical description of all Britain, set forth with the most ancient names, as well Latin as British (wherein I must much disagree from the opinions of learned men), I thought it expedient first in a few words to disclose the effect of my purpose to all, and by what arguments and authorities of the learned I am moved partly to change, and partly to ascribe unto other (otherwise than those which wrote before me have done), the names of countries, towns, rivers and other places. Which before I take in hand to do, I purpose to entreat a little of the knowledge of the British tongue,[68] of the signification of the letters, and the manner of pronouncing the same.[69] Whereby the true name both of the whole island and of many places therein may be manifest. The ignorance of which tongue hath driven many notable men to such shifts that, endeavouring to wind themselves out of one, they have fallen into many mo, and those more grosser errors.

The order, and signification of the letters is this, as followeth:

A, B, D, E, H, L, M, N, O, P, R, S, T. They have the very same pronunciation in the British tongue which they have in the Latin well-pronounced.

C and **G** have the same force and signification being placed before all the vowels that they have before *a* and *o* in the Latin tongue.[70]

CH expresseth the nature of χ, called *chi* among the Grecians, and hath no affinity with the pronunciation in French or English of the same aspiration, but is sounded in the throat, like *chet* in the Hebrew.

Double **DD**, as it is commonly written amongst our countrymen, or amongst the learned after this manner **DH**,[71] is pronounced like the Greek *delta*, or like the Hebrew *dalet* without *dagesh*.[72]

---

[68] British tongue] Welsh language
[69] Llwyd's guide to Welsh pronunciation largely accords with William Salesbury, *A playne and a familiar introduction, teaching how to pronounce the letters in the Brytishe tongue, now commonly called Welshe* (London: Henry Denham, 1567).
[70] That is, Welsh *c* and *g* are hard consonants.
[71] Though Twyne follows Llwyd in his use of the 'more learned' forms *dh* and *lh*, this edition employs the modern Welsh forms *dd* and *ll*.
[72] *dalet* without *dagesh*] The dagesh is a diacritic indicating hard pronunciation.

We use **F** always for *v* when it is a consonant, as *Llanfair* is in reading called 'Llanvair', for **V** is always a vowel.[73] Instead of the Latin *f* we use **PH** or **FF**.

We make **I** continually a vowel as the Greeks do, and is pronounced as the Italian *i*, or rather as the barbarous and unlearned priests in times past sounded *e*.

We have also a peculiar letter to ourselves, which the ruder sort fashion like **LL**, but the better-learned write with **LH**. I am not ignorant that the Spaniards have in use *ll*, and so have the Germans *lh*, as in the proper names of Lhudovicus and Lhotharius the Emperor in Panvinius is evident. But neither of these expresseth ours; howbeit, I take it rather that the Mexicani[74] which inhabit the new-found world do use that letter, which the Spaniards express by *ll*, but because I was never amongst them I doubt whether it be so or not, for ours is sharp in the hissing. For this letter **LL** is pronounced with a strong aspiration, putting the tongue hard to the teeth, being half-open, holding the lips immovable, the right pronunciation whereof is not easily learned, but by much exercise.[75]

U hath always the force of a vowel, and hath almost the sound which the French *u* hath, or the Hebrew *kibbutz*. For *v* we use single **F**, the consonant.

Besides the five vowels which the Latins use, we have other twain wherein we follow the Greeks. First **W**, and soundeth not much unlike the Latin *u* or (to speak more plainly) as the simple heretofore were wont in Latin falsely and barbarously to pronounce *o*. The last of the letters and vowels is **Y**, which we must examine, hard to be pronounced somewhat like *ypsilon*, as the learned of the University of Oxford do pronounce it.[76]

L, **X**, and **Z** are nothing needful to the writing of our words.

---

[73] V is always a vowel] That is, 'v' is always 'u'.

[74] The comparison would seem to link to Llwyd's theory that the medieval Welsh prince Madoc and his followers had settled in Mexico centuries before the arrival of the Spanish. See below, pp. 157-59.

[75] The advice in Salesbury's guide to Welsh pronunciation is similar, although, as Salesbury acknowledges, 'Ll cannot be declared anything like to the purpose in writing, but only by mouth' (sig. D1ʳ).

[76] Cambridge, where John Cheke had been Regius Professor, held the lead in Greek studies in the sixteenth century; yet Llwyd and Twyne had both attended Oxford, where Twyne's son Brian would later become Lecturer in Greek.

For *k* we use **C**, as we said before. We have also many diphthongs, in which both vowels – yea, if there be three, as it chanceth often – keep their full sound, or some part thereof.

Having thus much foretasted of the number and nature of the letters, let us draw near to the propriety° of the tongue, where we must note that, like as the Greeks and Latins in the ends of their words have variations and cases, so this tongue contrariwise hath the same changing in the beginning of the words.[77] Whereby it cometh to pass that even the best learned, through ignorance of the language, have been very much abused in the names of provinces, countries, and other things. Let us therefore briefly run over this propriety.

Every British word whose first radical° is *p*, *t*, or *c* hath in writing or discourse of talk (to avoid evil sound) three variations, so that radical *p* is sometimes turned into *b*, into *ph*, and into *mh*; *t* into *d*, into *th*, and into *nh*; *c* into *g*, *ch*, and into *ngh*; as appeareth in these examples: a 'head' is called *pen* in our tongue; 'out of the head', *o ben*, or 'his head', *ei ben*; 'with a head', *â phen*, or 'her head', *ei phen*; 'my head', *fy mhen*. Here you see a strange mutation of this letter, when it is called in one place *pen*, in another *ben*, in the third *phen*, and last of all *mhen*. Likewise, 'fire' in British is called *tân*; 'out of fire', *o dân*; 'with fire', *â thân*; 'my fire', *fy nhân*. In like manner *c* is changed. For 'love' is called in our tongue *cariad*; 'out of love', *o gariad*; 'with love', *â chariad*; 'my love,' *fy nghariad*.

Also *b*, with *d* and *g*, radicals, have their peculiar variations, as for example sake: *bara*, which signifieth 'bread'; 'out of bread', *o fara* (where *f* hath the force of *v* consonant); 'my bread', *fy mara*. And like as *b* is changed into *f* and *m*, so is *d* into *dd* and *n*, as *Duw*, with us the name of God (which is so likewise pronounced by the Frenchmen, though it be not written with the same letters); 'out of God', *o Dduw*; 'my God', *fy Nuw*. *G* in the first place vanisheth away, in the second place it is turned into *ng*: as *gŵr*, which signifieth 'a man'; 'out of a man', *o ŵr*; 'my man', *fy ngŵr*.

Besides these, *l*, *m*, and *rh*[78] have one only variation, as *llyfr*, a book; 'out of a book', *o lyfr*. *Môn*, the Isle of Anglesey: 'out of Anglesey', *o Fon*. *Rhufayn*, Rome: 'out of Rome', *o Rufain*.[79]

---

[77] Initial consonants in Welsh are subject to various mutations (soft, nasal, and aspirate), a feature also found in other Celtic languages.

[78] *rh*] As L.; T. mistranscribes or misprints as 'kh'.

The others be never radicals (as *d, f, th, l, r*), or else they be not changed (as *ph, ch, n*, and *s*).

The Description of Britain

480 This foundation being laid, which hath troubled many learned men, let us now come to the geographical description of the island. And first of all, let us briefly lay forth what divers men have diversely written of the name thereof.

Aristotle, a grave author, in his book *De Mundo* (Of the World),[80] which he wrote to Alexander, affirmeth that there be two very great islands in the ocean beyond Hercules' Pillars,[81] lying above the Celtae, which he calleth Brittanicas, namely Albion and Ierne. Which name of Albion, both ours and also the Roman histories do acknowledge as very ancient, and derived from Albion,
490 the son of Neptune, there reigning about the year of the world's creation 2220 – whereof (God willing) we will speak more at large in another place.[82] But whereas some say that it is so named by reason of the white cliffs, it is plain ridiculous.[83] And I wonder that men otherwise circumspect enough could be blinded in such light, as to have darkened all the names of places and men with Latin etymologies or derivations, seeing it is well known that the Latins at that time[84] possessed but the least part of Italy, and that the Apuli and the Calabri spake the Greek tongue, and the Tusci the Etruscan tongue, and almost the residue of Italy was possessed by the
500 Frenchmen,[85] whereby neither the Latin name nor their tongue was known to the borderers. Into which error Robertus Coenalis, a Frenchman, very well learned, with divers other hath fallen, while he endeavoureth to set forth the names of countries and cities of both Britains (the island and the continent) in expositions and

---

[79] *o Rufain*] As L.; T. has 'o Rhufain', failing to reflect the mutation of *Rh* to *R*.
[80] *De Mundo* (Of the World)] Today regarded as a pseudo-Aristotelian text.
[81] Hercules' Pillars] The Straits of Gibraltar
[82] The shadowy tradition involving the giant Albion had been promulgated in the Tudor era by Thomas Twyne's father, John Twyne (d. 1581), in his *De rebus Albionicis, Britanicis atque Anglicis* (prepared for the press by Thomas in 1590). Llwyd did not live to produce a further work dealing with the Albion tradition.
[83] In spite of Llwyd's protestations, this remains a widely accepted derivation of Albion, *albus* being Latin for 'white'.
[84] at that time] The age of Aristotle, the fourth century BC.
[85] Frenchmen] Gauls.

derivations from the Latin. Whereas the author, forgetting himself, sayeth in another place that first of all the Romans Julius Caesar beheld that part of France and this our Britain, and that the same places were so termed by the ancient inhabitants before ever they heard of the Roman name. Whereby I, as one not sworn to maintain the opinion of any man, but following reason, the faithful guide and leader of the wise, do constantly avouch that the derivations and deductions of the antique names of Britain and the parts thereof are not to be sought out of the Greeks and Latins, but forth of the most ancient British tongue. For, how shamefully the Latins have corrupted the names of the kings and places of the land, while they study for the finesse of their tongue, it is manifest to all those which being furnished with any skill of the tongues come to read the Roman histories. For so, very falsely, they have called Hermannus, Arminius; Ernestus, Ariovistus; Dictrichus, Theodoricus; and the invincible king of Britain, Meurigus, they have called Arviragus; and now of late years Polydorus hath termed Rhesus, the son of Thomas, Richard.[86]

Since therefore it is evident that we must not trust unto the Roman names, let us come to our own natural° tongue, by means whereof we shall bring the true name of Britain to light; which to accomplish the better, we must something say before.

Caesar, which first of all the Romans hath celebrated the name of this island in the Latin tongue, called it Britannia; whom almost all other Latin writers imitating have not changed the same name. Notwithstanding, only Sir Thomas Elyot,[87] a knight whose learning is not to be contemned, hath stood up of late amongst us, who contendeth not without good reason and probability that it was called in old time Prytannia, which he proveth by a very ancient copy that he had in his hands. But where he sayeth that it was termed so in Greek for the plenty and abundance thereof, surely I (which do quite reject such derivations) do not allow it; yet yielding rather to the name of Prytannia than Britannia, the authority of which ancient fragment I will endeavour to confirm

---

[86] Rhesus, the son of Thomas] Rhys ap Thomas (1449-1525), Welsh military leader and key ally of Henry VII.

[87] In his *Bibliotheca Eliotae* (London: Thomas Berthelet, 1542), Sir Thomas Elyot (d. 1546) tells the remarkable story of an ancient manuscript discovered in the foundations of a Wiltshire church in which almost nothing could be deciphered except the word 'Prytania'; Elyot concluded from this that Prytania must be the original Greek name for Britain, connoting a place rich in metals.

with weighty reasons. But because in so doing I shall appear to bring forth certain paradoxes and opinions not heard of before, the better to satisfy both my countrymen the Britons in Wales and others, I will lay forth my purpose before all men's eyes, not cleaving so precisely to mine own opinions but that if any man can bring me more better and more certain, I will quickly yield unto them. In the meanwhile (always reserving the judgement of the learned), you shall have mine opinion.

When I chanced of late years to come to the sight of Polydorus Vergilius the Italian and Hector Boethius the Scot, their British histories – whereof the first mainfully° sought not only to obscure the glory of the British name, but also to defame the Britons themselves with slanderous lies; the other, while he goeth about to raise his Scots out of darkness and obscurity, whatever he findeth that the Romans or Britons have done worthy commendation in this island, all that he attributeth unto his Scots, like a foolish writer – wherefore, being provoked by these injuries, that I might the better guard my sweet country from such inconveniences unto my small power, I began to peruse all such ancient histories, both Greek and Latin, as ever had written of Britain or the Britons, causing not only all such sentences, but each word also to be copied forth, to the intent that thereout, as of a thick and plentiful wood, I might gather sufficient timber to frame a British history. And not only continued in reading strange writers, but also the most antique fragments of our poets, which at this day (retaining therein, as in all other things else, the old name) are called *bardi*,[88] together with histories written in the British tongue, which of late so far as I suppose were by me first translated into English.[89] And not only conferred the deeds but also the names of kings and places in both tongues, where I have noted that Britannia was first called Prydain amongst us, as appeareth in the most ancient books of pedigrees. Wherein the Welshmen are too too curious, having amongst them

---

[88] *bardi*] Llwyd's attitude to the bardic order appears warmer than that of some other Welsh humanists, including William Salesbury, who were apt to condemn their diction and subject matter in equal measure. This positive image of the bards clearly influenced Michael Drayton in *Poly-Olbion*, and perhaps also Sir Philip Sidney, who writes admiringly of the longevity of the Welsh bardic tradition in his *Defence of Poesy*.

[89] The reference is to Llwyd's manuscript translation of the *Brut y Tywysogion*, subsequently revised and published by David Powel as *The History of Cambria* (1584).

continually certain registers of pedigrees and descents (which some call heralds) which perpetually do record in writing and memory the names of parents, with their children, contriving them into tribes as they were divided in old time. They think as well of themselves as either the Frenchmen, the Turks, or Latins, deriving their original from the Trojans.[90]

In these books (as I say) it is many times found that this island was called Prydain, as 'pen post Prydain', that is to say, the chiefest post or pillar of Britain. A certain writer also, which wrote many hundred years ago amongst the old valiant Britons, showeth the same, besides that the poets, and those which they call *bardi*, at this day do frequent commonly that word, as 'post Prydain oll, pryd a nerth', that is to say the pillar of all Britain, the beauty and strength. Moreover it is usually found in all our books 'Ynys Prydain', that is to say the Island of Britain, and 'Phrainc a Phrydain', that is, France and Britain. Whereby those that understand the tongue may easily gather that our Britons called this island *Prydain* in their language, which the Latins for the hardness and evil sound thereof have rejected, and have called the country Britannia, and the people Britanni, for the more gentle and pleasant sound's sake. Which I will prove by these strong arguments following.

Every British word (as we have said before) whose first radical is *p* hath three variations in construction, namely into *b*, *ph*, and *mh*. The name of Britain amongst us sometime beginneth with *B*, sometime with *Ph*, and sometime with *Mh*. Wherefore the first radical thereof must needs be *P*. And another infallible argument there is, that *B* is not the first radical of that name. There is no British word whose first radical letter is *b* that abideth any change into *p*, or *ph*. But the name of Britain among the Britons (as the propriety of the tongue requireth) sometimes beginneth with *P*, sometime with *Ph*, as I have showed before. Wherefore the name of Britain hath not *B* for his first radical letter. Neither is it necessary that we should seek the derivation of this name from the Greeks, since we may find the reason of it in our own tongue, wherein almost all names of men and places are of themselves significant. *Pryd* amongst us signifieth comeliness or beauty; *cain*

---

[90] As the Latins claimed descent from the Trojan Aeneas, so medieval scholars traced the origins of the Franks and Turks to the mythical Trojans Francus and Turcus.

signifieth white. So that by the joining of these two words together, and taking away *c* in composition for the better sound's sake, is made *Prydain*, that is to say a white or excellent beauty, or comeliness. As who should say, the first borderers thereto called it a fair and fertile land. But, seeing this is but a bare conjecture, I am not against it but that every man hold his own opinion. Neither am I ignorant that some very well learned men and expert in the British tongue do write the island's name with B – which I think they do rather following therein the Latins, than judging the same to be the true name, knowing the proofs which I have before alleged to be so undoubtedly certain that themselves cannot deny them.

Perhaps here will stand forth some enemy to the British name, saying that by these arguments I do disprove both the coming of Brutus into this island, and Polydorus himself with his British History.[91] But God forbid I should be so impious in such wise to despise the majesty of antiquity. Nay rather, when opportunity shall be offered I purpose to confirm (by bringing forth many weighty reasons, and authorities, which I have ready in store for a British History) both his coming and also to establish the credit of the British History. Nothing regarding the folly of those who, because they find not the name of it in the Roman histories, boldly deny that there is any such in the world at all; saying unto those that shall read Halicarnasseus[92] and Livius, so much disagreeing, and also considering the obscurity of the Latin name at that time when Brutus passed out of Italy into Greece, it shall easily appear that through the default of writers and negligence of such as wrote afterwards (among whom Livius, even of the Romans themselves, is touched with want of trust) many things of greater importance than the departure of Brutus are yielded to oblivion. And although Caesar call the Britons 'autochthonous',[93] that is to say, born in the same country where they dwell, and Diodorus Siculus sayeth that they were from the beginning, yet do I believe that Brutus came into Britain with his train of Trojans, and there took upon him the government of the ancient inhabitants and of his own men, and thereof were called Britons. For our countrymen unto this day do

---

[91] Llwyd's meaning is rather, 'deny, with Polydorus, both the coming of Brutus into this island and the British History'.
[92] Halicarnasseus] Dionysius of Halicarnassus, Greek historian of the first century BC, author of *Roman Antiquities*.
[93] autochthonous] 'αὐτόχθονός'; see Caesar, *De bello Gallico*, v.12.

call a Briton *Brituun* (which word cometh not from the ancient name of the island *Prydain*, but from Brutus, the king) and our histories call the Britons in the plural number *Brytaniaid*, and *Brython*, which words are derived from the name of Brutus. For in derivation of words our countrymen do often turn *u* into *y* (the ignorance whereof did very much trouble my friend Master Leland).[94] But because this which we have said touching the name of the island and the first inhabitants thereof seemeth sufficient for our purpose, we will now entreat of other matters.

The Division of Britain

Britain, which more rightly (howbeit more strangely) ought to be called Prydain, is divided into three parts: Lloegria,° Albania,° and Cambria.[95] Lloegria is called of our countrymen (reserving as yet the old name) that same part of Britain which, being possessed by the English Saxons and the Juti, peoples of Germany, is now of all nations called England. For when Britain by Maximus the Tyrant[96] was bereft of all the youth, a great part whereof was slain with him at Aquilaeia, the residue stoutly invaded and possessed a part of France called Armorica,° slaying and driving thence the country dwellers. Whereby that country at this day is called by the name of the Less, and the Continent Britain.[97]

And here I must not let pass with silence that Bede the Englishman, Volaterranus and Polydorus Italians, were shamefully overseen in saying that this island took his name of that other, being evident to all men that the same was termed Armorica (which in our tongue is as much to say, upon the sea),[98] and this ours, Britannia. Neither was there ever any of the ancient Britons, or Britons in France (so far as I know) before Sidonius Apollinaris,

---

[94] my friend Master Leland] L. 'nostro Lelando' (our Leland). Llwyd is unlikely to have been personally acquainted with the antiquary John Leland (*c.* 1506-1552), who had succumbed to incurable madness by the time Llwyd was out of his teens.

[95] On the legendary division of Britain among the three sons of Brutus, see below, p. 98, and Introduction, p. 1.

[96] Maximus the Tyrant] Magnus Maximus (emperor 383-88) seized control of the western empire from his power base in Britain, largely stripping the island of its legions; he features prominently in medieval Welsh historical tradition under the name of Macsen Wledig.

[97] the Less, and the Continent Britain] Names for Brittany.

[98] upon the sea] W. 'ar y môr'.

which lived a little after this migration, that left any remembrance of it. But in an epistle to Vincentius, of Arvandus's secretary, which accused his lord of high treason, thus he writeth:

> This letter seemed to be sent to the King of Goths, or Gutland, dissuading him from peace with the Emperor of Greece, and showing that the Britons upon Ligeris ought to be set upon.[99]

So far he. But if, as they dream (and also Coenalis which hath erroneously followed them), the Britons had possessed some part of France before that time, and such a part as should have been called Britain, as they do affirm impudently enough, it should not have escaped unspoken of, of all the Roman writers unto whom France was as well known as Italy. Howbeit our countrymen say that the Cornishmen and those were one nation, which both the kings' names being like in both countries (as Conan, Meriadoc – by which name a parcel of Denbighshire in North Wales is called to this day – Hoel, Alan, Theodore, Rywallon, with divers other), and also the proper words and names for all things almost one (although in their joining and construction of speech they seem a little to differ, as it chanceth sometimes in one country) do prove manifestly. Our countrymen call it in their mother tongue *Llydaw*, which word seemeth to me to be derived from the Latin word *littus*, signifying the shore, as who should say it were a country lying on the shore of France. For like as the Latins do change *d* in all our words into *t*, even so our countrymen do turn their *t* into *d*, and do always in words which begin with *l* write them with aspiration, as *lladron*, borrowing the word *latrones* from the Latins, that is to say in English, 'thieves'.

But to return again from whence we have digressed: when, as I have said before, the youth of Britain was led by Maximus into France, and those that were left at home were oppressed by the most cruel and savage nations the Redshanks° and Scots, looking for no succour from the Romans (which were then otherwise busied), about the year of Our Lord 450 they called unto them the Saxons, which were then practising piracy on the coasts of France and Britain, and gave them wages to aid them. And whereas some

---

[99] The quotation is from a letter written in 468 AD by St Sidonius Appolinaris (d. 489), Gallo-Roman bishop and author, to his friend Vincentius, concerning the treachery of Arvandus, Praetorian prefect of Gaul.

write that before that time the Britons never knew the Saxons, it may appear to be false out of sundry authors. For Claudianus, where he inveigheth against Eutropius, speaketh of them in these words, about the year of Our Lord, 400.

> What I may do, since thou my prince hast been,
> Things not far hence can show, for Tethis doth begin
> To wax more mild, since Saxons thou hast quelled, etc.[100]

720   Likewise, of the Fourth Consulship of Honorius:

> The Orcades° were wet with blood of Saxons slain.

And in another place Britain speaketh:

> And me [she sayeth], with countries near about who was
>   destroyed almost,
> Defenced well hath Stilico.
> By whose help now it is, that Scottish wars I do not doubt,
730   Ne do I dread the Picts, ne do I fear the Saxon rout,
> By standing on the shore, to see them come with doubtful
>   winds, etc.[101]

Also Sidonius Apollinaris, which wrote about their coming into England, handsomely describeth their piracy in an epistle to Lampridius:

> We may behold the wannish Saxons[102] here,
> Used to the sea before, to dread the shore;
740   From off whose heads, where outward they appear,
> Their bits content to hold not any more,
> The shears their tops of hair do clip and shore
> So that their locks, cut hard unto the skin,
> Do make their head decrease, but face to win.

And in his panegyric unto Socer:

---

[100] Claudian, *In Eutropium* [*Against Eutropius*], I (399 AD).
[101] Claudian, *De consulatu Stilichonis* [*On the Consulship of Stilicho*], II (400 AD).
[102] wannish Saxons] 'Saxona cærulum' (dark blue Saxons).

>   But also the Amorick coast, the Saxons' piracy
>   Well hoped for, to whom the British salts but play it was
> 750   All naked, and with clouted boat, the greyish sea to pass [...]

Moreover, Sextus Rufus in his book *De Notitia Provinciarum* (Of the Knowledge of Provinces) speaketh of the Earl of the Saxon shore, along both the Britains.

These[103] (I say) being sufficiently known to the Britons before, they sent them against the Scots and Redshanks, under the conduct of one Hengistus.[104] Whom when they had overcome, they entered a traitorous league with them, and like false men turned their face against their masters. And having slain the whole nobility of Britain by craft at Ambrose Hill,[105] and sending for aid from among the Englishmen, and Juti, being Germans, they usurped the same country which we call Lloegria. And after almost infinite battles they drave the ancient inhabitants into the ends and edges of the island, and parted the same between themselves, dividing it into many kingdoms, namely Kent, the South Saxons, the West Saxons, the East Saxons, East Englishmen,° the kingdom of March° (whom Lazius, a man very well learned and well deserving of posterity, in vain seeketh for in Germany, supposing the history of Bede to be written of the inhabitants of Germany and not of England), and Northumberland, which was also divided into twain, Bernicia and Deira.

Whose kings, being pagans, destroyed with fire and sword all churches, monasteries, and libraries.[106] And after that they had received Christianity by Augustine the monk, they fought many battles, both among themselves and against the Britons. Until that about the year of Our Lord 620,[107] Egbert, King of the West

---

[103] These] The Saxons

[104] Hengistus] Hengist, the semi-legendary Saxon conqueror of south-eastern Britain.

[105] Ambrose Hill] Mount Ambrius, site of a monastery on Salisbury Plain, where Hengist and his Saxon followers were said by Geoffrey of Monmouth to have slaughtered the nobility of Britain, leading Merlin to construct Stonehenge as a monument to the fallen.

[106] libraries] The destruction of Britain's ancient libraries was a perennial theme among early modern Welsh humanists, accounting, among other things, for the loss of the vernacular Welsh Bible which it was supposed must have existed in the early British Church.

[107] 620] 820; the error originates with L. Egbert of Wessex reigned 802-839.

Saxons, being made monarch of all, began to rule alone, and first of all commanded that the country should be called England, and the people Englishmen. Englishmen were a very famous people of Germany, whereof the captains and chief of Saxony (as Crantzius reporteth) were long time called Captains of Anglaria. And there remaineth yet (as I have read) a castle where they sometime abode, termed now Enger, in the frontiers of Westphalia, between Osnabruck and Herford.[108] Whereby it cometh that our countrymen, retaining the first name, do call all Englishmen *Saeson*, and their tongue *Saesneg*, and know not what these words 'England' or 'an Englishman' meaneth.

Shortly after, the Danes overcame the Englishmen and possessed this land until, the year of the incarnate word 1066, William, Bastard of Normandy, with his Normans, vanquishing both Englishmen and Danes, usurped the country. From which stock almost the whole nobility of this realm, unto this day, do fetch their descent.

The Description of England

But let us return to Lloegr, which in times past was environed with the British Ocean, the rivers of Severn, Dee, and Humber, but now, since the realm of England stretches forth beyond Humber to Tweed, we will also stretch forth the name of Lloegr so far. And although the Englishmen do possess beyond Severn Herefordshire, the Forest of Dean, and many other places, yet we hold that they dwell in Wales, not in Lloegr, and are taken almost everywhere of all other Englishmen for Welshmen.[109] But the river Dee is accounted at this day one of the ancient bonds, saving that in certain places both the people and the Welsh tongue have encroached more into England.

These things being thus presupposed, let us now descend to the particular description of Lloegr, or England. In which the country called Cantium of the Romans, of our countrymen Caint, of

---

[108] Enger [...] Herford] Enger, North-Rhine Westphalia, is the burial place of the Saxon leader Widukind (d. 808).

[109] There is some inconsistency in Llwyd's view of insular geography, in that the Anglo-Scottish border is deemed subject to change, whilst the Anglo-Welsh border is not.

Englishmen Kent, cometh first unto our view. From whence there is but a narrow cut over into France, to the haven Gessoriacus, which is now termed Boulogne, as S. Rhenanus[110] gathereth out of the ancient chart of warly descriptions. And not only Marcellinus, amongst the old writers, speaketh of the sea town of Boulogne in the life of Julian the Emperor, but also in his panegyric called 'Constantinus, the Son of Constantius', these are found:

820   Constantinus, the father being made Emperor, at his first coming, with an innumerable fleet of enemies, penned out the fierce ocean and environed the army, which lay upon the shore of the town Boulogne, etc.

Coenalis affirmeth the haven Gessoriacus is Cassel of Flanders – which town standing upon the top of a high hill, fourteen miles from the sea, sufficiently declareth the author's unskilfulness. And I take Iccius to be the same haven which now they term Caletum, for Calitium, Calais. But I cannot agree with those which make
830   Selusas of Flanders to be Iccius, being unlike that the Romans would have used so long a course by sea, when they might have passed over sooner and more commodiously from that place.

There were in Kent, in old time, three famous ports well known to the Romans: Doris, Rhutupis, and Lemanis. Doris undoubtedly is the same which both Englishmen and Britons, reserving the ancient name, at this day do call Dover. For we call water *dŵr*, or *dwfr*. And I am not ignorant that the Dovarians stoutly defend that their town heretofore was called Rutupium, and that Arviragus King of Britain builded there a noble castle. Yet I had rather give
840   credit to Antoninus who speaketh of both. And I suppose that to be Rutupium, which of the Englishmen is called Repcester,[111] nigh Sandwich, not far from the Isle of Thanet. For that island we call Ynys Rhuochym, as much to say Rutupina, whereof the shore deserved to be termed Rutupinum, and the Port Rutupis. Lemanis, or as some call it Linienus, is that river which is now called amongst the Englishmen Rother, and floweth into the ocean sea nigh Appledore. Moreover, besides these famous ports, are Rye

---

[110] S. Rhenanus] Beatus Rhenanus (1485-1547), humanist. Though 'Beatus' means blessed, Rhenanus was not a saint; T. appears to have misunderstood L.'s 'B. Rhenanus'.
[111] Repcester] Richborough

and Winchelsea, two towns, and farther within the main land Durobrevis and Durovernum. The same[112] Englishmen do call Canterbury, that is to say the court of the Kentishmen, and with us Caergant, and is chief metropolitan see of all England and Wales. The other is termed Rochester. But Antoninus placeth Vagniacum between London and Dorovernum, and between that and Durovernum, Durolernum, but what names they have at this day, I am altogether ignorant. Howbeit, it is manifest that these towns took their names of water, which is *dŵr* in British, and Durivern amongst us plainly signifieth water which floweth out of a place where alders grow;[113] whereby I am persuaded that the same town in times past thereof obtained his name.

But before I depart forth of Kent I must briefly touch that great wood whereof both British and English writers have spoken. The Britons call it Coed Andred, but the Englishmen Andredsweald. And Huntingdon affirmeth that it containeth in length one hundred and twenty miles and in breadth thirty miles, and that the worthy city called Caer Andred and Andredecester stood therein, which Dalla, King of the South Saxons, utterly overthrew, so that there remaineth no token nor rubbish thereof.[114] The Kentishmen and South Saxons to this day do call a place where wood hath been 'Walden', not knowing for all that whence the word is derived – when others, but falsely, call it Welden, others Wylden. For the English Saxons call a wood *walden*, as the Germans do now term a plain without trees *wolden*, as in these words 'Cottiswolden' and 'Porkewolden' it appeareth.

Next unto the Kentishmen, on the south side of the Thames, are those which in times past were the second kingdom of South Saxons, and were termed South Saxon, but is now divided into two shires, Southsex and Southtrey.[115] And I am of belief that Neomaguin[116] was their city, where Guildford now standeth. Chichester, the chiefest city of South Saxons, was called Caerceri in British.

After these come the Atrebates, which now are called the people of Berkshire, whose principal city in old time was called Calleva,

---

[112] The same] The latter
[113] Durivern [...] alders grow] W. 'Dŵr-y-wern' (water of the alder).
[114] According to Henry of Huntingdon's *Historia Anglorum,* Caer Andred was razed in 490 AD.
[115] Southsex and Southtrey] Sussex and Surrey
[116] Neomaguin] Noviomagus, now usually identified with Chichester.

but now Wallingford. Wherein I cannot consent to those which call Oxford Calleva, standing on the north shore of the Thames. There is also a village named Silchester, not far from Basing, which before time was called Caersegent, and Segontium of the Romans.[117] Antoninus also mentioneth Pontium, which appeareth now to be called Reading. The antique name of Spinae, which signifieth thorns, continueth to this day in the one side of Newbury, which is as much to say as New Court.[118]

From whence a good way off, upon the river Cunetio,[119] standeth a famous city called Cunetio by the Romans, but now Marlborough. Between these and the sea lie the Simeni, whose metropolitan or chief city is Venta, which in foretimes was a city of great renown, and of the Britons called Caerwynt, of the Englishmen Winchester. And at the sea there is the great port, called now Portsmouth, at whose mouth there standeth a city, called of old Caer Peris, but now Portchester. Also Tris Antonis, a haven, now Southampton, retaining the old name.

Over against these lieth the Isle of Wight, celebrated by the ancient Roman writers, and first subdued by Vespasian. The same is in length twenty miles and ten in breadth, in form like to an egg, in some places seven miles distant from the main shore, and in others but twain. It hath very rough and craggy cliffs; it is very plentiful of corn. The chiefest and only market town of all the island is Newport. There is also a castle called Caerbro,[120] that is to say, the tract for nets, expressing the British antiquity. The West Saxons, when they had driven away the Britons, added the same to their dominion, until Caedwalla, a Briton,[121] having slain Arwald, recovered it to himself. Englishmen call it the Wight, Britons term it *Gwydd*,[122] which in our tongue signifieth perspicuous or easy to be seen, as *gwyddgrug*, that is to say a perspicuous heap, *gwyddfa*, a perspicuous place (by which term the most highest mountain of

---

[117] Silchester in Hampshire, called Caer Segont by some medieval writers (not to be confused with Segontium in Caernarfonshire) is today accepted as the site of Calleva Atrebatum.
[118] **Marg.** 'Speenhamland nigh Newbury.'
[119] Cunetio] Kennet
[120] Caerbro] Carisbrooke Castle
[121] Caedwalla, a Briton] According to Bede, Caedwalla was descended of the royal house of the West Saxons; the name, however, is clearly Brythonic.
[122] *Gwydd*] W. 'presence'.

all Britain,[123] in Caernarfonshire, is called). The inhabitants of this island are wont to glory that their country is destitute of three great discommodities that are found in other countries, to wit foxes, begging friars, and lawyers. They are under the precinct and diocese of Southampton.

By the same seashore along follow the Severiani, called now the inhabitants of Wiltshire, whose chief city is Caer Severus, called also Caer Caradoc, and now by Englishmen Salisbury. Twixt these is St Ambrose Hill, celebrated by reason of the slaughter of the nobility of Britain there committed. Also Shaftesbury, known of old to the Britons by the name of Caerbaladin[124] and Caer Septon. At the west side of these lie the Durotriges, called of us Dŵr-gwyr, of the Englishmen Dorsetshiremen. From whence more westerly are the Damnonii, we call them at this day Dyfnaint, which signifieth deep and narrow valleys, and not of the Danes, as some affirm. These are called in English Devonshiremen; and they lie between two seas, the Severn and the British Ocean.[125] Their principal city is Isca, called also Augusta, before time Caer Yisc, of the water passing by, but now of the Englishmen, Exeter. Howbeit, I know well enough that some affirm that before it was called by the old Britons Pen-Uchel-Coed.[126]

Last of all cometh Cornavia, of the inhabitants and our countrymen called Cernico,[127] of Englishmen Cornwall. Here it is to be noted that the Saxons did thrust the relics of the ancient Britons into those straits. Who, because they used the British tongue, which the Saxons understood not, they termed them Cornwalas, that is to say Welshmen of Cornavia, or Cornwall, as they called also our countrymen Welsh Britons, after the German guise. This is the true etymology or cause of the name, and farewell to them which, pleasing themselves in the invention of the name, do call it 'Cornu Galliae', to say a horn of France, wherein Polydorus, as in other things also, uttereth his ignorance. As for mine opinion, very ancient books do confirm it, written in the Saxon tongue, and the name also whereby those which inhabit the

---

[123] Yr Wyddfa, the Welsh name of Mount Snowdon, signifies 'burial mound'.

[124] Caerbaladin] More commonly Caer Paladr; see *History of Cambria*, below, p. 155.

[125] British Ocean] English Channel

[126] Pen-Uchel-Coed] A high place with a wood; the name is more often associated by antiquaries with Lostwithiel, Cornwall.

[127] Cernico] The Cornish name for Cornwall is *Kernow*, in modern Welsh *Cernyw*.

country do usually call it. They speak the British language, and all their words almost are found like unto ours, but that they differ somedeal in construction of speech. The promontory of Cornavia, now Cornwall, is famous amongst our countrymen, commonly called Penrhyn Gwaed, that is to say, the promontory of blood, which I suppose to be called of Ptolomaeus Antivestaeum.[128] Beyond the Damnonii, or Devonshiremen, nigh the course of Severn, lieth sometime the region of Murotriges. We call it Gwlad yr Haf, Englishmen Somersetshire, where are many notable ancient places seen, as the mounts of Caermalet, otherwise called Camelot.[129]

There standeth also Iscalis, now Ilchester,[130] and the Isle of Avalonia, whose city is Venta, now Bristol, but in antique time the Britons called it Caer Oder yn Nant Badon, that is to say the City Odera in the Valley of Badon. Another town of the Belgae, with Ptolomaeus Aquae Calidae, that is of hot water, with Antoninus Aquae Solis, of water of the sun, the Britons call it Caerbadon, the Englishmen Bath, and is very renowned for wholesome baths of hot waters.[131] Of which thing I am a most certain witness. For whenas by the stroke of a horse which I had caught at Milan in Italy I was grievously pained with the sciatica continually the space of one whole year, and having assayed the help of many excellently learned physicians was nothing the better, I used these baths but only six days and was restored to my former health.

Between these and the Thames' head were the Dobuni, now Claudiani, whose chief town in old time was called Corinium, of the Britons Caer Cory, the Englishmen now term it Cicester.[132] And Claudia, commonly called Gloucester, a famous city standing upon Severn, the head of all the shire, I suppose not to have been known to the Romans, but was afterward (as Gildas reporteth) builded by Gloui a Briton, who after that the Romans were driven thence reigned there – and not so named by Claudius Caesar, as hereafter shall be shown. In the same shire also standeth Malmesbury, called before time Caer Bladon. These shires do

---

[128] Antivestaeum] Land's End
[129] Camelot] Llwyd follows Leland in linking the hillfort of Cadbury, near the villages of West and Queen Camel, with Camelot.
[130] Ilchester, Roman Lindinis, is not today identified with the Iscalis mentioned by Ptolemy.
[131] **Marg.** 'Commendation of the baths at Bath.'
[132] Cicester] Cirencester

make the third kingdom of Saxons in Britain, which they call West Saxons, whose king was Egbert, who, having subdued all the other, first of the Germans[133] obtained the monarchy of Lloegr.

Thus having described the countries that lie on the south side of the Thames, let us now come to the other in order. And first over against Kent, on the other side of the Thames, lie the Trinobantes, whose prince was Mandubracius, or as other write Androgorius; our countrymen call him Afarwy. The same sent for Caesar into Britain, and when he was come assisted him with his power, and followed him into Italy and Thessaly. Their chief city was builded by Brutus,[134] and was called Troy Newydd, that is to say New Troy; howbeit there be some which call it Trenovantum, because *Tre* signifieth in British a town. But afterward it was called of Belus,[135] which dwelt there, Dinas Beli, that is to say Belinus's Palace or Court. Last of all, of Lud, brother to Caswallan, which wonderfully adorned it with beautiful buildings, it began to be called Caerlud, and Llundain, that is to say Lud's City, and also London. And I am not ignorant how Polydorus seeketh Trinovantum about Northampton, but the authority of sacred antiquity is of more force with me than any bare conjecture of a strange° and unknown person. We yield these names to London, although Ptolomaeus lay them nearer to the Thames, and the negligence of the transcribers hath called London a city of Kent. And Marius Niger, afterward, 'the other part of the great bosom,[136] for the other side the Trinobantes do hold, into the middle whereof the River Thames doth flow'.

Polydorus Vergilius the Urbinate[137] goeth about to prove out of Tacitus by arguments of little force that the Trinobantes are inland people, when as his reasons seem to prove the contrary. For whereas he sayeth, 'if the Trinobantes had been nigh London, Suetonius should have had no safe passage thither' – nay rather, Polydorus, if it had been in the midst of the island, it had been harder for him to have come to London through the thickest of his enemies, for his way lay through them from the Isle of Anglesey, from whence he came. Wherefore it is more likely that the

---

[133] Germans] Anglo-Saxons
[134] **Marg.** 'The foundation of London.'
[135] Belus] Belinus, legendary king of Britain; see below, pp. 101-102.
[136] bosom] 'sinus' (curve).
[137] Urbinate] native of Urbino; Llwyd lays consistent stress on Polydore's foreign origins.

Trinobantes were inhabitants of Essex, as all saving a few obscure and unknown writers do affirm – who[138] suppose that with the Iceni their neighbours, which now be the people of Norfolk and Nordovolke,[139] they had conspired the death of the Romans, and had spoiled with fire and sword all that ever was in their way unto Verulam, slaying threescore and ten thousand Romans, and were returned back again safe and sound before Suetonius coming, as Tacitus avoucheth.[140] And that their rage extended not unto London, the cause was, as the same author reporteth, for that London was a colony of the Romans, and a great mart city of theirs, famous for plenty of travellers which resorted thither for traffic of merchandise, abounding with victual, and stoutly defenced with munition and garrisons against all adventures, as all men do know. Hereby it appeareth how weak Polydorus's arguments be, especially who so well knoweth that part of England, and that London was the city Trinovantum, which was afterward called Augusta, as Marcellinus reporteth.

With these reasons being sufficiently instructed, I say that the Trinobantes inhabited that part of Britain which after the coming of Saxons made up their fourth kingdom, which they called East Saxons, and another called Middle Saxons, whose principal city is London at this day, which sometime was under the kings of the Mercii, or March. Ptolomaeus mentioneth another besides this city Trinovantum, called Camudolanum, which I take to be all one with Camulodunum, as I judge by reading Roman histories (although Ptolomaeus speaketh of Camulodunum), for it stood not far from the Thames, and was by Claudius appointed the first colony of the Romans – and not near the Brigantes, as Polydorus, much less in Scotland, as Boethius dreameth.[141] And for the more plainness hereof, I think it good to bring forth the words of Dion, who had been sometime consul:

> Claudius, after that he had received the message, forthwith committed the matters appertaining to the city and the soldiers to Vitellius his colleague (whose consulship, as also his own, he

---

[138] who] That is, the majority of authors.

[139] Nordovolke] L. 'Nordovolcae', apparently a synonym for Norfolk.

[140] This refers to the revolt of Boadicea, discussed below pp. 132, 136.

[141] As William Camden would remark of Camulodunum, 'How strangely have some persons lost themselves in the search after this city!' (*Britain*, p. 416).

had prorogued for six months longer); himself departed from Rome to Ostia, where he took ship and arrived at Massilia, and taking the residue of his journey partly by land and partly by water, came to the ocean and passed over into Britain, and came to his army which lay by the Thames, looking for him. Whom when he had received in charge, he went over the water with certain barbarians which drew to him at his coming. He spread his banners, fought, and obtained the victory, and won Camulodunum, the regal seat of Cynobellinus, and took many prisoners, partly by force, and partly by yielding.

Hereby it appeareth evidently that Camulodunum standeth not far from the Thames, in which place Ptolomaeus placeth Camudolanum.

And I suppose that this was the colony of Claudius Caesar, famous for the church, which they call now Colchester, the old name being made (as I think) by joining the water and the church together – a common custom among the Britons, as Henllan, that is an old church, Llanelwy, a church standing upon the river Elwy or the Church Elwy, which the Englishmen and bishops nowadays call (but not well) the See of St Asaph. Besides an infinite number mo, whereby I am persuaded that those places which in Latin begin or end in these terminations, *Lan* or *Lam*, were of old so termed of churches in the British tongue. Moreover, out of this place of Dion it is gathered how much a man without shame that Polydorus Vergilius is,[142] who doubteth not to affirm that Claudius Caesar vanquished the Britons without any battle, and most impudently calleth them dastards,[143] whom Caesar himself, Tacitus, Dion, and Herodian term by these names: 'most warlike', 'cruel', 'bloodthirsty', 'impatient both of bondage and injuries'. But an infamous baggage groom, full fraught with envy and hatred, what dareth he not do or say? I omit his schoolmaster Boethius who, besides these lies, speaketh of a mighty war which Claudius made upon the people of the Orcades, affirming the same to be true, too too impudently. For thou mayst easily judge (good reader) how much land and sea the Roman Emperor with a great army could march over in sixteen days only, during which time he abode in

---

[142] **Marg.** 'Polydorus reproved.'

[143] Polydore had drawn pointed attention to Gildas's complaint that the Britons were neither courageous in war nor faithful in peace.

Britain, when Tacitus also, a most faithful writer, affirmeth that in the first years of Agricola the island of Britain was known, and the isles called Orcades were then unknown, but first found out and subdued by him. This Dion testifieth to be true in the *Life of Titus the Emperor*, neither speaketh Suetonius against it, where he sayeth that Claudius tarried in Britain but a very few days. Howbeit Eutropius, and after him Orosius, seem to think otherwise, not knowing exactly how far distant the Orcades be from Kent. But since reason and truth certainly persuade us to the contrary, let us stick unto them, as unto two most faithful guides, neglecting the judgement of Polydorus, with his Hector.

Next to the Trinobantes were the Iceni, whom I suppose to have inhabited that region which maketh the fifth kingdom of Germans, which is the East Englishmen, and their city Venta, which now of the Englishmen is called Norwich. And I am privy also that there are thought to be other Iceni in the West, but I think it more probable that these Iceni are put for Tigeni, of whom I will speak hereafter. And the kingdom of East Englishmen comprehended not only the Iceni but also Cambridgeshire, whose chief city in old time the Britons called Caergrawnt, the Englishmen Grantchester, of the water that passeth by, but now corruptly is commonly called Cambridge, and is a noble university, wherein flourisheth all good learning. Not far off is the Isle of Willows,[144] not of Eels as some have written. For *helig* in the British tongue signifieth willow trees, wherewith those fens do abound. All these in foretimes were called Girvii.[145] Joining to these are the Parisi, whose chief city Petuaria[146] is now begun to be called Peterborough.

Beyond the Midland Saxons, westward, were the Catuvellauni, now Hertfordshiremen and Buckinghamshiremen on the hill, whose cities are Salinae and Verulamium, whereof this last took name of a river Wer, for before time it was called in British Gwerllan that is to say, a church standing upon the River Ver, afterward Caer Municip, because it was a *municipium*, or incorporate town belonging to the Romans; Englishmen term it Verlamcester and Watlingchester. This city was destroyed through the rage of the Saxons, howbeit there remain the tokens and

---

[144] Isle of Willows] Ely
[145] Girvii] The Gyrwas, Anglo-Saxon inhabitants of the Fens.
[146] Petuaria] Not Peterborough in Cambridgeshire, but Brough-on-Humber, Yorkshire, almost 100 miles further north.

foundations of the walls to this day, near to St Albans Church on the other side of the water. But whereas some do think that the Thames sometime ran that way, it is to be laughed at. Howbeit, it is certain, that there was a great standing water hard by the city walls, where now are pleasant flourishing meadows in which, as I am informed, there was an anchor of a ship found of late,[147] whereby, and also by the corrupt copy of Gildas, that conjecture is risen.

After these come the Oxfordshiremen, on the north side of the Thames, whose city is called by Englishmen Oxenford. Our countrymen term it Rhydychen, that is to say, the Ford of Oxen, but what name it had in old time, it is altogether unknown. Yet some affirm that it is Caer Vortigern,[148] that is, Vortigern's City, and by him builded, whereto I cannot agree. For Gildas writeth that the same city was builded in the west part of the island, and I think it be in the kingdom of Wales, being called now after his name Gwrtheyrn.[149] Our friend Master Leland the antiquary earnestly defendeth that it should be called Ouseford, that is to say the Ford of Isis, against whom (as one having very well deserved of the Britons, and much exercised in ancient histories) I dare not contend. For it is certain that it standeth upon Isis, and that tract of time corrupteth the names of many places it is also evident. But whatsoever name it had at the beginning, it hath a very beautiful and healthsome situation, and a country which ministereth all things necessary abundantly, and a most famous school of all good learning, as all do confess which have seen the other universities of Europe.[150] Not far from this city stood Caer Dor, so called of the Romans, a city not unknown to the Englishmen, a bishop's see now called Dorchester, whereas the Thame dischargeth himself into Isis, from whence the name of *Tamesis*, the Thames, proceedeth.

Towards the north be the Buckinghamshiremen, and beneath them the Bedfordshiremen, and more northerly the Huntingdonshiremen, whose ancient names are not known. After

---

[147] an anchor [...] late] Llwyd may refer to Matthew Paris's account of excavations at St Albans in the eleventh century, led by the abbot Ealdred, in which rusty anchors and seashells were unearthed. If so, it is something of a stretch to refer to the discovery as having taken place 'nuper' (of late).
[148] Vortigern] Semi-legendary king of the fifth century AD, held responsible for first inviting the Saxons to Britain.
[149] Gwrtheyrn] Gwrtheyrnion, Powys, associated with Vortigern in Nennius's *Historia Brittonum*.
[150] **Marg.** 'A worthy commendation of Oxford.'

these are the Lincolnshiremen, of old Coritani, so far as the river Trent. The Britons in old time called it Caer Lwytgoed, the Romans Lindum, the Englishmen Lindecolyn, and at this day Lincoln. Notwithstanding, afterward, the Normans called it corruptly Nychol, as I have many times noted in ancient charters and records of the earls thereof written in the French tongue, and all that province was called Lyndesey. Next unto these at Trent be the Leicestershiremen, so called of Leicester, which in old time were called Caerbier.[151] At the south appear the Northamptonshiremen, so called of the River Avon which cometh along by the town; for *afon* in British signifieth a river, and the Saxons hearing the Britons so term rivers supposed that it had been the proper names thereof, whereby it came to pass that many notable rivers in England were called by that name. After these, at the west, follow the Warwickshiremen, whose principal city Caer Wythelin was founded by Guthelinus, a King of Britain; afterward of the Roman legions which went no farther, Caerleon, lastly of a noble Briton, which beautified it with many fair buildings, Caer Gwayr, and of the Englishmen is called Warwick.

Next after these are the Staffordshiremen, amongst whom is Lichfield, a bishop's see, that is to say, the Field of Dead Folk. For the northern Englishmen call death 'lich', and the unlucky night ravens, 'lich-owls'. Some affirm that here, not in Legancester,[152] Etheldred King of Northumberland most cruelly slew two thousand monks of the famous monastery of Bangor, men excellently learned, and such as (contrary to the custom of others) got their living with travail of their own hands. Which bloody war he would never have begun, had it not been at the motion of that bloodthirsty monk whom they call Augustine.[153] The cause was for that in some points they seemed to disagree from the Church of Rome, and refused to be under the jurisdiction of the Archbishop of Canterbury, having already of their own the Archbishop of Legion.[154] This was the charity and religion of that man, to make away such good and godly men as could not abide his intolerable

---

[151] Caerbier] L. 'Caerbeir'. Probably an error for Caer Leir; Leicester was said to have been founded by King Lear.
[152] Legancester] Chester
[153] **Marg.** 'An horrible fact of Augustine's the monk's.'
[154] Legion] Caerlleon-on-Usk

pride. But touching these matters, God willing, we will speak in another place.[155]

On the other side of Warwickshire are the Worcestershiremen, next to the Dobani. Their city, Vigornia, was of old time called of the Romans Brangonia, of the Britons to this day Caerwrangon, and of the Englishmen is commonly called Worcester, and is builded at the east side of Severn. Where is to be noted, that all the greater cities that lie upon the east shore of the rivers Severn and Dee were builded to resist the irruptions of the Britons into Lloegr, that is England. Like as the Romans erected many notable cities on the west shore of the Rhine, to restrain the forcible invasions of the Germans into France.

Adjoining unto these are the Shropshiremen, whose ancient city is Viroconium, called afterward of the Englishmen Wrekecestre, and short Wroxeter, all razed down to the ground in the Saxon war; from whose relics four miles off lieth Salopia, the head city of all the shire, notable for two bridges, and almost compassed with the Severn. The same in old time was called Pengwern, that is to say, the head of a place where alders grow, and was the seat of the kings of Powys, from whence the English name Shrewsbury is derived – although I remember that in ancient records I read it termed Salopsbury, and Slopesbury. Our countrymen call it Amwythig at this day. Next after these are the Devani, or Cheshiremen upon the River Dee, where as be certain wells out of whose liquor very good and pure white salt is sodden.

Besides the city itself, famous for the Roman monuments therein, which by reason that the Roman legions wintered there is called by the Britons at this day Caerlleon-ar-Dyfrdwy, that is to say, the City of Legions upon the River Dee (for difference sake betwixt that and another of that name upon the River Osca). It appeareth out of Antoninus that the same in times past was called in Latin Deva, of the river which we term Dyfrdwy, to say, the Water of Dee. The Englishmen call it Legancester, and afterward clipping the name shorter called it Chester, and the citizens do glory that they have the body of Henry IV Emperor, whom they affirm to have yielded up the Empire, and have betaken himself to

---

[155] But touching [...] another place] Augustine's crimes are further detailed on pp. 118-19.

a hermit's life. And so are they likewise persuaded of Harold, who was the last king of the Danish blood.¹⁵⁶

More east from these are the Dorventani, now Derbyshiremen, so termed of their chief city Dwrgwent, which is as much to say as White Water. All these shires and convents,° with a great part of Wales, as far as the renowned ditch of King Offa (of which we will speak hereafter), made up the sixth kingdom of English Saxons in Britain, which of the river Mersey was called the kingdom of Mercia, or March.¹⁵⁷

Here now I cannot sufficiently marvel how Wolfgangus Lazius, a man excellently learned and very well-deserved of all that be studious of antiquity, in his great work *Of the Migration of Nations*, should be so much deceived as to say that the Mertii, or people of March, were Marcomanni, and that their kings Penda, Offa, with all the rest, reigned in the lower Germany. Being most evident in all histories that there was never any such kingdom there, and that these kings and peoples whom he affirmeth to have dwelled in Germany, inhabited that country of Britain which we now describe. Likewise, while he endeavoureth to link together the descents and pedigrees of the Norman blood of the kings of England, he handleth them so confusedly, and so far besides truth, that it seemeth he never read either the names, or order, or deeds of the kings; but it is rather likely that he learned them by hearsay of some babbling unlearned fool, that had no regard of his good fame or honesty. As another hath done of late days, a man famously learned in the mathematics, in his geographical chart of this island.¹⁵⁸ And besides these, Hieronymus Ruscellus, in his *Ptolomaeus* lately printed at Venice, while he goeth about to set forth new names correspondent to the old, confoundeth places an hundred miles distant one from another, namely Colchester and Winchester.¹⁵⁹ Neither in other places are his guesses anything more certain, wherefore I exhort men not to trust him in this behalf.

---

¹⁵⁶ Henry IV, Holy Roman Emperor (d. 1106), is buried at Speyer. The burial place of Harold Godwinson (d. 1066), usually considered the last Anglo-Saxon rather than the last Danish king, is unknown. Llwyd's source for both these traditions is Gerald of Wales, *Itinerarium Cambriae*.

¹⁵⁷ of the river Mersey [...] Mercia, or March] The name of Mercia is more often considered to derive from the Old English *mearc*, meaning 'border' or 'marches'.

¹⁵⁸ As another [...] chart of this island] Gerard Mercator produced his wall map of the British Isles in 1564.

¹⁵⁹ **Marg.** 'A foule error.'

There remaineth the seventh and last kingdom of Saxons in England, which they termed Nordan Humbrorum, because it standeth at the north coast of Humber. The same was afterward divided into two kingdoms, of the Deirans and Bernicians. The kingdom of Deira contained all the country from Humber and Trent to the River Tyssa.[160] Bernicia reached from Tyssa to the Scottish Sea, which they call now *Fyrthew*;[161] the Britons term this same Brennich, and the other Deifr. The inhabitants of this region, especially southward, are called Snotingomenses, but now most commonly Nottinghamshiremen. Next unto these are Yorkshiremen, who of the Romans were called Brigantes, of whom Tacitus writeth thus:

> Petilius Cerealis fought many battles, whereof some were not unbloody, against the city of the Brigantes, which is reported to be the place of resort to the whole populous province, and obtained a great part of the Brigantes, either by victory, or else by fight.[162]

All these, the lying champion of the Scottish name, Hector Boethius, sticketh not to put into his Gallovidia,[163] and to prove the same by arguments gathered out of Ptolomaeus and Tacitus.

But how much Ptolomaeus was deceived, trusting to the report of others in describing the length and breadth of places in Britain (for he writeth that Scotland lieth forth to the east, and that the farthest promontory thereof is eight degrees more easterly than any place of England, which in this parallel do make about 240 miles, which is altogether untrue, seeing England standeth more to the east than Scotland doth), is as clear as daylight to all those that have tasted of cosmography. But Ptolomaeus is to be pardoned,[164] being an Egyptian born, and excellently well learned in mathematics, who hath done the best he could – but not foolish and impudent Boethius, born and brought up no farther off than Scotland. He speaketh thus of Tacitus, that he, being a grave author, affirmeth that the Brigantes were a Spanish brood dwelling

---

[160] Tyssa] Tees
[161] *Fyrthew*] the Firth of Forth
[162] Tacitus, *Agricola*, 17.
[163] Gallovidia] Galloway
[164] **Marg**. 'Ptolomaeus excused.'

in a far corner of Britain, farther than any durst avouch that at his time the Britons had passed. O impudent face, whereabout did Tacitus speak thus of the Brigantes?

He seemeth to derive the Siluri by a colour from the Spanish brood, because they lie over against Spain – Gallovidia is farther from Spain then any region of England or Wales. And that in Tacitus's time the Brigantes were first known to the Romans, I confess it, but he findeth it not in Tacitus, and – not mindful of himself, as it behoveth a liar to be – he calleth not to remembrance that he wrote in another place that Claudius the Emperor adjoined also unto his empire the Orcades, which lie beyond Scotland. But let us bid faithless Hector *adieu*, and let us now also see what the ancient writers have written of the Brigantes. Ptolomaeus reciteth the cities of Brigantes: Eboracum, Epiacum, Calatum, Bimonium, Caturactonium, Rhigodunum, Isurium, Olicana, with others. All men know that Eboracum is that city which the Britons call *Caer Efrog*, the Englishmen Everwyke, and now short York. Of the rest we do but conjecture, as Bimonium to be Bincester; Calatum (which Antoninus and Bede call Calcaria) to be Helicaster, now Tadcaster; Rhigodunum, Ripon; and Olicana, Halifax; and that Isurium is called Aldborough. There was never any man that dreamed that these cities were in Scotland. But Antoninus ascribeth them to the Brigantes, and placeth them in the way which leadeth to London from the Valley Praetorium,[165] for that there was a valley from the river Solvathianus° to the mouth of Tyne, all do know. I conclude, therefore, that it is impossible that the Brigantes were ever in Scotland. In so much that the remembrance of this name remaineth until this day amongst us. For when we see any man not duly obeying laws and commandments, him we call *Chwarae Brigans*, that is to say, one that playeth the Brigant, and like as they were rebels against the people of Rome, so doth he contemn the laws of magistrates and of elders. And surely I am of belief that all Deira before time was called Brigantia.

Ptolomaeus placeth the Venicones and Taexali between the Rivers Tyne and Tweed. This country alone now retaineth the name of Northumberland, when all the region before time, from that river to the Scottish Sea, was called by that name. For there is no river in all Britain that hath the name of Humber, but only that

---

[165] Valley Praetorium] The *vallum* or earthen rampart associated with Hadrian's Wall.

water into whom many notable streams do flow. Whereby our friend Master Leland, not without good cause, supposed that the same should be called Aber, which among the Britons signifieth an arm of the sea, either swiftness or fall of any water either into the sea (as Aberconwy, Aberteifi, Abertawe, that is to say, the mouth of Conwy, Tibius, and Tobius) or into some great river (as Aberhodni,[166] Abergavenny, to say the fall of Hodnus and Gevenus into Osca). Moreover, we call mouths, and entrances of rivers *Aber*, without adding anything more thereto, as in Caernarfonshire between Canovium[167] and Banchorium,[168] in the same manner, so that I think *aber* to signify as much as *aestus* doth, which is the rage, fall, or force of water, as is most agreeable with Ptolomaeus. Above these, were the Damnii,[169] whose chief city Antoninus maketh Vanduara to be, not far from the Valley Ofdam,[170] whereby I conjecture that they be those which we call now Westmorlandshiremen.

The Selgovii and Otadeni in times past inhabited Cumberland. At the very brim of the valley standeth a most ancient city; Ptolomaeus calleth it Leucopibia, Antoninus, Luguballia, the Britons and Englishmen term it Caer Luel,[171] and it standeth in the frontiers of the Novantes. Not far from this city, as Malmsburiensis reporteth, there was a stone found with this inscription: 'In token of Marius victory'. Which token of triumph I suppose to have been erected by Meurigus (whom some of the Romans have termed more aptly Arviragus, othersome Marius) in token that the Redshanks were there vanquished, Rodericus being their king, which at that season, as the Saxons did, exercised piracy in our seas, until at length one part of them settled in Albania and other in France. And it is well known that these countries, together with Gallovidia, so far as the River Cluda,[172] unto the year of Our Lord 870 were in the Britons' possession, at what time being by the Scots, Danes, and Englishmen disquieted with many battles, and in

---

[166] Aberhodni] Aberhonddu, or Brecon
[167] Canovium] Roman fort in the Conwy valley
[168] Banchorium] Bangor
[169] Damnii] Also known as the Damnonii.
[170] Valley Ofdam] L. 'vallo of dā'; here, as on p. 84 below, 'vallo' should rather be 'rampart' or 'entrenchment', and the reference is to Hadrian's Wall.
[171] Caer Luel] Carlisle
[172] Cluda] Here, the River Clyde (Llwyd will also use 'Cluda' to refer to the Clwyd in Wales).

the end their King Constantinus slain at Lochmaba in Anandra, they were enforced to return into Wales to their countrymen; and driving away the English Saxons, forcibly challenged to themselves the greater part of the country which lieth twixt Conwy and the water of Dee, which they possessed, and there appointed a kingdom, which of the river Cluda, on whose shore they dwelt, is of our countrymen called Ystrad Clwyd, of Marianus Scotus corruptly Streadiylead of the Wallanes. They had many conflicts against the kings of England, as the same author reporteth, until at length their last king dying at Rome they submitted themselves to the princes of Gwynedd. This Marianus, the chiefest historiographer of his time, one of late hath caused to set forth in print, being imperfect and lacking the better part, of set purpose (as himself confesseth) because of the ambiguity of the British History.[173] In like manner Sleidan, while he turneth his abridgement of Froissart into Latin,[174] being too too much partial to the Frenchmen, either overpasseth with silence the most noble and valiant deeds of the Englishmen or, varying from his author, reporteth them otherwise than Froissart hath written. Wherefore, me seemeth that the saying of Martial the poet very well agreeth with them:

> That which thou now dost turn,
> O Fidentine, the book is mine.
> But when thou turnest him ill,
> then he begins for to be thine.[175]

But this much by the way.

The last of the Northumberlandshiremen (and almost of all Lloegr) follow the inhabitants of Lancashire to be entreated of, whom the river called of the Englishmen Mersey divideth from the Kingdom of March, of whom the kingdom of March in England was so called. It is soon proved out of Ptolomaeus that these were called Ordovici in old time. 'For the Ordovici,' sayeth he, 'lie more south-west than the Brigantes do.' Since, therefore, that Yorkshire

---

[173] The universal chronicle of Marianus Scotus (d. 1082/83) was printed at Basel in 1559.
[174] In like manner Sleidan [...] Latin] Johann Sleiden's Latin epitome of Froissart, published in 1537.
[175] Martial, *Epigrams*, I.38.

is the kingdom of Brigantes, in vain with Boethius we seek them in Scotland, and much more in Norfolk with Polydorus. Wherefore, renouncing these fables, for my part I am persuaded that the Ordovici are not only the Lancashiremen, but also the Devani, or Cheshiremen and Shropshiremen, being recounted of Tacitus for a great city. In this place I call a 'city', as Caesar doth, a whole convent, or kingdom. For look how many cities there are, so many kingdoms in old time were in Britain, which severally° waging battle against the Romans were all the sooner overcome. Amongst the cities of these kingdoms, Ptolomaeus reciteth Mediolanum, called now Lancaster. Mancunium, as appeareth out of Antoninus, is called Manchester. Their king in times past was Caratacus, whose fame was known above the skies, who the space of nine continual years very much molested the Romans with war, at length was taken by treason of a woman[176] and led to Rome in triumph. And Claudius the Emperor deserved no less praise for vanquishing Caratacus than did Scipio for Syphax, or Lucius Paulus for Perseus, as Tacitus writeth, two most puissant kings brought home in show to the people of Rome.

And here can I not marvel enough what came in mind to that Boethius – not the Trojan but the Scot,[177] for:

Alas, what one was he, how far from that same Hector? Sore
He changed was, that in Achilles' spoils came home before – [178]

impudently to affirm that he[179] was a Scot, seeing that there was no such nation at that time in the world! But if there were, it was so enfolded in darkness that it was unknown to the Romans and Britons; or, as Haymo Armenius writeth of a certain nation, it had so bleared the eyes of all peoples and countries, that the Scots were invisibly conversant between the Romans and Britons. Polydorus

---

[176] treason of a woman] Caratacus was betrayed by Cartimandua, Queen of the Brigantes (see below, p. 82), an event portayed on the early modern stage in R. A.'s *The Valiant Welshman* (1612)

[177] not the Trojan but the Scot] T. spoils L.'s joke; the intended play is upon the chronicler's first name of Hector, not the surname Boethius.

[178] Virgil, *Aeneid*, Book 2, ll. 274-75. Llwyd alters the Latin text slightly, giving the phrase 'quantum diversus ab illo / Hectore' (how different from that Hector) in place of Virgil's 'quantum mutatus ab illo / Hectore' (how changed from that Hector). This tweaking of the text is lost in Twyne's translation. Virgil, *Opera*, ed. by R. A. B. Mynors (Oxford: Clarendon Press, 1969).

[179] he] Caratacus

1430 also writeth that he was king of the Ordulacae, when neither Tacitus nor Ptolomaeus mentioneth the same, but of the Ordovici. And Tacitus reporteth that he was not only governor of the Ordovici, but also of the Siluri.[180] Which Siluri dwelled not in Scotland, but in South Wales, as in another place it shall be proved more plainly.

And I remember very well that a few years ago, when I was in the frontiers of Shropshire with others, about certain business of my Lord's (the right honourable Earl of Arundel), where some part of his inheritance lieth, I chanced to fall into the view of a place 1440 exceedingly well fortified both by nature and art.[181] The situation whereof was upon the top of a high hill, environed with a triple ditch of great depth. There were three gates, not directly but ashosh[182] the one against the other, and on three sides steep headlong places, and compassed with two rivers, on the left hand with Colun, or Clun, on the right with Temis, which our countrymen call Tefeidiad, and accessible but on the one side thereof. These things when I beheld, I understood by the inhabitants that this place was called Caer Caradoc, that is to say the City Caradoc, and that there have been many fierce battles 1450 fought there against a certain king called Caradoc, who at last was vanquished and taken of his enemies. For our countrymen call not only walled cities and towns, but also all manner places which are entrenched and walled, by the name Caer, as I will prove afterward by example of many and divers places of Wales. Wherefore, when I perceived that this place was within the confines of the Siluri and the Ordovici (for it is scarce two miles distant from Colun, or Clun Castle, which is the patrimony and inheritance of the most noble and ancient family of Fitzalans in England), and that it so agreed in all points with the description of Tacitus that nothing could be 1460 wanting, I dare boldly affirm that this is the very selfsame place in which Ostorius contended with Caratacus in battle, and vanquished him – from whence flying, and putting himself in trust to the faith and credit of Cartimandua, the queen of Brigantes, was by her betrayed.

---

[180] **Marg**. 'Ann. lib. 12.'
[181] Llwyd describes the late Bronze Age or Iron Age hillfort of Caer Caradoc, Church Stretton, Shropshire.
[182] ashosh] The word seems to be otherwise unknown, but it is clear enough what Twyne means by 'a shoshe', in translation of Llwyd's 'obliquo'.

Moreover, that name of Caratacus is at this day so peculiar to the Welshmen that many princes and noblemen are called by that name. Amongst whom, at that time Trahernus the son of Caradoc ruled North Wales,[183] Fleanchus (as the Scots say) son to Banguho, after that king Macabaeus[184] had slain his father, by flight escaped into Wales, on whose daughter by secret access (but unfortunate and miserable to the parents) he begat Walter, who was the first of the Stuarts in Scotland that was of renown – from whom, unto this day, the kings of Scotland do vaunt themselves to have descended.[185] But I suppose it more likely that he whom they report to be the nephew of Trahernus the Scot,[186] born of his daughter, and his father a Scot in North Wales (a thing much disagreeing from the truth), rather to be one of Trahernus's own children, which by Griffin son unto Cynan,[187] together with Caradoc, Griffin, and Maelor Rhiwallon's sons, was vanquished and slain. And that this Walter escaped by flight into Scotland, and there attained to great honour. And this can be no great fraud or disgracing to the name of the Stuarts, that they are descended from the blood of the most noble and antique British kings, from which also most honourable family the same Owen Tudor, grandfather to King Henry the Seventh of that name, king of England, lineally descended by the father's side, as we will declare in our description

---

[183] Trahernus [...] North Wales] Trahaearn ap Caradog (d. 1081), ruler of Gwynedd.
[184] Fleanchus [...] Banguho [...] Macabaeus] Shakespeare's Fleance, Banquo, Macbeth.
[185] Boece's account, in John Bellenden's 1536 translation, is as follows: 'Fleance, escaping in this wise, and seeing new watching laid for his slaughter, fled in Wales; where he was pleasantly received by the prince thereof, and made so familiar with the prince's daughter, that he made her with child. The Prince of Wales, finding his daughter deflowered, pursued this Fleance with such hatred, that he finally slew him; and held his daughter in most shameful servitude, because she consented to her defloration with uncouth blood. At last, she was delivered of a son named Walter, who within a few years became a valiant and lusty man.' (Though raised in low estate, Walter eventually escapes to Scotland, where he rises to become steward of the realm.)
[186] whom they report to be the nephew of Trahernus the Scot] A muddled translation of L. 'quem Scoti Traherni esse nepotem [...] affirmant' (whom the Scots report to be the grandson of Trahernus).
[187] Caradoc, Griffin, and Maelor Rhiwallon's sons] 'Caradoco Gruffino & Meylerio Rywallonis filiis' (Caradoc ap Gruffydd and Meilyr ap Rhiwallon). Those named, allies of Trahaearn ap Caradog, fell with him at the Battle of Mynydd Carn (1081), where Gruffydd ap Cynan attained the rule of Gwynedd.

of Wales (and not from any mean or base degree, as false and impudent Meyerus, a Fleming, sticketh not to affirm).

The Description of Scotland

Now that we have wandered over all England, called Lloegr, let us next in order proceed to the second region of Britain, which of our countrymen is called Albania, of the inhabitants Scotland. This same in old time was of the Romans called the Second Britain. For Sextus Rufus reciteth five provinces of Britain:

I. *Maxima Caesariensis*, which I do take to be that part of Britain which by Julius Caesar was made tributary to the Romans, to wit Kent, the Kingdom of South Saxons, and the Region of Atrebates.
II. The second is *Flavia*, which by like conjecture being thereto moved, I suppose to be that which by Vespasian (who descended of the family Flavia) was by him set upon and subdued, that is to say, the Isle of Wight, which afterward was made part of the West Saxons' kingdom.
III. The third I judge to have been termed by the name of the First Britain, which lieth forth from the Thames to the valley or trench.[188]
IV. The fourth, being the Less and the Second Britain, compriseth Scotland.
V. It remaineth then of necessity that Wales be contained under the name of *Valentia*, which maketh up the fifth province. (Howbeit Ammianus writeth that that province which by Theodosius, captain to Valentinian, was taken, when he had driven thence the Redshanks and Scots, was then of the Emperor's name called *Valentia*.)[189]

And that the Britons inhabited these provinces, both our own and the Roman writers have left in memory. Neither was there ever any writer of name that made mention either of Scots or Redshanks

---

[188] valley or trench] As above, referring to the *vallum* associated with Hadrian's Wall.
[189] The five provinces have been set out as a numbered list in this edition, for the sake of clarity.

before Vespasian's time, about the year of Our Lord's incarnation threescore and twelve, at what time Meurigus (or Mavus,[190] or Arviragus) reigned in Britain. For our chronicles do report of a nation which lived by piracy and roving on the sea coming forth of Suevia° or Norway, having one Rhythercus to their captain, and landed in Albania, wasting all the country with robbing and spoiling so far as Caer Luel, where he was discomfited and slain by Meurigus, and a great many of his men also, and those which escaped fled to their ships and so conveyed themselves into the Orcades and the isles of Scotland, where they quietly abode a great while.

They call them Phichtiaid, that is to say Phichtiani in their mother tongue, and so are they likewise called in the Scottish and in their own tongue. Wherefore it is not likely that they were so called of the Romans for painting of their bodies, since they were called by that name before that they were ever known to the Latins.[191] Neither were they these, but the Britons, of whom Caesar and others do report that they were wont to paint their bodies blue with woad, that they might appear the more terrible to their enemies. And with us at this day, which seemeth to argue antiquity, blue colour is called *glas*, by which name also that herb (not altogether unlike a plantain, very well known now to merchants) is called. Besides all this, the Romans which first made mention of this people termed them not Picti, but Pictones.

These, as I have said before, after that they had taken heart of grass[192] and were grown to some power, out of these islands in their little leathern boats (such as our fishermen do use nowadays) along Scotland were want to rob and spoil shepherds and husbandmen. Until that about the year of Our Lord 290, when the Romans and Britons were both encumbered with civil wars for the purple robe (which Carausius wore, and after him Allectus), they entered generally into Cathanesia° and Caledonia, and driving thence the British shepherds and herdsmen, and calling unto them the Gatheli out of Ireland, which are now called the Scots, were so bold as to provoke the Britons in open war. For the Scots come of

---

[190] Mavus] L. 'Mavo'; T. 'Maus'.
[191] The Latin *Picti*, painted ones, is a probable origin of the name of the Picts.
[192] taken heart of grass] The phrase may play on the proverb 'take heart of grace'.

the Irish brood,[193] as they themselves and others do know very well, and are termed amongst our countrymen by the same name, to wit *Gwyddel*, which as their own histories do testify was the most ancient name of that nation. And that the same nation came forth of Cantabria, now Biscaya, and passed over the sea into Ireland, and there chose them a place of abode, both ours and their own writers have left in memory. But by what cause or occasion they were called Scots, truly I do not know. For I do quite reject the Egyptian fables of Scota.[194] And the selfsame language and the very same manners and behaviour with the Irishmen, and that they be called of the Britons by one name, declareth sufficiently that they came from thence. For the Southernmen[195] of them are not true Scots, but born and begotten rather of Englishmen, whereof a great number, flying at the coming of William Duke of Normandy, departed into Scotland, and do boast to this day that they come of Englishmen, whereas they, and the Englishmen, count the other Scots but rude and barbarous.

These nations, as I say, until that Honorius came to the Empire, which was about the year of the Lord 420, molested the north part of Britain with incursions and robberies. At which time, having called a power out of Ireland to help them (as Gildas and Bede do avouch) under conduct of Reuda, established themselves a kingdom[196] in the west part of Albania. But the Redshanks possessed the east region, whereas first they made war against the Romans and the Britons, and afterward with the Englishmen, and Danes, sometime they were confederate, sometime they warred diversly, until about the year of Our Lord 840, all the Redshanks were destroyed by Kennethus, King of Scots, insomuch that their name and kingdom ceased to be any longer in Britain. Whose country the Scots added unto their own, which to this day is renowned in Britain.

This much I had to say of the Scots and Redshanks, according to the verity of the history. Howbeit I know well how Boethius, a most vain reporter of fables, impudently affirmeth that they reigned in Britain three hundred years before Christ was born. And he

---

[193] **Marg**. 'Scots original.' As Spenser's Irenaeus observes in *A View of the Present State of Ireland,* 'Scotland and Ireland are all one and the same.'

[194] the Egyptian fables of Scota] Medieval Scottish historians traced their nation's origins to an Egyptian princess, Scota, and her Greek husband, Gathelos.

[195] Southernmen] Inhabitants of Lowland Scotland.

[196] a kingdom] Dál Riata

feigneth that there were so many kings, so many wars by them most valiantly waged against the Romans, so many wholesome laws and statutes in Britain by them instituted, as neither Lucian in his fabulous narrations, neither the author of the book of *Amadis of Gaul*, nor witty Ariostus in his *Orlando Furioso*, have ever commended unto us in fables.[197] But to the intent that I may set forth the most beastly man in his colours, and that the sleight and subtlety wherewith he endeavoureth to blear all men's eyes may be displayed, I will briefly touch certain of his most vain trifles, and such as all men of wit and understanding may easily perceive to be stark lies. And here I let pass Egyptian fables, and of the stock and race of Scottish kings in Britain before Caesar's coming. Where he affirmeth that Caesar was vanquished by the Scots and fled out of Britain, who afterward sent ambassadors unto the Scots and Redshanks to request their friendship, and that at last he conducted his Roman army into the Forest Caledonia; also that Augustus sent his messengers unto Metellus, King of Scots, to entreat him for peace. Moreover, he maketh Caratacus (a Briton, and son to King Cunobelinus, as Dion a most famous author reporteth) King of Scotland. He sticketh not to avouch that the Brigantes, Siluri, and Ordovici were Scots. He showeth how dangerous the expedition was of Claudius the Emperor, and describeth great wars between him and Canus the king of the Orcades. He writeth that Voadicia, the most renowned queen of Iceni, whose valiant deeds against the Romans Tacitus and also Dion have made known to the world, Venusius Earl of Brigantes, Cartimandua the Queen, were all Scots. And finally, there is no one thing wherein the Romans or Britons behaved themselves courageously or wisely in Britain which this monster doth not ascribe unto his feigned Scots, and which at that time were unknown to the world.

And he hath not only transcribed the mind, but also whole sentences and orations of Tacitus into his book, always changing the names of nations and cities, like a malicious falsifier without all shame or honesty. He sayeth Caesar and Tacitus wrote these things of the Redshanks, and those of the Scots, and that these nations made such and so many wars, whenas indeed the names of Scots or Redshanks are not at all to be found in these most noble writers. And truly, it is not like that Caesar, being a very wise gentleman,

---

[197] *Amadis of Gaul* [...] *Orlando Furioso*] Popular sixteenth-century romances, the latter a particular influence on Spenser's *Faerie Queene*.

when he had thoroughly learned the state and manners of the Britons and Irishmen, would with silence have overpassed the names of the Scots and Redshanks, specially having sent ambassadors unto their kings. Neither is it probable that Tacitus, a famous man and very expert in the state of Britain and other countries, when he describeth the expeditions of Agricola his father-in-law in to Britain, and as it were depainteth forth the shires, peoples, ports, and rivers of that region by their proper names, and maketh mention of a certain Earl of Ireland taken by Agricola, knew not also the names of Scots and Redshanks, with whom Boethius feigneth he waged that war, whenas in every place he seemeth to call the inhabitants of Albion Britons. And it had stood much more with Agricola's honour, being a worthy man, whom Tacitus also by his works endeavoureth to make more noble, to have subdued unknown nations, and such as feed on man's flesh (such as it shall be proved that the Scots were, long time after), rather than the Britons, which were sufficiently known to the Romans.

Also Dion, a man which had been consul and familiar with Severus the Emperor, and unto him dearly beloved, whilst he declareth his expedition into Britain at large, not once speaketh of the Scots or Redshanks, being very well known to all men that he conveyed all his force and power into Albania or Scotland. For, quoth Dion, the Meati and Caledonii, two diverse kinds of Britons, revolted from the Romans, and Severus calling together his soldiers commanded them to invade their country, and kill all that ever they met, and thus he charged them in these words:

>   Let none escape your hands away,
>   nor cruel bloody broil.
>   No tender imp, though in her womb
>   the dame therewith do toil:
>   Let him not scape a woeful death.[198]

When Severus came into Caledonia he fought never a battle, neither saw he any power of his enemies in a readiness, and so passing throughout all his enemies' land, having not lost in fight, but by water and hunger, fifty thousand men, returned unto his fellows. If the Scots had been in Britain at that time, the reporter

---

[198] Homer, *Iliad*, VI.

hereof, being a friend (neither after him Herodian, who in sufficient long discourse hath set forth that voyage), would have defrauded an Emperor so ambitious and thirsty of honour as Severus was of his due praise. Wherefore it is as evident as noon days that at this time, which was about two hundred and two years after the incarnation of Our Lord, the Scots had no seat in Britain. Over and besides all this, neither Eutropius, neither Spartianus, neither Capitolinus, neither Lampridius, neither Vopiscus, nor Aurelius Victor, who have all written the expeditions and wars of the Roman emperors in Britain, have in any place made mention of the Scottish or Redshank name.

Although therefore, I suppose that these arguments are sufficient to improve° and condemn the mere trifles of Boethius, notwithstanding I will lightly touch two of his histories, which by the author are set forth at large enough, with words a foot and a half long. But I pray you, 'when ye be let to look, your laughter (friends) you would refrain'.[199]

In the second book of his fables, he writeth how that Ptolomaeus Philadelphus, King of Egypt, sent forth his orators unto Reutha, King of Scots, that by the view taken and report of his near countrymen, namely such as had come lineally from the Egyptians, he might understand the situation and form of the country, together with the conditions and manners of the people, to the intent that he might set down the same in his work of cosmography, which he had then in hand. Which orators, being right courteously entertained, were afterward led through all the regions and towns of Scots and Redshanks; at last, being largely rewarded, returned into Egypt. O noble and worthy deed of a gentleman, but most unthankful Ptolomaeus, and unmindful of so great rewards! Who, after that he had sent his ambassadors into countries so far distant, hath left no shire, yea almost no town in all Britain in that worthy work of his unspoken of (which was set forth, not by the King, but long time after by another Ptolomaeus Pheludensis, a philosopher very well learned), only his well-beloved cousins the Scots and Redshanks he hath left raked up in their own darkness, neither once vouchsafed in his book, wherein he made a most perfect

---

[199] 'Spectatum admissi risum teneatis amici?' Horace, *Ars Poetica*, l. 5, in *Epistles*, ed. by Augustus S. Wilkins (London: Macmillan, 1965). This might be translated, 'when you are admitted to this view, could you refrain from laughing, friends?'.

description of all Albania, to express so much as their names. Nay rather Boethius, it is a sin to believe that such a king, when he had sent thither his legates and recited all the cities and people of Albania, to have been ignorant of the nation's name, and in describing the situation of the region so to have varied from the truth. For he, which set forth that noble work about the year of our redemption 140, appeareth in no place to speak of the Scots and Redshanks, which at that time were unknown to the world.

This being omitted, let us come to the second fable, wherein (gentle reader) whether I shall move thee to laughter or loathsomeness I am uncertain. He writeth that one Gillus usurped by force the kingdom of Scotland, before the coming of Caesar into Britain, who after that he had committed many cruel deeds, at length by Ewenus the lawful heir, one Cadallus being captain, was in Ireland vanquished in bloody fight, and afterward slain. 'Of this slaughter, by reason that the Irishmen were afflicted with the force and arms of the Albion Scots, the poet Claudianus and other writers have entreated.'[200] Whereby he maketh the noble poet Claudianus, which lived under Honorius 410 years after the incarnate word, author of the Scottish war against Gillus – which unto him seemeth no inconvenience, who in other places most impudently fathereth his follies and fables upon Caesar the Dictator and Tacitus. In very deed, Claudianus hath written of the Gildonic War made in Africa by Mascezel, brother to Gildo, chieftain therein, and of the expedition which Honorius took in hand against the brother that rebelled.[201] But I beseech you my friend Hector, tell me whether you affirm this gear in jest or in good earnest, that thereby we may judge of the residue? Or whether that you thought you could deceive all men with your lies? This Gildo was a Goth, no Scot, the war was in Africa, not in Ireland. This visible tyrant lived in the year of Our Lord 398, but their feigned and invisible Gillus is devised to have flourished 400 years before.

Besides these insults and unsavoured lies, he affirmeth that all the knowledge and learning of the Druids came first unto the Scots, whenas it plainly appeareth unto such as are exercised in the reading of histories, that philosophy and the liberal sciences were known to the Celtae and Britons long before they were to the

---

[200] Boece, *Scotorum Historia*, II.49.
[201] Gildonic War] In 398 AD, the African commander Gildo rebelled against the Western Empire and was subdued by an army led by his brother, Mascezel.

Greeks and Latins.²⁰² But as touching the wholesome laws and institutes which he falsely attributeth unto the Scots, unto those which read Solinus and Mela, depainting forth the manners and nature of the Irishmen, the truth will appear. Likewise out of St Jerome, whom we may better credit then Boethius, it is evident that at his time (that is as much to say as in the year of Our Lord 400) the Scots were accustomed to eat man's flesh. For, sayeth he:

> what shall I say of other nations whenas I myself, being but a young man, saw in France Scots which feed on man's flesh. And whenas they chance to find in the woods any herds of hogs, also any droves of cattle or beasts, they use to cut off the buttocks of the herdsmen and keepers, and the paps of women, accounting those parts for a most delicate dish. These Scots, as though they followed Plato's commonwealth, have no peculiar wives of their own, but as their lechery moveth them (sayeth he) run lasciviously about, after the manner of beasts.²⁰³

This much St Jerome.

Since, therefore, it is certainly proved out of this true author that they were so barbarous at his time, it is not like that so many hundred years before, as Boethius doth feign, they were ruled with so many good laws and wholesome institutes. Neither do I, for my part, write this to the intent I would detract anything from the Scottish glory, insomuch as I know very well that this nation, after that it had departed from barbarousness and embraced Christian religion, and obeyed laws and rights precisely like other people, was so firmly joined in league of friendship with our Britons that we read how in many wars the one nation aided the other. I acknowledge also that many things have been by them done both wisely and valiantly in Britain, France, and Italy, and that the Englishmen, howbeit a strong nation, seldom assayed the Scots in war but that they were always ready with all their force to join with them in battle, which is no sign of a cowardly or heartless people. But I write this only to this intent, that the truth of the history may

---

[202] According to legends associated with pseudo-Berosus, propagated in sixteenth-century Britain by John Bale among others, Britain had been ruled in the centuries after the Flood by the Samotheans or Celtae, who excelled all other peoples in wisdom and learning. The Samotheans were eventually displaced by the giant Albion.

[203] St Jerome, *Adversus Jovinianum* [*Against Jovinianus*], 2.7.

be known, and that the Scots themselves may contemn this fabler, and hold themselves contented with this: that together with the Saxons, Frenchmen, and Englishmen, most noble nations, they were first known to the Roman world. And now let us see what substantial and approved writers, whom both we and they must credit, have transported to memory touching the Scots and Redshanks.

The first, therefore, of the Romans (so far as I know), Mamertinus in his panegyric called 'Maximianus' maketh mention of the Redshanks by these words:

> And truly not, like as there is but one name of Britain, so should the loss be but small to the commonwealth of a land so plentiful of corn, so flourishing with numbers of pastures, so flowing with rivers of metals, so gainful for revenues, so well beset with havens, so wide in circuit. Which when Caesar, first of the Romans and the beginner of this your name, entered into, wrote that he had found another world, supposing it to be so big that it seemed not to be compassed with the ocean, but rather to compass the ocean about. But at that time Britain was nothing furnished with ships for war by sea, and the Romans, after the Punic and Asiatic wars, had lately been busied against pirates, and afterward by the Mithridatic fight were very well practised by sea and land. Besides, this nation was then but rude, and the Britons being accustomed but only to the Redshanks and Irishmen their enemies, as yet but half naked, soon yielded unto the Roman arms and ensigns – that Caesar almost in all that expedition could vaunt himself but of this one thing, that he had sailed upon the ocean.[204]

He affirmeth that the Britons only dwell in an island, and termeth them Hibernenses, who afterward were called Scots. Also another panegyric unto Constantinus the Emperor speaketh of the Redshanks, called Pictones, as followeth:

---

[204] The quotation is from a panegyric of 289 celebrating the proposed British campaign of the Emperor Maximian; though associated with the name of Claudius Mamertinus, it cannot be by the same author who flourished in the mid-fourth century.

> For neither he [speaking of his father Constantius] after such and so many notable acts which he hath done, vouchsafeth to get not only the woods and marshes of the Caledones and other Pictones, but neither Ireland which lieth nigh, neither the farthest Thule, neither yet the Fortunate Islands, if there be any such.

Thus far the panegyric. This he wrote about the year after Christ was born 320, at what time it seemeth that the Pictones or Redshanks began first to inhabit the furthermost parts of Scotland.

After him, Ammianus Marcellinus[205] first of the Latins made mention of the Scots, in the year of our salvation 364, in the tenth consulship of Constantius and the third of Julianus, whenas in Britain, by excursion and breaking forth of the Scots and Redshanks (being wild nations), peace being broken, the places about nigh to the frontiers were spoiled. And afterward, in the life of Valentinian and Valens,[206] he sayeth:

> At this time, as though alarm were sounded throughout all the Roman dominions, the most fierce and savage nations arose, and forcibly invaded their near neighbours. The Alemanni or Almains spoiled the country of France and Rhetia together; Sarmatae, the Pannoniae, and the Quadi (now Bohemians); the Redshanks, Saxons, Scots, and Attacotti much molested the Britons.

And afterward:[207]

> At that time the Redshanks being divided into two nations, Deucalidonae and Vecturiones, also the Attacotti, a very warlike nation, and the Scots wandering uncertainly about here and there, wasted and spoiled very much. And as for the coasts of Gallia, they were spoiled by Frenchmen and Saxons, etc.

Hereby it appeareth in what darkness the Scottish state is drowned. For Boethius in no place maketh mention of the Attacotti, who appear by this author to have dwelled in Albania, and to have been

---

[205] **Marg**. 'Lib. 20.'
[206] **Marg**. 'Lib. 26.'
[207] **Marg**. 'Lib. 27.'

1850 of the Scottish race. Wherefore it is most likely that, a little before that time, the Scots and Attacotti (who afterward vanished into the name of the Scots) forth of Ireland and from the Hebrides, the Redshanks out of the Orcades, whereas they lurked before, by one consent entered into Albania, and there provoked by war the Romans and Britons, and that they departed out of the field sometime conquerors and sometimes conquered. For shortly after, Ammianus reporteth that after that these nations were by Theodosius, a valiant captain under Valentinian, vanquished and driven out of the Roman province, they were at quiet. And this can
1860 be no disparagement, but rather a great glory to the Scottish nation, that rather at that time than before that, forcibly against the Romans' will they planted them seats in Britain. Which is proved not out of vain and fabulous writers, such as is Boethius and other such like, but out of substantial authors and such as do very well know the state of Britain.

After all these Claudianus, a poet singularly learned, in divers places maketh mention of these nations, as for example *Of the Getic War*:

1870   A power also there came, against the farthest Britons bent,
Which bridled hath the Scots so fierce, and notes with iron brent
Then failing reads, whilst Redshanks' blood and breath is spent.[208]

And in his panegyric to Honorius:

The nimble Moors hath he, and Picts (so termed by name full true)
Subdued, and he the Scots with blade at random did pursue.

1880 And of the Fourth Consulship of Honorius.

[...] were wet with Saxons slain
The Orcades, and Iceland[209] eke was hot with Redshanks bane,

---

[208] These lines from Claudian's *De Bello Gothico* are translated by Maurice Platnauer as 'next the legion that had been left to guard Britain, the legion that kept the fierce Scots in check, whose men had scanned the strange devices tattooed on the faces of the dying Picts' (London: Heinemann, 1922, p. 157).

And frozen Ireland eke, dead heaps of Scotsmen wept amain.

Who did ever set forth more plainly the natural country of both nations? For he showeth how Redshanks came from Thule, that is to say islands of the north, and the Scots but lately out of Ireland. And in another place in his panegyric, Britain speaketh unto Stilicho:

> And me (she sayeth), with countries near-
> about who was destroyed
> Almost,[210] defensed well hath Stilicho,
> when Ireland's soil on every side
> The Scots do move, and seas
> with noisome sails do foam about.
> By whose help now it is,
> that Scottish force I do not doubt,
> Ne do I dread the Picts, etc.[211]

Hereby it appeareth manifestly that at this time (that is to wit the year of our salvation 410) the Scots possessed no certain place in Britain, but many times used to make irruptions out of Ireland, and by little and little subdued the north parts of the island; and at length, having driven thence the inhabitants, established their kingdom there under Valentinian the younger, the year of God incarnate 444, whenas now the Romans had left off the charge and care of Britain.

This much I had briefly to say touching the original of the Scots and Redshanks. Now I will address myself to the description of Albania or Scotland. It is separate from England by the River Tweed, the hill Cheviot, and certain little rivers running down into the channel Solvathianus. The first people which come to hand are Gallovidiani, of old time called by the Romans Novantes (and not Brigantes, as we have showed before). Ptolomaeus called their city Leucopibia, which we term now Caer Luel, and standeth in the

---

[209] Iceland] Twyne has 'Island', the usual early modern spelling of Iceland, in translation of the Latine *Thyle*; Iceland was often identified with the semi-legendary northern land of Thule.
[210] with countries nearabout [...] destroyed / Almost] That is, almost destroyed by neighbouring peoples.
[211] Claudian, *De consulatu Stilichonis*, II. Llwyd omits Claudian's personification of Britain as a savage, tattooed and clothed in animal skins.

    entrance of both kingdoms. Next unto these were the Gadini, nigh the river Glota, which some do better call Cluyda; howbeit, that name (by reason of the propriety of the tongue) is sometime pronounced Gluyda, whereby grew that error of calling it Glot. Upon this river's side sometime there stood a noble city of the Britons called *Caer Alt Clut*, or *Archuyd*, that is to say, a city standing upon Cluyda, which is now of the Scots called *Dùn Breatainn*,[212] because it was restored again by the Britons, about the year of our salvation 800.

    Above these, towards the East Sea, lieth a region which now is called Laudonia[213] and Mercia (March), but in times past Bernicia, and of the Picts, called also Redshanks, Pictlandia. The Maeatae are placed here by Dion. 'For', sayeth he, 'the Maeatae dwell beyond the wall, unto the Caledonii'. Ptolomaeus layeth the Vacomagi beyond Tueda. This limiting wall (as Spartianus reporteth) was first builded by Hadrian the Emperor, fourscore miles in length. And Capitolinus is author that Antoninus erected another made of turves, between the Britains. And, last of all, that Severus by a trench which was cast from sea to sea divided the Roman province from the other Britains all men do generally agree. Whereby our countrymen call it *Mur Severus*, that is to say, Severus's wall, and in another place *Gwal Severus*, Severus's valley,[214] at this day.

    In this region standeth Edinburgh, the seat of the kings of Scotland, sometime builded by Eboracus, king of Britons, called also *Castell Mynyd Agned*, that is to say, the Castle of St Agnes Hill, and afterward the Castle of Virgins. The water there, which is now called Forthea, was called the Picticum Sea, and afterward the Scottish Sea, and thus far stretched the kingdom of Northumberland. Tacitus calleth the same Bodotria, howbeit Polydorus so termeth the River Levinus,[215] which out of the Lake Lomundus floweth into Cluyda. 'For', saith he, 'Glota and Bodotria, two divers arms of the sea running forth a great length, are kept asunder with a narrow piece of ground.' Wherefore Bodotria floweth not into Glota, neither is it any river, but an arm

---

[212] *Dùn Breatainn*] Dumbarton
[213] Laudonia] Lothian
[214] Severus's valley] Rather, Severus's palisade or entrenchment, the correct translation of 'Vallum Severi'. W. *gwal* means 'wall'.
[215] River Levinus] River Leven

of the sea – therefore it cannot be Levinus by any means. Beyond these arms of the sea dwelled the Caledonii, the most noblest nation of Albania, where now the inland Scots inhabit. At the east part was Horestia, now Angusia, Fisa, and Mernia.[216] At the west were the Epidii, and more towards the north the Creoni. And after these the Canvuaci, where now Lennosia, and Argadia, and Lorna[217] are. The Caereni possessed Loguhabria; the Lugi, Strathnavernia; and, at the other sea-coast, the Cauti, Moravia, and Rossia. And the Cornabii, which are farthest off all, inhabited Sutherlandia and Cathanesia.

And whereas Boethius writeth that in the time of Claudius the Emperor the Moravi came by a whole navy into Scotland, it is most false, as appeareth in histories.[218] For the nation of the Slavi, whereof the Moravi took their beginning, was altogether unknown to the world until the time of the Emperor Mauritius, about the year of Our Lord 600. The Marcomanni also, and the Quadi, inhabited those places which afterward, the year of Our Lord 900, being under Arnulphus, began by Zuentebaldus king of the Slavi[219] to be called the kingdom of Moravia.

Beyond Scotland in the German Ocean are the islands called Orcades, whereof the biggest is called Pomonia.[220] And on the other side of Albania, in the sea Vergivium (which the Britons call *Môr Iwerddon*, as who should say the Irish Sea, from whence I conjecture that the antique name Vergivium was derived), lie the Isles Hebrides, in number two and forty, of others called Euboniae. The Isle of Anglesey is none of these, as I will show in another place. And not far hence lieth Ireland, an island also, which our countrymen call Iwerddon, the inhabitants Vernia.[221] Whereby in my opinion they do far better which term it Ivernia (as Mela, and Juvenal in his second Satire), or Ierna (as Claudianus, and Dionysius), rather than Hibernia, now Ireland. The Britons and Scots do call the inhabitants by one name, *Gwyddel*.

---

[216] Angusia, Fisa, and Mernia] Angus, Fife, and Kincardinshire, or Mearns
[217] Lennosia, and Argadia, and Lorna] Lennox, Argyle, and Lorne
[218] And whereas Boethius [...] appeareth in histories] In Boece, the Moravians of Germany unite with Queen Voada (Boudica) in revolt against the Romans.
[219] Zuentebaldus king of the Slavi] Svatopluk or Zwentibold I, King of Great Moravia (d. 894).
[220] Pomonia] Mainland, Orkney
[221] Vernia] The Gaelic name for Ireland is *Éire*.

The Description of Wales

Thus having ended the description of Scotland, with the islands lying thereabout, let us now proceed to Wales, the third part of Britain. The same is divided from Lloegr,° that is England, by the rivers Severn and Dee, and on every other side is environed by the Vergivian, or Irish Ocean. And it was called Cambria, as our chronicles do report, of Camber, the third son of Brutus, like as Lloegr of Locrinus, and Albania of Albanactus, his other sons also.[222] This same only, with Cornwall, a most ancient country of Britons, enjoyeth as yet the old inhabitants. The Welshmen use the British tongue, and are the very true Britons by birth. And although some do write that Wales doth not stretch forth on this side the River Vaga, or Wye, this can be no fraud to us. For we have taken in hand to describe Cambria and not Wallia, 'Wales' as it is now called by a new name, and unacquainted to the Welshmen. In North Wales, the Welshmen keep their old bounds. But in South Wales the Englishmen are come over Severn, and have possessed all the land between it and Wye. So that all Herefordshire, and the Forest of Dean, and Gloucestershire, and a great part of Worcestershire, and Shropshire on this side Severn are inhabited by Englishmen at this day.[223]

These regions, with certain corners of Flintshire and Denbighshire, were sometime under the kings of March. And our countrymen unto this day do call their near borderers *Gwyr y Mers*, that is to say, the Men of March. For Offa, a most mighty king of March, the year of the incarnate word 770, to the intent that the bounds of his kingdom towards the Britons in Wales might the better be known, caused a very deep ditch with an exceeding high wall to be made, from the water Devanus,° a little above the castle called Filix,[224] through high hills and deep valleys, fens, rocks, cliffs, and rivers, unto the mouth of the River Wye, about an hundred miles long. The same, reserving the old name (for of our

---

[222] The story of the division of Britain among the three sons of Brutus is found in Geoffrey of Monmouth's *Historia regum Britanniae*. The event was depicted on the Elizabethan stage in the anonymous play *Locrine* (1580s).

[223] Llwyd's insistence that the Severn marked the true boundary of Cambria would influence English literature from Drayton's *Poly-Olbion* to Milton's *Comus* (see Introduction, pp. 25-26).

[224] the castle called Filix] L. 'Filicis castrum', translatable as 'the castle of the fern or bracken'.

countrymen it is called *Clawdd Offa*, that is to say, Offa's Ditch), it may easily be seen of all, throughout the whole coast. And all the towns and villages almost which be on the east side thereof have their names ending in these terminations, *-ton* or *-ham*, whereby it appeareth that the Saxons sometime dwelled there. Howbeit, now the Welshmen in all places beyond that ditch towards Lloegr have planted themselves.

The inhabitants of this region are called in their mother tongue, Cymbri. In which word, the force of the sound of the letter B is scarcely perceived in pronouncing. And it is very likely that this was the most ancient name, and that Cambria a region of England was thereof so called.

When I perceived that the Cymbri, which fought with the Romans so many bloody battles, were called by the same name that ours are, it came into my mind to inquire and search what good writers have thought of the beginning of that nation. And having read much thereof, I found also very much, whereby I am so persuaded that I dare avouch that it was this our British nation.[225] First, the name is all one with ours; then their tongue, which is a very great argument. For Plinius in his Fourth Book, and thirteenth chapter, sayeth that 'Philemon was of the Cymbri called *Mori marussium*, that is to say, *Mare mortuum*, the Dead Sea, unto the promontory Rubeas,' etc.[226] And our countrymen call the Dead Sea in their tongue, *Mor Marw*. And as for these words, neither the Germans, neither the Danes, neither Sueones,° neither the Slavi, neither the Lithuani, nor the Livones,[227] do understand them. Wherefore it is manifest that the Cymbri were none of these nations. But our Cymbri do speak so: wherefore it is evident that they were of the same name and tongue.

Moreover, Plutarchus in the 'Life of Marius' affirmeth that they departed out of a far country, and that it was not known whence they came, nor whither they went, but that like clouds they issued into France, and Italy, with the Almains.° Whereupon the Romans supposed that they had been Germans, because they had big bodies,

---

[225] Llwyd is among the first, but certainly not the last, to propose a link between the Welsh or *Cymry* and the ancient Cimbri, inhabitants of Jutland.

[226] Twine struggles with Llwyd's abbreviated quotation from Book 4 of Pliny the Elder's *Natural History,* wherein Philemon is quoted as a doubtful authority on the extent of the domains of the Cimbri.

[227] Livones] A Finno-Ugric-speaking people inhabiting parts of modern Latvia and Estonia.

with sharp and horrible eyes. Thus much he. Since therefore he hath left their original unknown, and our chronicles do testify how that the Britons had always great familiarity with the Northern Germans, it is like enough that the British Cymbri passed over into Denmark, whereby it was termed Cymbrica, and so joining with the Almains° made war upon the Romans. And first vanquished Papirius, with his army in Illyrica; afterward overcame Aurelius Scaurus with his legions in France, himself being slain by King Belus (which name is also familiar amongst the Welshmen at this day). Besides that, Manlius and Caepio were discomfited nigh Rhodanus, when there were 12,000 of the Romans slain.[228]

In the end, at Athesis in Italy, they were overthrown and almost all slain.[229] And those which remained after the battle escaped into Germany, and were divided into two parts. Whereof the one, returning into Britain, gave name to the country Cymbria; the other, departing out of Germany, rested nigh to the sea Balteum, and afterward were called of the Germans Aestiones, whose tongue, as Tacitus writeth, is like the British.[230] And to confirm all this, I read of late in a most ancient fragment of the British tongue[231] how that long since there departed a very great army of Britons into Denmark, which, after many valiant wars, stoutly made in most parts of the world, never returned again.

But whereas divers do affirm that these were the indwellers of the Danish Chersonesus,[232] hereby it appeareth false, that the Danes long before that time, possessed that land, as their histories do declare. Neither is there any Danish or Suetish writer, that ever made mention of the Cymbri. Othersome affirm that they descended of the inhabitants of Cimmerius Bosphorus.[233] But neither the nation's name, neither their manners, neither their kings' names do agree. Which, if you respect ours, are all one. For Clodic, Lhes, Bel, Lhud, Thudfach, Berich, by which the kings of

---

[228] Llwyd here summarizes the action of the Cimbrian War, 113-101 BC.
[229] almost all slain] The Cimbri were defeated in battle on the banks of the Athesis (Adige) in 101 BC.
[230] See Tacitus, *Germania*, 45.
[231] The reference to an ancient fragment in the British tongue inevitably recalls the *liber vetustissimus Britannici sermonis* which Geoffrey of Monmouth claimed as the source for his fabulous history of ancient Britain.
[232] Chersonesus] 'peninsula' (Greek); Jutland was known as the Danish or Cimbrian Chersonese.
[233] Cimmerius Bosphorus] The Strait of Kerch, which links the Black Sea with the Sea of Azov.

the Cymbri were called, be very common names amongst the Britons. Their neglecting of gold and silver, the shape of their bodies, their shields, armour, swords (yea, made of brass, whereof I saw twain which of late were found in hollow rocks in North Wales),[234] their reverence towards women and priests, their custom to sacrifice men unto Mercury, declareth that they were British Cymbri.

Neither will I deny that which many do write, that the Sicambri,[235] and afterward the Franci, were of their brood, unless that their own historians affirmed, that they were so called three hundred years before, of one Cambra daughter to Belinus, which was king of Britain, and married to Antenor their king. Wherefore I conclude that the Cymbri either departed forth of Britain about that time, or else were the remnants of the great army which was gathered in Britain and France, and settled with Brennus in the marches of Greece, at the same time. For it is undoubtedly known that Brennus was a perfect Briton, and brother to King Belinus, and son to Dunwallus, which not only our chronicles do testify, but also the country's name, where the ambitious man fought with Belinus his brother, and was called of him Brennich.[236] Divers rivers also amongst us called by that name, and also a most ancient castle, standing upon the top of an exceeding high hill in Gwania, called Dinas Bran, that is to say, Brennus's Court or Palace, are a very good argument hereof. Besides this, there remain most ancient rhymes in the praise of Cornwenna their mother, because that when Brennus came forth of France with aid against his brother, with her naked breast and paps she reconciled them together, which one hath thus interpreted:

> O out alas, what meaneth this?
> Do you my bowels harm?
> What wicked cause doth move
> Two brothers' powers to be so warm?
> Cannot all Britain you contain?
> Since it is very sure,

---

[234] hollow rocks in North Wales] This is one of Llwyd's relatively few references to archaeological evidence.
[235] the Sicambri] An ancient Germanic people, forerunners of the Franks, mentioned by Caesar.
[236] Brennich] The Anglo-Saxon kingdom of Bernicia, known in Old Welsh as *Bryneich*.

2120   That both you twain, within this
       Womb of mine, did once endure?
       May not your mothers tears,
       Nor torn hairs from purpose pluck?
       Nor naked doleful breasts,
       In tender age, which both did suck? [237]

Who then joining their armies ran over all France and Italy, vanquished the Romans and took the city, and departed out of Italy, as Polybius reporteth.[238] And Belinus returned into Britain, but Brennus with 15,000 footmen and 61,200 horsemen, as Pausanias writeth, set upon the Greeks.[239] And, having subdued the Macedonians, Thessalians, Thracians, and the Poeonians, all the other people of the Greeks he overthrew at Thermopylae, in a most horrible bloody battle. In fine, whenas he was about to sack the Temple of Apollo of Delphos, his army was, wholly almost, miraculously slain by the fall of a mighty great cliff, and a wonderful rain from heaven. Wherewith Brennus being struck with sorrow – a most courageous gentleman as he was – slew himself.

And I wot well, how Polydorus complaineth of the supputation° of years, whenas indeed the time agreeth very well with the British History. But whereas he maketh two Brennuses, that is altogether beside credit, since no writer before him ever yielded the same to memory. And as concerning the true supputation of the age of the world, divers authors have diversly written. Besides these reasons, by their own tongue, which is the best proof that may be, we will easily convince that they were Britons – and that Brennus's soldiers spake the British tongue, we will likewise soon declare.

Pausanias in his tenth book writeth thus:

---

[237] The Latin verses translated here are the work of John Castoreus, also known as John Bever (d. 1311), appearing in his condensed version of Geoffrey's *Historia*, the *Tractatus de Bruto abbreviato*.

[238] vanquished the Romans [...] as Polybius reporteth] The sack of Rome by the Gauls under their chieftain Brennus in 386 BC is described in the histories of Polybius and Livy; where Polybius reports that the Gauls departed in safety, Livy records that they were subsequently annihilated by a Roman army under Camillus. Llwyd's controversial claim that Brennus was a Briton would cause the young Philip Sidney some difficulties in his correspondence with Hubert Languet; see the Introduction, pp. 8-11.

[239] Brennus [...] set upon the Greeks] The Gallic invasion of Greece under a leader named Brennus or Brennos occurred in 280 BC, more than a century after the sack of Rome which Llwyd attributes to the same man.

Brennus had with him forth 20,400 horsemen, which were all fighting men, for the truer number of them indeed were above threescore thousand and two hundred. For there followed every horseman, two servants on horseback. These, when their masters were fighting, stood always in the rearward and assisted them, that if by chance they were unhorsed they should set them on theirs, and if the man were slain the servant should succeed in his place; but if they were both killed by force of fight, then was the third at hand ready to supply for them that were dead. If the first and chief had received a wound, one of these other conveyed him out of the battle, and the third fulfilled the room of him that was hurt. And this practice of fighting on horseback they term in their country language, *trimarchisia*, for they call a horse *marcha*.

Thus far Pausanias. What can be spoken more plainly? Our Britons at this day call *tres* in the masculine gender *tri*, and in the feminine *tair*, that is, *three*. And a horse they call *march*. Whereby *trimarch* unto them signifieth three horses. Hereby, therefore, all must needs confess either that the Frenchmen spake the British tongue (which almost all histories do deny), or that these were natural Britons. And afterward he sayeth that the Frenchmen call a shield *tyren* in their country speech, which word we do likewise use at this present, calling a shield *tarian*.

Moreover Athenaeus writeth that the relics of the Frenchmen, under Bathanasius their captain, took up their dwelling about Ister, and after that were parted into twain, whereof the one were called Scordisci and dwelled in Hungary. The other, by the name of Brenni, possessed part of the Alps, by the Mount Brennerus in Tirolensis shire, whom Appianus calleth all by the name of Cymbri – which do all show that they were Britons. For *bathynad* in our country language signifieth a formed judge. For *bath* is beauty or form; *ynad*, with us, is a judge, in authority next to the king. For when Brennus was dead, they chose him to their captain. Farther, *ysgar* with us is to separate, and *ysgaredig* signifieth those which be separated. Whereof this part of France, when it departed from the residue, was termed *ysgaredig*, from whence Scordisci is derived, retaining the name of Brennus's captain. And *bryn*, in British, is a mountain or hill, of which word Brennerus was so called. Over and besides this, Gatheli, or the Irishmen, when as

2190 about this time they departed out of Cantabria, now Biscay, wandering upon the sea to seek new dwellings, called all Britons *Brennach*, of Brennus their famous captain, by which name they call our countrymen to this day. And thus much sufficeth to have said of Brennus.

But whereas some affirm that the Frenchmen used the British tongue, by certain French words cited by Rhenanus, Sidonius, and Lazius, it appeareth to be most false. Notwithstanding, I cannot sufficiently marvel that of the tongue of this most mighty nation, whose bounds are comprised by the Rhine, the Pyrenees mounts, 2200 Apennines, and the ocean, there is almost no show or token to be found remaining.[240] And that it was most ancient, it appeareth out of Berosus, Annius, Giambularius, and Postellus. Whereby Gallia, now France, was so called of rain, which the Hebrews call *gal*, and the Britons *glaw*, as who should say, berained, or overflowed by the deluge.[241] Notwithstanding the Spaniards – although they were afflicted by the Romans, the Catti, the Alani, the Vandali, the Goths, the Suevi, and Mauri, or Moors – yet in Cantabria, called now Biscay, and Asturias (for these are only the very true Spaniards, and Hiberi) they have preserved their ancient speech.[242] 2210 For that which is commonly called the Spanish tongue is but a medley made out of the Latin, Gothic, and Arabic.

But let us omit all these things, and return again unto our Cambria, called Wales, which we in our mother tongue do term *Cymru*. This, more than four hundred years since, as Giraldus hath very well noted, the Englishmen, after the fashion and manner of the Germans, have called Wallia, that is Wales. For when the ancient Almains had sometime joining next unto them of foreigners, the Frenchmen, whom they called *Walli*, it came to pass, that afterward they called all strangers, and those which dwelt 2220 in other provinces, *Walli* and *Wallisei*. Like as at this present, as well Frenchmen, as Italians, and Burgundians, they call *Walli*, and all things that come forth of strange countries, *Walsh*.

This country, I say, which (that I may use the words of Giraldus):

---

[240] **Marg.** 'The bounds of France'
[241] **Marg.** 'Etymon of Gallia'
[242] their ancient speech] Apparently a reference to the Asturian language or dialect, still spoken in parts of northern Spain.

by a false name, yet most frequented at these days, but less proper, is called Wallia, Wales, containeth in length two hundred miles, and about one hundred in breadth. For it reacheth in length from the haven Gordwr in Mona, called Anglesey, unto the haven Eskewyn[243] in Wenta, eight days journey. In breadth from Porth Mawr, that is to say the great haven of Menevia,° unto Rhyd Helig, which the Britons call Vadum Salicis, the Englishmen Willowford, about four days journey. A land much abounding, and very well fortified, with high mountains, low valleys, great woods, waters, and fens. In such sort that, from time the Saxons first usurped this island, the residue of the Britons which departed into those coasts, neither by the Englishmen long ago, neither since by the Normans, could be altogether subdued. As for those which betook themselves to the south corner, which of their captain's name was called Conavia, because it is not so well defenced, were not able to resist. For the third part of the Britons which do now remain, possessing the southerly sea-coast of France, a singular good country, was not translated thither after the destruction and conquest of Britain, but long afore that by Maximus the Tyrant, who, after many sharp battles which the British youth sustained under him during those wars, was with this farthermost shore of France rewarded by the Emperor's liberality.[244]

Thus far Giraldus.

This country sometime° was inhabited only by the Britons, but afterward the Englishmen began to possess it, unto Offa's ditch, against whom the Welshmen made infinite wars, until the coming of William the Norman. Under whose son, Henry, the Flemings (being then driven out of their country by breaking in of the sea) took upon them the possession of Roose, a province of Demetia.° Who, in many wars were provoked by the Princes of Wales, but always valiantly defended themselves and theirs, and at this day, differing from the Welshmen in tongue and manners, are yet in the same place recounted° for Flemings.

The kings of England, especially Henry the First, the Second, and Third of that name, calling unto them the Scots, Irishmen, and

---

[243] haven Eskewen] Portskewett, Monmouthshire.
[244] The passage quoted is the opening of Gerald of Wales's *Cambriae descriptio*.

Cantabrian Gascons, did very much provoke and molest this nation with continual wars. But the Welshmen, being divided under three kings, whom they called princes (which was the very cause of their destruction),²⁴⁵ defended themselves and their own stoutly. Howbeit certain regions of South Wales, as Roose, Glamorgan, Wenta,° Brecknock, and part of Powys, by Robert, son to Hammon, and certain worthy earls of Gloucester, the Brussii, the Bohuns, Brian Guilford,²⁴⁶ Adam of Newmarch, but specially by Roger Montgomery and his sons, Hago which was slain in Anglesey, Robert of Belisine, and Arnulf which builded the castle of Pembroke, and the Fitzalans, Lords of Oswestry and Clun, were quelled and tamed in many battles, and came into the right and possession of the conquerors. And Gwynedd, although that part thereof which lieth on this side Conwy²⁴⁷ was first weakened by the earls of Chester, and afterward by the forenamed kings which, at the River Cluda,²⁴⁸ sundry times wasted all with fire and sword, notwithstanding after the departure of the kings they drave the Englishmen thence, and razed their castles down to the ground, and always defended their bounds. Until the year of Our Lord 1282, Edward the First of that name, leading a mighty army against Prince Llywelyn, and another arriving in the Isle of Anglesey and vanquishing the same, from whence they entered into Arfon (a region exceedingly well fortified by natural situation) by a bridge made of boats, in the very same place where sometime Agricola lead over his soldiers.²⁴⁹ Where the two armies, joining together, vanquished a great multitude of the Gascons and Biernes, with divers other noble men, and brought them in subjection to the Englishmen.²⁵⁰ Whenas also at the same time his third army, under

---

²⁴⁵ Compare David Powel's comments on the dissension of Welsh princes, below, p. 152.
²⁴⁶ Brian Guilford] Brian fitz Count, Lord of Abergavenny in the early twelfth century; mentioned again on p. 129.
²⁴⁷ on this side Conwy] 'cis Conovium'; the phrase does not require an Anglocentric perspective, as both England and Llwyd's native Denbighshire lie on 'this' (eastern) side of the Conwy.
²⁴⁸ River Cluda] River Clwyd
²⁴⁹ Agricola had crossed the Menai Strait in the opposite direction, conquering Anglesey from the Welsh mainland. This reversal of direction disrupts any easy identification of English with Roman conquerors.
²⁵⁰ A muddled and inaccurate account of the battle of Moel y Don, which was in fact a Welsh victory. See the longer account in *History of Cambria*, below, pp.

the Earl of Gloucester and Roger Mortimer, sacked and spoiled South Wales, being accompanied with many earls and lords of Wales which loved not the Prince. Until that the Prince himself, being forsaken by many of his own men, was by the men of Builth betrayed, not far from the river Vaga, or Wye, whither he came with a very few soldiers. And by one Adam Francton, which fought under the conduct of Elias Walwyn, far from the residue of his own power – being accompanied with one only page, and unarmed, with certain other noblemen of that country, which had told the same before to his enemies – was there slain most dishonourably. After whose death, the Welshmen came in subjection to the Englishmen, and had always afterward to their prince the King of England's eldest son, or daughter if male issue failed.

This King built certain towns and castles there, which he compassed with stone walls, and left garrisons in them to keep the Welshmen in awe; and provided by special laws, for that intent made, that Welshmen should enjoy no such liberties nor freedoms as they and their posterity had granted unto the Englishmen. But by many edicts and decrees set forth against the Welshmen, especially by Henry IV (who by reason of a rebellion made by one Owain, which dwelt near the valley of Dee, was very highly offended with all that nation),[251] the kings of England kept them under the yoke of servitude and, abolishing their own proper laws, brought in the English laws, providing by general commandment that no man should use the Welsh tongue in any court or school. Howbeit, the honour of the most ancient tongue so much prevailed that not only the Welshmen themselves but also the inhabitors of the English towns through Wales, being now called by the name of Welshmen, do gladly frequent the same. And hath removed the bounds into Englandwards, over the River Dee, chiefly since the beginning of the reign of Henry VII, a most prudent prince, until this day – who, lineally descending from his grandfather, Owen Tudor, a Welshman born in the Isle of Anglesey, quite delivered all the Welshmen from such laws of bondage as in other kings' days they

---

176-77. In Oxford Douce L. 533, the word 'vanquished' is crossed out and 'slew' written in the margin by an early hand.

[251] a rebellion made by one Owain [...] all that nation] The only reference in the *Breviary* to the rebellion of Owain Glyndwr. On the Penal Laws of 1402, see below, p. 149.

were subject unto.²⁵² And the most mighty prince, King Henry VIII, his son, delivered them wholly from all servitude, and made them in all points equal to the Englishmen.²⁵³ Whereby it cometh to pass that, laying aside their old manners, they who before were wont to live most sparingly are now enriched and do imitate the Englishmen in diet and apparel.²⁵⁴ Howbeit, they be somedeal impatient of labour, and overmuch boasting of the nobility of their stock, applying themselves rather to the service of noblemen²⁵⁵ than giving themselves to the learning of handicrafts. So that you shall find but few noblemen in England, but that the greater part of their retinue (wherein Englishmen exceed all other nations) are Welshmen born. For men chiefly brought up with milk meats,° being nimble and well set of body, are very apt to do any kind of business. Besides, being somewhat high-minded and in extreme poverty, acknowledging the nobility of their family, are more given to the culture and trimming of their bodies (like Spaniards) than to riches or the belly, and being very apt to learn courtlike behaviour, are therefore by the English nobility preferred before Englishmen.

Howbeit also of late they have very commendably begun to inhabit towns, to learn occupations, to exercise merchandise, to till the ground well, and to do all other kinds of public and necessary functions as well as Englishmen. And in this one thing surpassing them, that there is no man so poor, but for some space he setteth forth his children to school, and such as profit in study sendeth them unto the universities where, for the most part, they enforce them to study the civil law.²⁵⁶ Whereby it chanceth that the greater sort of those which profess the civil or canon laws in this realm are Welshmen. And you shall find but few of the ruder sort which cannot read and write their own name, and play on the harp after their manner. And now also the Holy Scriptures and daily service are printed in their tongue.²⁵⁷ And like as this nation (as Tacitus

---

[252] Llwyd rather over-praises Henry VII who, though he showed favour to the Welsh in some respects, did not repeal the Penal Laws.
[253] in all points equal to the Englishmen] Llwyd refrains from noting that one aspect of the equality legislated by the so-called Acts of Union was the banning of the Welsh language from courts of law and public offices.
[254] **Marg.** 'Commendation of Welshmen'
[255] **Marg.** 'Their skill in service'
[256] **Marg.** 'Their studies in learning'
[257] Holy Scriptures [...] printed in their tongue] As MP for Denbigh, Llwyd had been instrumental in securing the passage of Act of Parliament calling for the translation of the Bible into Welsh (1563). William Salesbury's translations of the

reporteth) being very impatient of injuries was always at variance in continual wars and slaughter within itself, so now, through fears of laws which they do very civilly obey, they strive in actions° and controversies unto the consuming of all their goods. And thus much touching the manners and demeanour of the Welshmen at this day.

But now hear of their old, out of Giraldus, which writeth thus:

It is a light nation, a sharp nation rather than a rough, a nation wholly given unto wars. For here, not only the noblemen but all the multitude is ready to armour. For the trumpet no sooner soundeth alarm but the husbandman cometh as speedily to battle from the plough as doth the courtier from the court. For not here, as in other places, 'the ploughman's toil in circle round doth run';[258] for in March and April only they steer once for oats, but they fallow not twice in summer, and the third winter after for wheatland. The most part of the people is fed with rudder beasts[259] for the pail. They feed on oats, cheese, milk, and butter, on flesh more abundantly, on bread more sparingly. They trouble themselves with no merchandise, with no travel by sea, with no handicrafts, neither with any affairs else, saving martial. And yet they seek for preservation of peace, and their liberty. They fight for their country, they labour for their liberty, for which, not only to blade it out, but also to lose their lives they count it sweet. Whereby it cometh that they think it shame to die in their beds, and an honour to die in war. And these, being now the remnants of Aeneas's train, would run forth headlongwise in armour for their liberty. Of whom this is very notable to be marked, that many times, being naked, they dare encounter with those which bear weapon,[260] unarmed with those which are armed, and footmen with horsemen. In which conflict, many times, only through their nimbleness, and courage of mind they become the conquerors. And are not

---

New Testament (*Testament Newydd*) and the Book of Common Prayer (*Y Llyfr Gweddi Gyffredin*) had appeared in 1567, published by Humphrey Toy, a London stationer of Welsh descent.

[258] 'the ploughman's toil in circle round doth run'] Gerald quotes Virgil, *Georgics*, 2.401.

[259] rudder beasts] rother beasts, cattle.

[260] those which bear weapon] 'cum ferro vestitis' might better be translated 'those clad in armour'.

unlike unto those in place, and nature, of whom the poet speaketh:

> Subject unto the Northern Bear,
> Most happy folk by their mischance, on whom those heaps of fear,
> And chiefest dread of death doth nothing daunt. Whereby doth rise
> To them a ready mind to run to fight, and death despise,
> Accounting for to spare life, that will come again, great cowardice.[261]

And in another place:

A nation slenderly armed, trusting rather to their agility than the force of their men. For if they be overcome today, and shamefully turned in to bloody fight, notwithstanding tomorrow they prepare a new expedition, not mindful of their loss nor shame. And although they prevail not when war is proclaimed with open meetings, yet in secret ambushments and breakings in by night they will vex their enemy. So that being nothing troubled with hunger nor cold, neither wearied with martial affairs, neither falling into desperation by adversity, but soon ready to rise up after a fall, and pressed by and by again to assay the peril of war, as in battle easy, so in continuance of war hard to be overcome. Whereby Claudianus seemeth to speak of the nature of the same nation, saying:

> If that their hearts you let a while
> To rest, so many slaughters they
> Devoid of sense do seem
> To take, and of small price the loss
> Of so much blood to deem.[262]

---

[261] *Cambriae descriptio*, I. 8, quoting Lucan, *Pharsalia*, Book 1.
[262] *Cambriae descriptio*, II.4, quoting Claudian, *In Eutropium*, Book 2. Llwyd quotes judiciously from a chapter chiefly concerned with the weakness and cowardice of the Welsh in battle.

Thus much he, and more which shortly, God willing, shall be set forth.[263]

Now let us come to the description of the land. This land, after the British destruction, was divided into six regions – as I read of late in a very ancient book written of the laws of the Britons. For (sayeth that book) after that the Saxons had vanquished the Britons and obtained the sceptre of the realm and the crown of London, all the people of Wales assembled together at the mouth of the River Dyfi to choose a king. 'Ac yno y doethant gwyr Gwynedd, a gwyr Powys, a gwyr Deheubarth, a Reynnwc, ac Esylluc, a Morganuc.' That is to say, and thither came men of Gwynedd, and men of Powys, and men of Deheubarth, and of Reynnucia, and of Syllucia, and Morgania,[264] and they chose Maelgwn, whom others call Maglocunus of Gwynedd, to be their king.[265] This was about the year of Our Lord 560.

Howbeit, afterward, in the lamentable conflict against Ethelfredus King of Northumberland, are recited the kings of Dynetia, which falsely they call Demetia, of Gwenta, of Powysia, and of North Wales. And in another place mention is made of the kings of Ystrad Clwyd. So that hereby it is easily gathered that this country was subject unto divers petty-kings or earls, unto the time of Roderick the Great,[266] who obtained the monarchy of all Wales, the year of Our Lord 843, dividing it into three parts, which he left in possession of his three sons. For unto Mervinius (as Giraldus termeth him, to whom I consent), his eldest son, he gave Gwynedd; to Anarawdus (whom some make the eldest), Powys; and to Cadellus, the youngest, Deheubarth. And that I may use the words of Gildas:

> South Wales was allotted to Cadellus with the blessing and goodwill of all the people, which they call Deheubarth, which is

---

[263] more which shortly, God willing, shall be set forth] Llwyd apparently intended to publish an edition of Gerald's writings about Wales, as David Powel would eventually do in 1585.

[264] Reynnucia [...] Syllucia [...] Morgania] Reinwg, Seisyllwg, and Morgannwg were all divisions of Deheubarth, or South Wales.

[265] Maelgwn [...] their king] Maelgwn of Gwynedd, who reigned in the mid-sixth century, is bitterly disparaged by Gildas in *De Excidio et Conquestu Britanniae*, where his name is given as Maglocunus.

[266] Roderick the Great] Rhodri Mawr (d. *c.* 878) peacefully united most of Wales under his rule in the third quarter of the ninth century.

as much to say as, the right side. Which, although in quantity it be far the biggest, notwithstanding, by reason of noblemen (which in the Welsh tongue are called *uchelwyr*, that is to say, high men, wherewith it aboundeth) which were wont to rebel against their lords, and to defy them in armour, it seemed to be the worser.[267]

This division (whilst their posterity contended among themselves in civil war, and each of them alone with the Englishmen in external) at last destroyed the kingdom of Wales.

The chiefest of these kingdoms, which the inhabitants call Gwynedd, Englishmen North Wales, and the Latin writers corruptly Venodotia, had in ancient time these limits: on the west and north sides it hath Vergivium, or the Irish Ocean, at the southwest and by south the River Dyfi, whereby it is cut off from South Wales. On the south and east sides it is severed from Powys and England with high hills, and sometime with waters unto the force of the River Dee. The same also was parted into four regions which contained fifteen *cantrefi*,° which signifieth an hundred villages.

The principalest of these regions was the Isle of Anglesey, of whom we have spoken in another place, and in the same was a king's palace, the seat of North Wales, in Aberffraw, whereof the kings of Gwynedd, have the name of the kings of Aberffraw. For in the laws of Hywel Dda (that is to say, Good Howel), of Wales both king and lawyer,[268] which I have seen written both in the British and Latin tongues, it was decreed that like as the King of Aberffraw ought to pay threescore and three pounds for tribute unto the king of London, so likewise the kings of Dinefwr and Mathrafal were severally bound to pay so much. Whereby it appeareth that this king was the chiefest prince of all Wales. About Anglesey be divers little islands, as Ynys Adar, that is to say, the Isle of Birds sometime, but now it is called Ynys Moelrhoniaid, to wit the Isle of Whales, in English the Skerries.[269] Also Ynys y

---

[267] The quotation is from Gerald of Wales, *Cambriae descriptio*, I. 2, and not from Gildas, who lived three centuries before Rhodri Mawr.
[268] lawyer] lawgiver
[269] Ynys Moelrhoniad [...] Isle of Whales [...] Skerries] Ynys Moelrhoniad in fact means the Isle of Seals, as Llwyd's 'insula phocarum' makes clear; Twyne, apparently unfamiliar with The Skerries, simply transcribes the word 'Ysterisd' from the *Commentarioli*.

Llygod, that is, the Isle of Mice, and the isle Seiriol, in English Priestholm.

The second region of Gwynedd, called Arfon (as who should say 'above Anglesey'), the best fortified part of all Wales, for it containeth the highest mountains and rocks of all Britain, which we term Eryri, the Englishmen Snowdon, because they carry snow. For height and plenty of cattle scarce inferior to the Alps, it hath in it many rivers and standing waters; beyond whose farthest promontory, called Llŷn, lieth an isle which Ptolomaeus termeth Lymnos, our countrymen Enlli, the Englishmen Bardsey, that is to say, the Isle of the Bardi. In Arfon over against Anglesey stood an ancient city, called of the Romans Segontium, of the Britons Caersegont, of a river which passeth thereby. But now out of the ruins thereof there is a new town, and a castle founded by Edward the First of that name, King of England, called Caer Arfon, that is to say, a town upon Anglesey. And not far from thence, over against Anglesey, lieth the bishop's see of Bangor. And upon Conwy water, which there ebbeth and sloweth, standeth Conwy, of our countrymen called Aberconwy, a walled town builded by the same king.

Then followeth Meridnia, with us Meirionnydd, and Giraldus calleth it the land of the sons of Conavius. 'The same', as he sayeth, 'is the most roughest and sharpest of all Wales, having in it most highest mountains. The people use long spears, wherewith they be of great force, as the South Wales men with their bows, so that a harness cannot bear it off.'[270] So much he. The sea-coast there, by occasion of great herring taking, is much frequented by people of divers countries. In the same standeth the town Harlechia, by the seaside. And within the land is the great Lake Tegid, through which the river Dee, which we call *Dyfrdwy*, (that is to say, the water of Dee) floweth. Where it is worth the noting that there is in that pond a peculiar kind of fish which is never found in the running water; neither the salmons, whereof the river is full, do ever enter into the lake. In this country and in Arfon are seen great multitude of deer and goats upon the high hills. And these two countries, of all Wales, came last into the power of the Englishmen. Neither did the people of this country ever frequent domestical

---

[270] a harness cannot bear it off] That is, iron mail cannot deflect it.

incursions, but before our time always seemed to obey laws rightfully.²⁷¹

The farthest and last part of Gwynedd is called of our countrymen Y Berfeddwlad, that is to say, the inward and midland region, and is severed from Arfon by the river Conwy, of whom Antoninus and Ptolomaeus do speak under the name of Novius. In this, besides the forenamed river, standeth a most antique city of the Britons called Deganwy in Rhos, of the Englishmen Gannock, and famous in Tacitus by the name of Cangorum, whereof the people of that country were called of the Romans Cangi. And Ptolomaeus mentioneth the promontory of the Iangani, which they call now Gogarth – a place so fortified by nature that it can scarce be taken by man's strength. This city (as I say) was the seat and palace of the later kings of Britain, whenas now their power began to quail, as namely of Maelgwn, Cadfanus, Cadwalla (whom Bede termeth a most cruel tyrant, because he persecuted his enemies very fiercely), and of Cadwaladr, who was the last king of Britain of the British blood. This city, the year of our redemption 816, Cynan Dyndaethwy reigning in Wales, was struck with lightning from heaven, and burned in such sort that it could never be afterward restored. Howbeit, the name remaineth to the place to this day, out of whose rubbish Conovia was builded.

Moreover, in this territory, in Rhyfaniacum,²⁷² Henry Lacy, Earl of Lincoln, to whom the conqueror thereof, Edward I, gave that land, erected a very stout castle, not only by natural situation but also by a wall of wonderful thickness, made of a very hard kind of stone, in my opinion the strongest and best-defenced thing in England.²⁷³ Adding also thereto a town walled about, which by the ancient name he called Dynbech, although those which came afterward termed it Denbigh. This fine town (and my sweet country), being compassed well nigh about with very fair parks and standing in the entrance of an exceeding pleasant valley, aboundeth plentifully with all things that are necessary to the use of man. The hills yield flesh and white meats; the most fertile valley, very good

---

²⁷¹ If Tudor Meirionnydd seemed less law-abiding than in times past, this was in part due to its recent incorporation of the district of Mawddwy; the 'red bandits of Mawddwy' were responsible for various notorious crimes, including the murder of Lewis Owen, Sheriff of Meirionnydd, in 1555.
²⁷² Rhyfaniacum] Rhufoniog
²⁷³ England] 'totius Angliae' seems a remarkable slip on Llwyd's part; Denbigh Castle is not in England.

corn and grass. The sweet rivers, with the sea at hand, minister all sorts of fish and foul. Strange wines come thither forth of Spain, France, and Greece, abundantly. And being the chief town of the shire, standing in the very middle of the country, it is a great market town, famous and much frequented with wares and people from all parts of North Wales. The indwellers have the use of both tongues and, being endowed by kings of England with many privileges and liberties, are ruled by their own laws. The valley nigh whereto this town standeth is termed amongst us Dyffryn Clwyd, that is to say the Valley of Clwyd. It is almost eighteen miles in length, and in breadth in some places four miles, in othersome six. On the east, west, and south sides it is environed with high hills, on the north with the ocean sea. In the midst it is cut in twain by the River Clwyd, whereof it taketh name, into whom divers other little streams, falling out of the hills, do discharge themselves, by reason whereof irriguous and pleasant meadows and plentiful pastures do lie about the banks thereof. In the entrance of which valley, Ruthin, an ancient town and castle of the Greys, from whence the most noble family amongst the Englishmen took beginning, is to be seen. And not far from the sea standeth Rhuddlan, in Tegeingl, sometime a great town but now a little village. In the same province is a cathedral church, of our country men called Llanelwy, of the Englishmen, St Asaph, builded between two rivers, Clwyd and Elwy.

I remember that I have read that there was one Elbodius, Archbishop of North Wales, preferred unto that honour by the Bishop of Rome. Who first of all, the year of our salvation 762, reconciled the Welshmen to the Romish Church, from which before they had disagreed. For the Britons, imitating the Asiatic Church, celebrated their Easter from the fourteenth day of the moon unto the twentieth; when the Romans, following the Nicene Council, keep their Easter from the fifteenth to the one and twentieth. Whereby it cometh to pass that these nations have celebrated that feast on divers Sundays. But let the bishops take regard how far they do err from the decrees of the Nicene Council while they follow that uncertain rule of the motion of the sun and moon which they call the Golden Number,[274] being therein very

---

[274] **Marg.** 'The Golden Number reproved'. The Golden Number, used in calculating the date of Easter, refers to a given year's position within a 19-year cycle of 235 full moons.

foully deceived. Which thing in times past was objected for a crime against the Britons by the over-superstitious monk Augustine, and likewise by Bede, which too much attributed unto such trifles, insomuch that for the same cause he durst term them heretics. But now, howbeit under curse of the Nicene Council, it be otherwise commanded: it is rejected by the prelates themselves, and the whole Church of Europe. But let us return to our purpose.

In that place where the See of St Asaph is, was sometime a college of learned agonists,[275] that I may use Capgrave's words, celebrated for multitude, under Kentigern a Scot, which was called Elguense (or Eluense) of a river. This province, Tegenia, is called of the Latins Igenia, and after being vanquished by the Englishmen began to be termed Tegeingl, that is to say, the Englishmen's Tegenia. Afterward, being inhabited by Britons – coming forth of Scotland and driving the Englishmen thence – with the valley of Clwyd, Ruthin, and Rosse, make one kingdom, which Marianus calleth Streudglead, our countrymen term it Ystrad Clwyd, that is to say, the Soil of Clwyd. For this word *ystrad*, with the name of some river joined thereto, doth usually signify amongst the Welsh men, a vein or soil of land nigh to a river, as Ystrad Alyn, Ystrad Towyn, with many such like. Their last prince, called Dunwallo, forsaking his kingdom when the Danes afflicted all Britain, departed to Rome the year after the incarnation 971, where shortly after he died.[276]

In Tegenia is a well of a marvelous nature which, being six miles from the sea, in the parish of Cilcain, ebbeth and floweth twice in one day. Yet have I marked this of late, when the moon ascendeth from the east horizon to the south (at what time all seas do flow), that then the water of this well diminisheth and ebbeth. And not far from this place is the famous fountain taking name of the superstitious worshipping of the virgin Winifred, which boiling up suddenly out of a place which they call Sychnant, that is to say a dry valley, raiseth forth of itself a great stream, which runneth immediately into Devanus. This water, besides that it breedeth moss of a very pleasant savour, is also most wholesome unto man's body both for washing and drinking, and of very good taste, in so much that many being washed therein were cured of divers

---

[275] agonists] strugglers (against sin and ignorance).
[276] Dyfnwal III, King of Strathclyde (d. 975), ruled over the region in Scotland, not over Ystrad Clwyd in North Wales.

infirmities wherewith they were born. Moreover, in Tegenia there is a certain ancient monument of an old building, in a place called Bodfari, sometime renowned by Roman letters and arms. The town which they call Flint, standing upon the water Deva, is known not only to be the head of Tegenia, but also of the whole shire.

After the description of Gwynedd, let us now come to Powys, the second kingdom of Wales. Which in the time of German Altisiodorensis,[277] which preached sometime there against Pelagius's heresy,[278] was of power, as is gathered out of his life. The king whereof, as is there read, because he refused to hear that good man, by the secret and terrible judgement of God, with his palace and all his household was swallowed up into the bowels of the earth, in that place whereas, not far from Oswestry, is now a standing water of an unknown depth, called Llynclys, that is to say, the devouring of the palace.[279] And there are many churches found in the same province dedicated to the name of German. The city of Shrewsbury in old time was the prince's seat of this kingdom. But when the Englishmen had taken it, it was translated to Mathrafal, a place five miles from Pool° of Powys. This region had on the north side Gwynedd; on the east, from Chester unto Hereford, England; on the south and west, the River Wye and very high hills whereby it was disjoined from South Wales. And because the land was plain and near to England, and much vexed with continual war by Englishmen, and afterward by the Normans, this part of Wales did first experiment° the yoke of English subjection. Which brooding stout men, and such whose nature could not abide to be at rest, but given to murder and excursions, not only procured infinite trouble unto the kings of England, but wrought also great injury unto their neighbours the Welshmen. But afterward, being parted between two brothers, as was the custom of the Britons, it began to wax weak. And the part which lieth on the north side of Tanat, Murnia, and Severn befell unto Madoc, whereof it was called Powys Fadog. The other part came both in name and possession of Gwenwynwyn.[280]

---

[277] German Altisiodorensis] St Germanus of Auxerre

[278] Pelagius's heresy] The British monk Pelagius, active in the late third and early fourth centuries, denied the doctrine of original sin and hence the need of divine grace.

[279] Llynclys [...] devouring of the palace] From W. *llyn* (lake) and *llys* (palace).

[280] See *History of Cambria*, below, p. 162.

The first lost the name of Powys, for being subdued by the Normans it came into the power and right of the conquerors. The first region thereof, Maelor, is divided into twain by the River Dee, namely the Saxon and Welsh, whereof the first appertaineth unto Flintshire, and the other unto Denbighshire, in the which standeth the Castle of Lion, now commonly called Holt. And not far from thence are seen the rubbish and relics of the most notable and famous monastery of Bangor, while the glory of the Britons flourished. In the same were two thousand and one hundred monks, very well ordered and learned, and divided into seven sorts, daily serving God. Amongst whom, those which were simple and unlearned by their handy labour provided meat and drink and apparel for the learned, and such as applied their study. And if anything were remaining they divided it unto the poor. That place hath sent forth many hundreds of excellently well-learned men (amongst whom it hath also vomited forth to the world the most detestable arch-heretic Pelagius). And afterward, through the envy and malice of Augustine – not the Bishop of Hippo, but the most arrogant monk – and the most cruel execution of his minister Aethelfrith,[281] worthy men, of far more perfect order than he was of, were made away, and the whole house from the very foundations, together with their most noble library, more precious than gold, was razed down and destroyed with fire and sword.[282]

It were overlong to repeat what Latin and British chronicles do report of the intolerable pride of this man. For when he, sitting in his regal seat, disdained to rise up unto the British bishops, which came unto him humbly and meekly as it became Christians to do, they beholding the same both judged and said that he was not the minister of the most gentle and meek lamb Christ, but of Lucifer, as they had learned in the Holy Scriptures, and so they departed home again. For which contempt and reproach, and partly also because they agreed not in some points with the Archbishop of Canterbury, which he had appointed,[283] and with the Church of Rome, he so stirred the hate of the Englishmen against them that shortly after, as I said, by Aethelfrith, through the aid and help of

---

[281] Aethelfrith] King Aethelfrith of Northumbria, who was deemed to have slaughtered the monks of Bangor Yscoed in a battle near Chester at the instigation of Augustine of Canterbury.
[282] **Marg**. 'A wicked deed'
[283] which he had appointed] i.e. to which office he had been appointed.

Ethelbert King of Kent, provoked thereto by Augustine, the monks which desired peace were most cruelly slain. And afterward the Britons, under the conduct of Brochwel King of Powys, were vanquished. Until that at length, being aided with power from Belthrusius Duke of Cornwall, Cadfan King of North Wales, Meredoc King of South Wales, and heartened forward by the oration of their most learned abbot Dunetus,[284] who commanded, as our chronicles report, that everyone should kiss the ground in remembrance of the communion of the Body of Our Lord,[285] and should take up water in their hands forth of the River Dee and drink it,[286] in commemoration of the most Sacred Blood of Christ which was shed for them, who[287] having so communicated, they overcame the Saxons in a famous battle and slew of them, as Huntingdon writeth, a thousand, threescore and six, and created Carduanus their king in the City of Legions.

Next ensue Yale and Chirk, hilly countries. In this last standeth that antique castle which at this day is called Brennus's Palace. And these appertain unto Denbighshire. But more to the north are Ystrad Alyn, so named of the River Alyn, and Hope, of Flintshire. Towards Shrewsbury lieth Whittington and Oswestry, a noble market, and enwalled round at the charges of the Fitzalans, a most ancient family of England whose inheritance it is, and these belong unto Shropshire. Above these in the west are the Edeirnion men, joined now unto the Meirionnydd men, upon the River Dee. And all these, at this present, are called Gwyneddii, or men of Gwynedd, for the name of the men of Powys is perished amongst them.

The second region of Powys contained the same province,[288] which now only enjoyeth the name of Powys, and sometime stretched very wide, but now containeth only three *cantrefi*, lying wholly on the north side of the River Severn – which is the second river of Britain, falling from the high mountains of Plymnonia, and rising forth of the same head with Wye and Rheidol, and running through Arwystli and Cedewain in Powys, maketh speed to

---

[284] Abbot Dunetus] Saint Dunod, Abbot of Bangor-on-Dee.
[285] **Marg.** 'Note this place'
[286] Spenser in *The Faerie Queene* refers to 'Dee, which Britons long ygone / Did call diuine, that doth by Chester tend' (4.11.x).
[287] who] The subject of the sentence is the Britons of Powys.
[288] The second region [...] province] i.e. the same province contained the second region of Powys (Powys Wenwynwyn).

Shrewsbury, and so floweth forward through Bridgnorth, Worcester, and Gloucester, from which, not far off, it ebbeth and floweth,[289] and between Wales, Devonshire, and Cornwall beareth name of the Severn Sea. Our countrymen term it Hafren, and not Severn as the Englishmen do. The chief town and king's seat of Powys, called Mathrafal, retaineth the ancient name, howbeit the buildings be defaced and worn. And one mile from Severn standeth a town, the only market of all that region, of the Englishmen Pool, of the Welshmen called Trallwng, that is to say, the town of the standing water, so called of the lake whereto it is nigh, where there stand aloft two castles builded sometime by the princes of Powys. This princedom came by inheritance unto a woman called Hawise who, being married unto one Charleton an Englishman, made him Lord of Powys,[290] from which house at length it descended unto the Greys in the north.

Next unto that standeth Cadevenna, a new town,[291] above whom towards the rising of Severn are Arwystli and Llanidloes, countries well known by reason of the towns. And more by west and by north, at the head of Dyfi, Mawddwy, now a portion of Meirionnydd, and Cyfeiliog, known by the town Machynlleth. On the other side of Severn, beneath the region Kerry, there is a castle by a little town which Welshmen call Trefaldwyn, that is to say Baldwin's town, but the Englishmen term it Montgomery, of the builder Roger of Mont Gomer.[292] From this town, all these regions being joined together are called Montgomeryshire, a country breeder sometime of noble horses (now it sendeth forth but few), and by the forenamed Roger and his sons, very valiant and warlike gentlemen, very sorely afflicted, until that Robert being accused of high treason was enforced to fly his country.[293] The region is hilly, and by reason of plentifulness of pastures very good for grazing of cattle, abounding with many waters, and bringing forth tall men,

---

[289] ebbeth and floweth] The Severn becomes a tidal river a few miles above Gloucester.
[290] Hawise [...] Lord of Powys] Hawise Gadarn [the Strong], heiress to Owain ap Gruffydd ap Gwenwynwyn or Owen de la Pole, Lord of Powys, married John Charleton in 1309.
[291] Cadevenna, a new town] That is, Newtown in the *cantref* of Cedewain, founded under Edward I.
[292] Roger of Mont Gomer] Roger Montgomerie, 1st Earl of Shrewsbury (d. 1094).
[293] Robert [...] enforced to fly his country] Robert de Bellême, 3rd Earl of Shrewsbury, was deprived of his English lands and titles after rebelling against Henry I in 1101.

very well-favoured, much addicted unto idleness and unprofitable games. Whereby it cometh to pass that you shall find many rich English farmers amongst them, whenas the landlords themselves, which will take no pains, do become very poor. These six shires, namely Anglesey, Arfon, Meirionnydd, Denbighshire, Flintshire, and Montgomeryshire, Englishmen comprise under the name of North Wales.

There remaineth yet that part of Powys which stretched sometime unto Wye, whose first region taketh name of the River Colunwy,[294] and of the castle and possession of the Fitzalans. Next to Maelienydd and Gwrtheyrnion, hilly countries, and at the south, Radnor, called of the Welshmen Maesyfed, head of the shire. Joining unto these are the Elfael, with the Castle of Pain,[295] by Wye, which our countrymen call Gwy. Beyond all these are Presteigne, which we call St Andrew's Church, and Kington, with the Castle of Huntington. And upon Temis, of us called Tefeidiad, standeth the fair town and castle of Ludlow in Shropshire, in old time called Dinau, the work of Roger Montgomer; and above that, the castle of Wigmore, the patrimony of the Mortimers. And at Severn, Bridgnorth and Bewdley, in old time very well known by the castle Tychil.[296] And on the south-west side, upon Logus,[297] which we call Llugwy, on a passing fertile plain standeth Llanllieni, of the Englishmen Leominster. And not far thence is the ancient city Henffordd, that is to say, an old way, of Englishmen in old time called Ferleg, now Hereford, standing upon Wye, or more truly upon Gwy.

Towards Severn are Malvern Hills, and in the very corner between Severn and Wye, not far from the town of Ross, is that renowned wood which of the Danes is called the Forest of Dean. These regions, with all Herefordshire beyond Wye, before they were possessed by the Englishmen, in old time were termed in British Euryennwc, and the inhabitants Eurnwyr – of which name there remaineth yet some signification apparent in one place of Herefordshire. For that which the Englishmen called Archenfeld, the Welshmen called Ergyng, and afterward Ergengl. And no

---

[294] Colunwy] Clun, Shropshire
[295] Castle of Pain] Painscastle
[296] the castle Tychil] Tickenhill Palace, Bewdley
[297] Logus] The River Lugg

marvel, since the least portion thereof retaineth now (as I have said) the name of Powys.

There remaineth the third kingdom of Wales, of the English called South Wales, of our countrymen which inhabit the land Deheubarth, that is to say the right or south part, for so we use to term the south. The same is wholly compassed with the Irish Sea, the stream of Severn, and the rivers Wye and Dyfi. And although the country be very fertile and the land rich, and far more bigger then Gwynedd, notwithstanding, as Giraldus sayeth, it was counted the worser. And that not only because *uchelwyr*, that is to say the noblest and chiefest men, refused to obey their kings, but also by reason that the sea-coasts thereof were continually molested by the Englishmen, Normans, and Flemings. Whereby the prince was compelled to forsake Carmarthen his seat, and to appoint the principal place of his regality at Dinefwr in Cantref Mawr. And although these princes were of great authority in Wales, yet after that Rhesus the son of Theodore the Great[298] was slain through the treason of his own men, they were no longer termed dukes, nor princes, but *arglwyddi*, that is to say lords. Until at length, through civil wars, by dividing of their lands amongst many, and also by external (while the Englishmen endeavoured to possess all by force and craft), they were so weakened, that after the death of Rhesus the son of Gruffudd[299] (a very noble and valiant gentleman) they lost both the authority and name of princes and lords.

Now let us descend unto the description of the province, whereof the first region which cometh to hand is that, which Giraldus calleth Ceretica, our countrymen Ceredigion, the Englishmen Cardigan. (Where it is to be noted, as in all other, that C and G have the force of *Cappa* and *Gamma*.) This region on the north hath the Irish Sea, on the east the river Dyfi, whereby it is divided from Gwynedd, and towards Powys very high hills, on the south, Carmarthen, and on the west, Dynetia. Their tongue (as Giraldus affirmeth) is esteemed the finest of all the other people of Wales. And Gwynedd's the purer, without permixtion, coming nearest unto the ancient British. But the southern most rudest and coarsest, because it hath greatest affinity with strange tongues.

---

[298] Rhesus the son of Thedore the Great] Rhys ap Tewdwr Mawr (d. 1093).
[299] Rhesus the son of Gruffudd] Rhys ap Gruffudd (d. 1197); see *History of Cambria*, below, p. 159.

The sea-coast of this part Richard de Clare, a very noble man, coming in with a navy and building castles at the mouths of Dyfi and Ystwyth, possessed it for his own, and leaving garrisons there returned into England. But when he understood that his men were besieged by the Welshmen, being boldened by his great power, he intended by an over-rash enterprise to go aid them by land. But at Coed Grano, not far from Abergavenny, he was slain with all his army by Iorwerth of Caerlleon. And so those forts returned again unto their old lords.

I suppose that the mouth of Ystwyth is of Ptolomaeus called Rotossa, and Aberdyfi, Tibium, but that through negligence of the transcribers they were confounded into one.[300] Not far from this place standeth Llanbadarn Fawr, that is the Church of Paternus the Great, which in old time was had in great veneration. For Welshmen, above all other nations, were accustomed to reverence churches and attribute much honour unto ecclesiastical persons. For (as Giraldus reporteth) they used not once to touch the most deadliest foes they had, and such as were accused of treason, if they escaped unto the church. Yea, not so much as their enemies' cattle, if they fed in any pastures or leazes which appertained unto the Church. Moreover, when they be armed and going unto battle, if they fortune to meet with a priest on the way, they will cast down their weapons and require benediction with a stooping head. In the same region is a place in which (they say) under Dewi's feet, whom in Latin they call David, while he inveighed against the Pelagians, the earth billowed and rose up in a hill, which they term Llandewi Brefi. In the other part of the region is the principal town of the shire, upon the river Teifi, which we term Aberteifi, to say, the mouth of Teifus; the Englishmen call it Cardigan. This river only of all Britain, as Giraldus reporteth, aboundeth with otters,[301] but now our countrymen know not what they are. The bare name, which is *afanc*, they take for a monster of the water.

Passing forth along by the same sea-coast, there cometh unto our view a region of ancient time termed of our countrymen Dyfed, of Ptolomaeus, Demetia (for Dynetia), in English, West Wales, and now Pembrokeshire. The same reacheth from sea to sea, the farther

---

[300] confounded into one] Ptolemy writes of a river Ratostabius in South Wales.

[301] with otters] 'castoribus' should rather be translated 'with beavers'. In 2011, the Wales Wild Land Foundation announced plans to reintroduce beavers to Ceredigion for the first time since the twelfth century.

promontory whereof Ptolomaeus calleth Octopitarum, a little declining from the word Pebidion. By the northern ocean along lie Trefdraeth and Abergwaun,[302] and Cilgerran within the mainland, and in the west angle, is the bishop's see of Menevia,[303] sometime famous with an archbishop's see. For Dewi, who is called David, translated the Archbishopric from the City of Legions, where it was of antiquity, into Menevia. After whom there sat there five and twenty archbishops, whose names are found in Giraldus.[304] The last whereof, called Samson, in the time of a grievous plague of pestilence then reigning, fled into Armorica, or the Lesser Britain, with his pall,[305] where being chosen Bishop of Dol he left there his pall, which his successors have enjoyed unto this day, before whom the Archbishop of Tours hath prevailed. But ours, by occasion of the Saxon war and their own poverty, lost their ancient dignity, notwithstanding all bishops of Wales were consecrated by the Bishop of Menevia, and he of them, as his suffragans, until the days of Henry I, whenas Bernhard was consecrated by the Archbishop of Canterbury, and used himself long time after as Archbishop, until in the end his action fell at Rome. This much Giraldus.

Neither was there any Bishop of Menevia before Morgeneu (which was the thirty-third from David) that tasted any flesh. And he, the very same night when he first tasted flesh, was slain by pirates.[306] This church hath been very often spoiled and destroyed by English and Danish pirates. Here in the Valley Rosea[307] was born the great Patrick who endued Ireland with the Christian faith. Haverfordia, which they call now West Hereford, is distant from this see 21 miles, in old time called of the Britons Aberdaugleddau, that is to say, the Mouth of Two Swords. For so the chiefest rivers of all Britain, which make any haven, are termed. Englishmen call the same Milford, and some Alaunicum, by the Latin name. The Welshmen call this Town now Hwlffordd, and the haven reserveth

---

[302] Trefdraeth and Abergwaun] Newport and Fishguard, Pembrokeshire.
[303] Menevia] St David's
[304] *Itinerarium* II.1. Gerald campaigned tirelessly but without success for the restoration of the office of Archbishop of St David's or Menevia, with authority over the bishops of Wales.
[305] pall] pallium, the vestment worn by an archbishop.
[306] Gerald records that on the night of his death Morganeu appeared in a vision before another bishop, saying 'Because I ate flesh, I am become flesh'.
[307] Valley Rosea] Glyn Rhosyn, or the Valley of Roses.

his antique name. Upon the same crook or bosom standeth Pembroke, head of the shire, the work of Arnulph Montgomer, which Gerald of Windsor valiantly defended against Rhesus, son to Theodore. And after that peace was established (as Giraldus reporteth) he took to wife Nessa, the daughter of Rhesus,[308] on whom he begat worthy issue both male and female, by whom both the sea-coast of Wales remained unto the Englishmen, and the force of Ireland was afterward vanquished. At the south sea lieth Tenby, as Englishmen term it, but Welshmen, Dinbych-y-Pysgod, that is to wit, Fishing Denbigh, so called for difference twixt it and the other, which is in Gwynedd. This same part of Demetia, or Dynetia, is at this day possessed and inhabited by Flemings, sent thither by Henry I. The people, being stout and rough, defended themselves and theirs valiantly against the Welshmen. And although many times, especially by Cadwaladr, Cynan, and Hywel, sons of Owain, Prince of Gwynedd, and Rhesus, son to Gruffudd of North Wales, and lastly by Llywelyn the Great, as Parisiensis termeth him, who had in his army thirty thousand men, they were almost destroyed and slain. Yet have they always recovered their strength again, and unto this day are known from Welshmen by diversity of their manners and tongue.

The third province of South Wales, Maridinia, taketh name of Maridunum, a very ancient city whereof both Latin and Greek writers make mention. By which name it was so called and known, long before the birth of that very well learned man whom the Englishmen corruptly call Merlin, but our countrymen Myrddin. Neither did the city take name of him, but he of that, whereas he was borne. We call the same Caerfyrddin by reason of propriety of the tongue, whereby we change M into V (the consonant, for whom our countrymen do use F), in the castle and city of Myrddin. That same Ambrose, who was borne of a noble virgin (whose fathers name is of purpose suppressed), for his passing skill in the mathematics and wonderful knowledge in all other kind of learning was by the rude, common people reputed to be the son of an

---

[308] Nessa, the daughter of Rhesus] The princess Nest ferch Rhys, a famous hinge of Welsh genealogies, had numerous children, both in her marriage with Gerald de Windsor and through liaisons with various other Welsh nobles and marcher lords.

2940 incubus, or a male devil, which in similitude and likeness of men do use carnally to company with women.[309]

This town, as Giraldus writeth, was in old time compassed round with a fair brick wall. And upon the river Clarus, which Ptolomaeus termeth Tobius, we Towy, is said that the king's seat and palace of South Wales was builded, until that it was taken by the Englishmen. After what time it was removed unto Dinefwr upon the same river, a place very well fortified with woods and hills. In this region, by reason of the strong situation of places, the princes of South Wales made well-nigh their continual abode; 2950 which was divided from Ceretica by the River Teifi, by whose side standeth the noble castle of Emlyn. On the other sides it is environed with very high hills and with the sea.

Towards the sea is Catguilia, now Cydweli, a country sometime possessed by Mauritius of London. Next whom lieth Gower, which joineth unto Morgania, with a town at the mouth of Tawe, of us Abertawe, of Englishmen called Swansea. Morgania, of Englishmen Glamorgan, of us called Morgannwg and Gwlad Forgan, that is to say, the country of Morgan – of one Morgan which was there slain by his aunt's son Cuneda, who was King of 2960 Lloegr more than two thousand years since, so called.[310] It lieth on the Severn Sea, and was always wont to be rebellious against his prince. Wherefore, when it refused to obey his true and lawful prince, by the just judgement of God, which always revengeth rebellion and treason,[311] it was enforced to come in servitude unto strangers. For about the year of Our Lord 1090, when Iestinus, son to Gurgantus, Earl of Morgania,[312] refused to obey Rhesus, son to Theodore, Prince of South Wales, and sent Aeneas son to Cedivorus,[313] sometime Lord of Demetia, into England to take muster of soldiers, and there received a great army under the 2970 conduct of one Robert, son to Hamo, and joining with other rebels out of Wenta and Brechinia, met with Rhesus in Black Hill and

---

[309] Gerald of Wales follows Geoffrey of Monmouth in stating that Merlin's father was an incubus.
[310] According to Geoffrey of Monmouth, Marganus and Cunedagius were the sons of King Lear's two older daughters, Goneril and Regan. Some years after Lear's death, they overthrew their aunt Cordelia, and then made war upon each other.
[311] **Marg.** 'Treason and rebellion always punished'
[312] Iestinus, son to Gurgantus, Earl of Morgania] Iestyn ap Gwrgant (d. 1093), last King of Morgannwg.
[313] Aeneas son to Cedivorus] Einion ap Collwyn

there slew him; and so, paying the Englishmen their wages, discharged them. But they, taking regard unto the goodness of the soil, and the great variance which was then amongst the Welshmen, as in foretime the Saxons had done they turned their force of arms against those which entertained them, and soon displaced them wholly of all the champion,° and the best of the country. Which Hamo divided amongst twelve knights which he brought with him, reserving the better part to himself. Who, building there certain castles and joining their power together, defended their farms and lordships which they had possessed and taken. Whose heirs peaceably enjoy the same unto this day. But Iestinus scarcely reserved to himself and his the hilly country. The twelve knights names were these: London, Stradling, St John, Turberville, Grenville, Umfraville, St Quintin, Soarus, Sullius, Berkerollus, Siward, and Fleming. In this province are Neath, upon a river of the same name, Pontfaen, that is to say Stonebridge (Englishmen falsely call it Cowbridge), Llantwit, Ewenny, Dunwyd,[314] towns and castles, besides Caerphilly, a most ancient castle and fortress which, as report goeth, was erected by the Romans, and Caerdydd, the principal town of the shire, standing upon the river Taff (Englishmen term it Cardiff). And not far from thence is Llandaff, to say, a church standing on Tavus, ennobled with a bishop's see.

Next unto this region lieth Wenta, under Monmouthshire. This in old time was called Siluria, which may easily be proved, contrary unto the ridiculous authority of Boethius and Polydorus.[315] And first to begin with Tacitus, who affirmeth that the Siluri lie over against Spain – but these are far more near Spain than any part of Scotland, wherefore it is more like that they dwelt here, rather than in Scotland. Moreover, whereas in a fair discourse he describeth the expedition of Agricola against the Albani, or Scots, and there reciteth all the people and nations of Albania, he never maketh mention of the Siluri, which was the most warlike nation of them all. And undoubtedly, if they had been in Scotland he would never have passed them over with silence. Considering also how he telleth that there were exceeding great forests in Siluria, the tokens whereof remain as yet in Wenta.

Ptolomaeus also, and after him Marius Niger, layeth the Siluri next unto the Demeti and Maridunum, but somedeal more easterly.

---

[314] Dunwyd] St Donat's
[315] See above, p. 78.

3010 Besides these authorities, the most ancient book of the British laws mentioneth Syllwg, a province of Wales, whose inhabitants we must needs call in the British tongue Syllŵr, whereby they were of the Romans termed Silures. And one part of Wenta is at this day called Gwent-llwg, leaving out one syllable, as though it were Gwent Sillwg. Also Chepstow, a fine market town in Wenta, before a few years since passed was called by the name of Strigulia, which seemeth to come somewhat near to Siluria. Moreover Antoninus, a very grave author, maketh mention how Venta of the Siluri was not far from this, towards the ferry or place
3020 of passage over the Severn. Wherefore it were but a jest henceforth to seek for the Siluri in Scotland. And although that Plinius writeth that out of the region of the Siluri over into Ireland was but a very short cut, we must thus take it, that at his time Britain was not sufficiently known, nor the people of Albania long after that subdued. Whereby when certain of the Romans (as Englishmen use nowadays) had passed over into Ireland out of South Wales, others (which never saw Britain) supposed it to be a very short cut.

In this region is situate the most ancient and noble City of Legions which our countrymen call Caerlleon ar Wysg, that is to
3030 say, the City of Legions upon Usk (for difference sake between it and the other which is builded in North Wales, upon the River Dee). Of whom Giraldus writeth thus:

The same was an ancient and noble town, the tokens whereof remain as yet: a huge palace, a giantlike tower, goodly baths and hot houses, relics of churches, and places like theatres, compassed with beautiful walls, partly yet standing. Also buildings under the ground, conduits, secret passages, and vaults under the earth, stews[316] framed by wonderful
3040 workmanship. There lie two martyrs, Julius and Aaron, which had churches dedicated unto them. There was also a cathedral church of an Archbishop, under Dubricius,[317] which fell to David.

This much he.

---

[316] stews] hypocausts, for the heating of baths.
[317] under Dubricius] St Dubricius or Dyfirg, sixth-century evangelist of south-eastern Wales.

Also on the other side of Usk, in the way which leadeth to Strigulia, are seen ancient ditches and the remnants of town walls of the Siluri of Venta, which now also they call Caerwent, to wit, the city Venta, whereof the name grew to the whole country. At the mouth of Wye, which we call Gwy, is a famous market town, in old time Strigulia, but now called the Castle of Gwent. The Earls Marshal[318] and their heirs of this place, did very much weaken the state of Wales. Not far hence is Monmouth, of us Monwy, so called by the meeting of Mona and Wye together, the head of the whole shire. Above, at Osca, are the castle of Osca called Brynbuga, and in the upper Wenta, at the meeting of Usk and Gevenna, is Abergevenny, the lord whereof, Brian Guilford, wrought much mischief against the Wenti. But afterward, Willus Brustius, Lord of Brecknock,[319] under pretence of love and friendship called the nobles of Wenta into this castle to feasting and banqueting. Who coming thither with Seisyllius, son to Dunwallan, chief man of all that region, and his son Gruffudd, suspecting no deceit and unarmed, were every one most cruelly slain by Brustius's guard, which were put ready in armour for that purpose.[320] And afterward suddenly breaking into Seisyllius's house, the unmerciful butchers murdered the young infant Cadwaladr his son despiteously before the mother's face. Whose sons notwithstanding, taking the castle, and having slain Ranulf Poerius with many other noble men at Llanddingad,[321] manfully revenged their father's death. But Brustius, being reserved unto greater mischief, was famished to death with his mother in the castle of Windsor.[322]

And here I thought good to note that the name of Seisyllius, being common among the Britons and Welshmen, ought to be written not with C (which always expresseth the nature of the English K) but with S.[323] For else it should be read amongst the Welshmen 'Kyllius'.

---

[318] William Marshal, 1st Earl of Pembroke (d. 1219), was lord of Chepstow Castle and improved its fortifications.
[319] Willus Brustius] William de Braose (d. 1211).
[320] **Marg**. 'A cruel deed.'
[321] Ranulf Poer, Sheriff of Herefordshire was killed at Dingestow (Llanddingad) in 1182, an incident described by Gerald of Wales, *Itinerarium* I.4.
[322] **Marg**. 'A just revenge'. It was not the William de Braose responsible for the Abergavenny massacre but his wife and son (also named William) who were said to have been starved to death at Windsor by the orders of King John.
[323] The remark is aimed at the leading Elizabethan statesman William Cecil, who had anglicized his father's surname of Seisyllt.

There remaineth yet the last inland region of South Wales, which maketh the shire of Brecknock, the head whereof, Brecknock, or as the Welshmen term it, Aberhodni, standeth in Usk, upon the fall of Hodni.[324] Bernard of Newmarch, first of all Englishmen, by force of arms subdued the same. Above this region lieth Boguelth, which they term Builth, a rough and hilly country, reaching from Wye to Tobius. Beneath is Ewias, won by the power of Paganus, the son of John. Which afterward was parted in twain, Harold and Lacy. And not far thence is Hay, well known by Roman monuments, called Tregelli, that is to wit the Town of Hazels. These seven shires – Ceredigion; Dynetia,[325] called also Demetia and Pembrokeshire; Carmarthen; Morganica, now Glamorgan; Gwenta, called also Monmouth; Brycheiniog; and Radnor – are by Englishmen ascribed unto South Wales.

Thus much when I had written of the true, antique, and now-accustomed names of the regions and cities of Britain, I determined here to have ended, lest by this my unpolished and barbarous writing I should become tedious to the impatient reader. But when I called to my remembrance how Polydorus Vergilius, whose works be in all men's hands, doth in all places nip and gird at the Britons, endeavouring in words to extenuate the glory of the British name, and to obscure them with a perpetual blot, in his history often terming them a cowardly and false generation, I thought it worth the travail to bring forth a few authorities out of the books of famous writers and approved historiographers. Whereby the indifferent reader may easily judge, what credit is to be given to the said Polydorus; and that such as are of the learnedest writers of the state of Britain, either he read them not, or else (that is more like), being incensed with envy and hate of the British name, passed them over with silence.

Caesar himself, who first all the Romans made mention of Britain (howbeit, no man is accounted an upright judge in his own cause), confesseth that at the first encounter the Britons fought valiantly against the Romans, and that they troubled them very much, and afterward that the legion which was sent for provision of corn and victual was so pressed by their enemies that they could scarce endure it. And that at his coming, for fear (as he sayeth) they

---

[324] Aberhodni [...] Hodni] More commonly Aberhonddu, and Honddu.
[325] Dynetia] L. and T. both have 'Dwetia'; probably a compositor's error for Dynetia, L.'s preferred spelling.

retired. And that I may use his own words: 'Caesar, supposing it to be an unfit time to provoke the enemy and to give him battle, kept himself in his own place, and after short time brought back his legions into their tents.' This retreat some termed a flight, which may also be proved because that shortly after, when it was past midnight, he took shipping privily and departed out of Britain. Neither was this the power of all Britain, but a band of Kentishmen suddenly gathered, as appeareth in his history.

After this, in his first book, he showeth that the British wagoners fought stoutly upon the way, and in another place that they entered forcibly into his camp. And that the Roman cohorts or bands, being afeard when Laberius the tribune was slain, safely returned back again. Which, what other can it signify, then that they escaped by flight? He confesseth also how Cassivelaunus by the falling from him of Mandrubatius and certain his cities was especially moved – not by battle wearied – to send ambassadors unto him to entreat of peace. All these things, spitefully, Polydorus dissembleth.

Also Diodorus Siculus, who wrote in the time of Augustus, sayeth:

> It is reported, that the inhabitants of Britain are aborigines, that is to say first born in the country, leading their lives after the manner of men in old times. In fight they use chariots, such as is said the ancient worthies of Greece used in the battle of Troy. In behaviour they are simple and upright, far distant from the craft and wiliness of men of our age. Their fare is nothing excessive nor costly, far from the dainty delicates of rich men.[326]

Thus much he.

Tacitus also, a worthy writer, doth wonderfully commend the puissant deeds of Caratacus against the people of Rome, and confesseth that after the taking of him they were oftentimes foiled and discomfited by one only city of the Siluri. And as for Venutius, whom he writeth to have been fierce and hateful against the Romans, he reporteth that he vanquished not only the Romans but such Britons also as aided them. His words be these: 'the kingdom

---

[326] Diodorus Siculus, *Bibliotheca historica*, V.21.

to Venutius, and unto us remained war.'³²⁷ And after it followeth, that he cannot deny, but when Queen Boadicea (whom Dion termeth Bundwica) was deservedly exasperated, she caused sixty and ten thousand Romans to be slain. Whose courage more than manlike, and noble deeds worthy to be extolled with praise unto Heaven, and equivalent to the acts of renowned emperors and captains, Tacitus and also Dion, men of great name, have celebrated in fair and large discourse. And in the life of *Agricola:*

3160 In wishing for dangers, there is like boldness in Britons and Frenchmen. And when they come unto the pinch, in refusing of them like dastardness. Howbeit, the Britons resembling more hardiness, as being such whom long rest and peace had not yet made soft or effeminate. For we have heard also that the Frenchmen have flourished in wars. But shortly after, cowardice crept in through idleness, whereby they lost both manhood and liberty, which likewise befell to the vanquished Britons, the residue whereof remain yet, such as the Frenchmen were.

They are strong on foot. Certain of them do fight in
3170 chariots, the drivers whereof are counted the worthier, whose clients and servants do fight and defend them. In foretime they were prepared for kings, but now through favour and faction every prince hath gotten them. Neither were there anything more profitable for our use, against strange and valiant nations, saving that they do not generally safeguard and defend all.³²⁸ It is seldom that two or three cities do join to withstand their common danger, so that whilst they fight severally, they are overcome universally.³²⁹

3180 Also in another place: 'the Britons do muster, pay tribute, and fulfil other commandments of the Empire without stay or grudging, so that there be no injury offered, which they can hardly abide. And

---

³²⁷ 'the kingdom to Venutius, and unto us remained war'] 'regnum Venutio, bellum nobis relictum'; Tacitus, *Historiarum Libri*, ed. by C. D. Fisher (Oxford: Clarendon Press, 1956), III.45.
³²⁸ Twyne appears to suppose the subject under discussion is still the use of chariots, when Tacitus has shifted his theme to political divisions amongst the Britons.
³²⁹ *Agricola*, 11-12.

now they be subdued to obey, but not yet to be slaves.'[330] And a little afterward:

> But now they begin to instruct the children of princes in liberal sciences, sayeth Agricola. And to prefer the wits of the Britons in study before the Frenchmen's. That they, which of late detested the Roman tongue, do now desire to be eloquent therein. Afterward, the majesty of our attire, and our gown was commonly worn, and by little and little, they came to the imitation of our vices and superfluities, as to have galleries, baths, and to use our niceness in feasting. Which amongst the unskilful was termed humanity, when as in deed it is part of servility.[331]

Dion Cassius, a man that had been consul among other things, hath left this in writing unto posterity of Caesar's expedition into Britain:

> The Britons durst not set openly upon the Romans, because they kept diligent watch and ward, but they took certain which were sent, as it were, unto their friends' and confederates' region, to provide victual, whom they slew all, excepting a few which Caesar coming with speed rescued. Then began they to assault the camp, wherein they prevailed not, but were repulsed, not without slaughter on their side. Howbeit, they never took peace, before that they had been many times put to the worst. Caesar, contrary to that he had purposed, ended the war, requiring yet mo pledges, of whom notwithstanding he received but few. So Caesar returned into the continent, and such things as were unquiet during his absence he appeased, gaining nothing to himself nor to the city of Rome out of Britain, but only the glory of the expedition taken in hand. Which both he himself did very much set forth in words, and the Romans extolled wonderfully at Rome. In so much that, in consideration of these deeds so happily achieved, they decreed a supplication or thanksgiving of twenty days.[332]

---

[330] *Agricola*, 13.
[331] *Ibid.*, 21.
[332] Cassius Dio, *Roman History*, XXXIX.51-52.

3220 And in another place:

> The Britons calling forth their fellows, and communicating the effect of their intent unto Suella[333] (who amongst all the petty-roys or earls of that island was of greatest power), they marched unto the Roman ships where they rode at anchor. With whom the Romans meeting at the first encounter were troubled with the wagons, but anon making a lane amongst them, and avoiding the wagons, they cast their darts against the enemy which came running in sidelong upon them, and so restored the battle. After this battle both parts stood still in the same place; and in another conflict, when the barbarous people had overcome the Roman footmen, yet being discomfited by the horsemen, retired back to the River Thames.[334]

Moreover Herodian, in the life of Severus, writeth thus of the Britons:

> For divers places of Britain (sayeth he) by common washing in of the ocean do become marsh. In these marshes, therefore, the barbarous people do swim and wade up to the belly, not regarding the miring and dirtying of their naked bodies. For they know not the use of garments, but they arm their bellies and their necks, supposing that to be an ornament and a token of riches, like as other barbarous people do gold. They paint also their bodies with divers pictures and shapes of all manners of beasts and living things. Wherefore they wear on nothing lest thereby they should hide the painting of their body. It is a very warlike nation, and greedy of slaughter, contented only with a narrow shield and a spear, and a sword hanging down by their naked side. They are altogether ignorant of the use of the breastplate and headpiece, taking them to be a let unto them in passing over the fens and marshes.[335]

---

[333] Suella] Cassivelaunus
[334] Dio, *Roman History*, LX.1
[335] Herodian, *Roman History*, III.14.

Besides these, Eutropius of the French war[336] writeth thus: 'Caesar passeth over into Britain, having thereto prepared eighty ships, partly for burthen, and partly to fight, and maketh war upon the Britons. Where, being first wearied, with a sharp battle, and afterward falling into a cruel tempest: returned into France [...]' and so forth. And afterward: 'Again, at the beginning of the spring: he sailed into Britain, where at the first encounter of the horsemen, he was vanquished, and there was Labienus the tribune slain, and at the second battle, with great peril of his own men: he overcame the Britons, and constrained them to fly.'

Suetonius Tranquillus affirmeth that Vespasianus overcame in battle two mighty and valiant nations of Britain, and that he fought thirty times with the enemy, which is a token of no cowardly, but of a most stout and warlike nation. Eutropius also in the ninth book of his history writeth thus: 'when notwithstanding war was in vain made against Carausius the Briton, a man very expert in martial affairs, in the end peace was concluded.'[337] And Sextus Rufus,[338] reciting the Roman legions, among the legions of the Master of the Footmen reckoneth up 'Britannicians', and 'British', and among the legions Comitalensis the 'Second British Legion'.[339] And again among the legions of the Master of the Horsemen, the 'French Britons', and again, 'Britons'. And afterward, with the worthy and approved Earl of Spain, the 'invincible younger Britons'. And in another place he numbereth the 'younger British carriers', with the Earl of Britain.

But what shall it be needful to turn over the works of so many learned men, that the glory of Britain may appear? Whenas so many puissant kings, so many invincible captains, so many noble Roman emperors sprung forth of the British blood have made manifest unto the world by their noble acts, well worthy immortality, what manner men this island bringeth forth. For what shall I speak of Brennus, the tamer of the Romans and Greeks, and almost of all the nations in the world? What of Caswallan, to whom, as Lucan reporteth, Julius Caesar did turn his fearful back?

---

[336] The following quotations do not come from Eutropius but from the opening paragraphs of Bede, *Historia ecclesiastica gentis Anglorum*.
[337] Eutropius, *Breviarium*, IX.21. Marcus Aurelius Carausius (d. 293) was not a Briton, but a Roman military commander who staged a revolt in Britain, declaring himself emperor.
[338] Llwyd quotes from the *Notitia dignitatum* (*c.* 400), not by Sextus Rufus.
[339] **Marg.** 'Bands of Britons'

What of Caratacus, who molested the people of Rome with war, the space of nine years? What of Bunduica, that valiant manlike dame, who to begin withal, and for hansel° sake,[340] slew 70,000 Romans? Of whom such fear invaded Rome and Italy (as Virunnius writeth) as never the like before, neither at coming of Brennus, nor of Hannibal. What of Arviragus, the invincible King of Britain? Who, in despite of the Romans, which were lords of all the world, preserved his liberty? What of those noble captains which fought thirty times with Vespasian? Who also with sorrow and anguish of mind killed Severus, the most valiant emperor, because he could not overcome them?[341] What (as I say) shall I speak of these, when as Britain hath yielded forth and communicated to the rest of the world Constantinus Magnus, not only a most valiant and fortunate captain but, that more is, a perfect good man, and the first emperor of the Christians, instructed by Helen his mother, a Briton also. How much France and Italy for their delivery from tyrants are indebted unto Britain for this man, which was brought forth out of the midst of the bowels thereof, all men do well know, only Polydorus excepted, and William Petit the monk,[342] his schoolmaster, of late brought to light (unworthy ever to have seen light) by the slanderers and detractors of the British glory. And for as much as a certain Frenchman of late days, and also an ancient Greek author of the name of Maior,[343] affirm that he was borne at Dyrrachium, called now Durazzo,[344] I mean to bring forth the most ancient words of the panegyric which was pronounced before Constantinus himself:

> O (sayeth he) most fortunate, and now above all lands most blessed Britain, which didst first behold Constantinus the Emperor. Nature hath worthily endued thee with all benefits of

---

[340] for hansel sake] because of a good omen; T. uses the same phrase in his continuation of Thomas Phaer's translation of the *Aeneid*: 'Æneas first the rusticke sort sets on / For happy hansils sake'; *The whole xii bookes of the Aeneidos of Virgill* (London: William How, 1573), Book 10, sig. Ee^r.
[341] Septimius Severus fell ill and died on campaign in Britain in 211 AD.
[342] William Petit the monk] William of Newburgh, known as William Parvus, twelfth-century chronicler and early critic of Geoffrey of Monmouth.
[343] of the name of Maior] The marginalist in Douce L. 533 is surely right to cross out this reference to an unattested Greek author and to substitute the phrase 'of a greater authority and fame' as a translation of Llwyd's *maioris nominis*.
[344] Dyrachium, called now Durazzo] Durrës, Albania. Constantine was indeed born in the Balkans, and not in Britain.

air and soil, in whom is neither overmuch cold of winter, nor heat of wummer. Where there is also such plenty of corn that it sufficeth for the use of Ceres and Liber (that is to say, for bread and drink). Where are also woods without wild and cruel beasts, the earth without hurtful serpents; contrariwise, of tame cattle an innumerable multitude, strutting with milk and laden with fleeces, with all other things necessary and commodious for our life. Very long days, and no nights without some light, whilst that uttermost plains of the sea shore raiseth no shadow, and the show and aspect of the stars of heaven do exceed the bounds of night, that the sun, which to us seemeth to go down, appeareth there but to pass by. Good Lord, what a thing is this, that always from some furthermost end of the world there come down new powers from God, to be worshipped of all the earth?[345]

Thus far he.

What of Bonosus, out of the captains of the bounds of Rheticus,[346] a more courageous then fortunate Emperor? What of Carausius Augustus,[347] who the space of seven years together wore his princely robes, contrary to the will of Jovius and Herculius?[348] What of Allectus Caesar,[349] for subduing whom Mamertinus seemeth to prefer Maximianus before Caesar Julius, whose words I will not stick to allege. 'And truly', sayeth he, and so forth.[350] After him sprang the Emperor Maximus, a Briton and nephew to Helen, a man both stout and virtuous, and worthy of Augustus but that in his youth, leading an army against Gratianus, whom he vanquished, he had sacked his country.[351] Who by Helen his wife, daughter to Euda, left his son Victor emperor. And as Paulus Diaconus writeth, 'Britain also acknowledgeth Marcus and Gratianus, the Emperors.' Moreover Constantinus with his son Constans, when Gratianus their countryman was slain, were created emperors in Britain – in

---

[345] Panegyric of Constantine, anonymous, AD 310.

[346] What of Bonosus […] Rheticus] The usurper Bonosus, who hanged himself to avoid defeat (281 AD), was the son of a British rhetorician.

[347] See above, p. 135, n. 337.

[348] Jovius and Herculius] Titles of the co-emperors Diocletian and Maximian.

[349] Allectus Caesar] Allectus, treasurer to Carausius, assassinated him in AD 293 and succeeded him as ruler of Britain and northern Gaul until his defeat and death in 296.

[350] Llwyd has quoted the passage above, p. 92.

[351] sacked his country] Maximus did not pillage Britain, but stripped it of its legions for use in his campaigns; see pp. 59-60.

name like to the above said, but not in happiness, against whom Gerontius their captain (of whose death there are extant very ancient British rhymes)[352] made another Maximus than the first was, Augustus. And, after all these, Ambrosius Aurelius is by Panvinius accounted the last emperor of the British blood.

Besides these twelve emperors, Britain hath also brought forth to the world the most puissant and invincible King Arthur, whose everlasting renown and most noble deeds our friend Master Leland hath set forth and made more apparent by infinite testimonies and most weighty arguments,[353] against the gnarring and doggish mouth, and hatred more than ever was Vatinian's,[354] of Polydorus Urbine, and of the greasy monk Rievallensis,[355] more conversant in the kitchen than in the histories of old writers. And not only our countrymen but also Spaniards, Italians, Frenchmen, and the Sueones beyond the Sea Baltheum (as Gothus reporteth out of their histories)[356] do celebrate and advance unto this day in their books the worthy acts of this puissant King. Cadfan also, who from Prince of Gwynedd became King of the Britons, and his son Cadwalla (whom Bede calleth a tyrant, because he persecuted the Saxons with cruel war), whilst the British Empire[357] was in decaying, were valiant kings. And after the British destruction there rose up noble gentlemen in Wales, not to be debarred of their due praise, as Roderick the Great and his nephew (by his son) Howell surnamed Good,[358] both famous as well in war as peace.

---

[352] Gerontius [...] British rhymes] A military hero named Geraint features in the early Welsh poem *Y Gododdin*, later becoming associated with King Arthur.

[353] John Leland, *Assertio inclytissimi Arturii Regis Britanniae* (London: R. Wolfe, 1544), translated by Ralph Robinson as *The Assertion of King Arthure* (London: John Wolfe, 1582).

[354] hatred more than ever was Vatinian's] Catullus uses the phrase 'odio Vatiniano' (Poem 14, line 3) as a byword for extreme hatred, with reference to the name of a despised official. *The Poems of Catullus*, ed. by Guy Lee (Oxford: Clarendon Press, 1990).

[355] greasy monk Rievallensis] William of Newburgh; an Augustinian monk, William was not an inmate of the Cistercian Abbey of Rievaulx, but dedicated his *Historia rerum Anglicarum* to Abbot Ernald of Rievaulx.

[356] Gothus [...] histories] Olaus Magnus, *Historia de gentibus septentrionalibus* (Rome, 1555); the Swedish historian described the conquests of Attila, not Arthur.

[357] British Empire] Albeit with reference to an ancient rather than a present or future imperium, this is the first appearance in English of this soon-to-be notorious phrase.

[358] Roderick the Great [...] Howell surnamed Good] Rhodri Mawr and Hywel Dda, see above, pp. 111-12.

Also Gruffudd, the son of Llywelyn, the son of Seisyllius[359] who most stoutly defended Wales his native country. And after him Owain, Prince of Gwynedd, who most hardily withstood at Cole[360] Henry II, the most mightiest king of all that ever reigned in England, thrice entering into Wales with great armies, whose son also he slew in Anglesey, and the greater part of his army, as Giraldus reporteth. And his nephew likewise, born of his son, Llywelyn the Great, whose innumerable triumphs (that I may use the words of Parisiensis, the Englishman) do require special treatises.

And not these only, but also the Cornishmen, being the remnants of the old Britons, as they are the stoutest of all the British nations, so are they counted to this day the most valiant in warlike affairs. Neither yet the Britons which dwell nigh France, a nation of the same brood, do any whit degenerate from their forefathers, whenas they did not only many hundred years prosperously defend, amongst the thickest of stout and sturdy nations, those seats which they had purchased with their manhood and prowess, but also have vanquished the Goths and Frenchmen in great battles, and stoutly withstood the most mighty prince Charles the Magne, put to flight the army of his son Louis the Emperor, which was sent against them under conduct of Murmanus, overcame Charles Calvus, then Emperor and King of France in open fight, twice vanquishing his army, Numenius[361] being king, the Emperor privily flying thence, leaving there his pavilions and tents and all other his kinglike provision, as Regino writeth. But Herispous,[362] son to Numenius, compelled the same Charles to make shameful and dishonourable truce with him. Whom Salomon also, son to Herispous,[363] a valiant and warlike gentleman, enforced to retire back when he was coming against him with a mighty army.

---

[359] Gruffudd ap Llywelyn ap Seisyll (d. 1063), the only monarch to rule over the entirety of Wales.

[360] Cole] The Battle of Coleshill or Ewloe (1157), in which Henry II's army was ambushed and defeated.

[361] Numenius] Nominoe or Nevenoe (d. 851), 1st Duke of Brittany, known in Breton as 'Tad ar Vro' (father of the country). He defeated the army of Charles the Bald (Charles Calvus) at the Battle of Ballon (845).

[362] Herispous] Erispoe, Duke or King of Brittany, reigned 851-57.

[363] Salomon also, son to Herispous] Salomon (Duke of Brittany 857-74) was not the son of Erispoe but his cousin, and his assassin.

But when Salomon was dead the Britons, through desire to reign, and contention who should next be king, fell unto civil wars among themselves,[364] as Sigisbertus sayeth, and so they were constrained to leave off the destruction and overrunning of France, which they had determined. What shall I speak of the noble deeds of Vurfandus, an invincible captain, against Hasting the Norman and Pastquitanus the Briton?[365] Of Judicael also, and Alan, who manfully drave the Normans out of their coasts, which pitifully wasted and spoiled all France? What shall I need to touch such wars as they made long after upon the kings of France, being therein aided by the impregnable power of the Englishmen, since it is well known to all men that it was always a most potent nation?

And, that I may at length stop Polydorus's mouth, together with his Gildas,[366] thus much I say: that if he stick in any point unto him, he was no historiographer but a priest and a preacher, whose custom is very sharply to inveigh against the faults of their hearers. Wherefore, if we seek authorities out of sermons, as Polydorus Urbine hath done, what parish, what town, what nation or kingdom may escape infamy? What hath Bernhard written of the Romans? Thus surely, terming them impious, unfaithful, seditious, dishonest, traitorous, great speakers but little doers. These things are by divines spoken in the pulpit according unto their manner, that the like faults might be amended and the life reformed, not that the Romans or Britons were such indeed. Neither is there any man, unless he be a shameless sycophant, that lieth in wait for all occasions to disprase and accuse, which will go about by wresting of sentences forth of the sermons of preachers, slanderously to tax and infamously to note any whole convent, shire, city, or people. Wherefore, let such idle and ill-disposed slanderers leave off, and suffer the true renown of Britain appear to the world – neither judge me, good reader, of too sharp a tongue. Seeing (so God help me) neither envy of any foreign name, neither thirst of vain glory, neither hatred of any nation, but alonely the love of my country

---

[364] **Marg.** 'Divisions are dangerous'

[365] Gurfand, Duke of Brittany (d. 876) fought a civil war against Pascweten, Count of Rennes. His son Judicael made peace with Alan the Great, younger brother of Pascweten, and these two leaders defeated the Vikings at the Battle of Questembert in 888/89, where Judicael died.

[366] Polydorus [...] his Gildas] Llwyd also made extensive use of Gildas, but resented Polydore's use of him to testify to the cowardice and treachery of the Britons.

which is evil spoken of undeservedly, and desire to set forth the truth, have provoked me to write thus much.

And touching this rude and disordered little treatise: truly I would not have suffered it to have come to light, had I not well hoped that all learned men would accept this my endeavour in good part, and also take occasion, by this which I have rashly enterprised first, to handle the same matter more at large, in fair discourse and finer style. And if they shall think anything herein spoken over-sharply or not well-advisedly, I submit myself to the judgement of those that be better learned. And if I be admonished of my faults, I promise to amend them when occasion shall be given. Thus fare you well.

Certain Welsh, or rather true British words, converted into Latin by the author, and now translated into English.[367]

a	with
aber	force or rage of water
Armorica	upon the sea
arglwyddi	lords
afanc	an otter[368]
afon	a river
bara	bread
bath	beauty, form, or comeliness
Britunn*	a Briton
bryn	a mountain or hill
caer	a city
cain	white
cariad	love
clawdd*	a ditch
da	good
dinas	a court or palace
Deheubarth*	the right side
Duw	God
dwfr, and *dŵr*	water
dyffryn	a valley
dyfnant* [369]	deep and narrow valleys
ei	his
fa	a place
fy	mine
fflint	a flint stone
gelli* [370]	hazel trees
glas	blue colour or woad
glaw	rain
grug	a heap
gŵr	a man

---

[367] In addition to translating Llwyd's Latin glosses into English, Twyne adds words to the glossary based on Llwyd's etymologies of British place names. The added entries, many of them misleading, are noted with a *.

[368] otter] 'castor, animal', that is, beaver.

[369] *dyfnant*] Added word, based on Llwyd's etymology of Dyfnaint (Devonshire); the plural form of *dyfnant* (ravine) is *dyfnentydd*.

[370] *gelli*] Added word, based on Llwyd's etymology of Tregelli. Hazel in Welsh is *collen*, plural *cyll*.

gwlad	a country
gwal*³⁷¹	a valley
gwyn	white
gwydd*	perspicuous
helyg*	willow trees
llan	a church
lladron*	thieves
Llydaw*³⁷²	the shore
llyfr	a book
mam	a mother
march	an horse
mawr	great
mur*	a wall
mynydd*	a hill
o	forth of
pen	a head
Phrainc*³⁷³	France
Phrydain*³⁷⁴	Britain
porth*	a haven
pryd	beauty or comeliness
rhyd	a ford
Rhufain	Rome
Saeson*	Englishmen
Saesneg*	English
strad*	a soil
sychnant*	a dry valley
tair	three (feminine gender)
tan	fire
taria*	a shield
tre	a town
tri	three (masculine gender)
ynys	an island
ynad	a judge, next the king
ysgar	to separate
ysgaredig	separate

---

[371] *gwal*] Added word, based on T.'s mistranslation of L.'s 'Pallum Severi' as 'Severus's Valley' rather than Severus's Palisade (see p. 96); W. *gwal* means 'wall'.
[372] *Llydaw*] Brittany
[373] *Phrainc*] The unmutated W. form is 'Ffrainc'.
[374] *Phrydain*] Prydain

The History of Cambria

The History of Cambria, now called Wales, a part of the most famous Island of Britain, written in the British language above two hundred years past. Translated into English by Humphrey Llwyd, gentleman; corrected, augmented, and continued out of records and best approved authors, by David Powel, Doctor in Divinity.

I. Introduction

Caradoc of Llancarfan (gentle reader) collected the successions and acts of the British princes after Cadwaladr to the year of Christ 1156.[375] Of the which collections there were several copies afterward kept in either of the abbeys of Conwy and Stratflur,[376] which were yearly augmented as things fell out, and conferred together ordinarily every third year, when the *beirdd*[377] which did belong to those two abbeys went from the one to the other in the time of their *clêra*;[378] wherein were contained besides such notable occurrences happening within this Isle of Britain as they then thought worthy the writing. Which order of registering and noting continued in those abbeys until the year 1270, which was a little before the death of the last Llywelyn who was slain at Builth. These collections were copied by divers, so that there are at this day of the same in Wales a hundred copies at the least, whereof the most part were written two hundred years ago.

This book Humphrey Llwyd, gentleman (a painful and a worthy searcher of British antiquities), translated into English and partly augmented, chiefly out of Matthew Paris and Nicholas Trivet. But before the book was polished (having yet many imperfections, not only in the phrase, but also in the matter and substance of the history) it pleased God to take him away in the flower of his time; who (if God had spared him life) would not only have set out this history absolute and perfect, but also have opened unto the world other antiquities of this land, which now lie hidden and unknown. The copy of his translation, the Right Honourable Sir Henry

---

[375] Concluding his *Historia regum Britanniae* in the year 689 with the death of Cadwaladr, the last king of the Britons, Geoffrey of Monmouth assigned the ensuing history of Wales to his contemporary, Caradoc of Llancarfan. His name became associated with the chronicle *Brut y Tywysogion*.
[376] Stratflur] The Cistercian abbey of Strata Florida, or Ystrad Fflur, Ceredigion.
[377] *beirdd*] bards
[378] **Marg.** '*Clêra* is their ordinary visitation which they use every third year.'

Sidney, Lord President of Wales (whose disposition is rather to seek after the antiquities and the weal public of those countries which he governeth, than to obtain lands and revenues within the same, for I know not one foot of land that he hath either in Wales or Ireland), had lying by him a great while, and being desirous to have the same set out in print, sent for me in September last, requesting me to peruse and correct it in such sort as it might be committed to the press. But I (knowing myself to be far unable to perform and accomplish those things which are requisite to the publishing of such an history, and being otherwise called and employed) was very loath anything to meddle therein, and so excused myself. Yet he conceiving a better opinion of me than there was cause, would needs have me to do mine endeavour in that behalf. Whose request I was not of duty to gainsay or withstand, and thereupon I promised to do my best – which travail two things have caused me to be the more willing to take it in hand.

First, because I see the politic and martial acts of all other inhabitants of this island, in the time of their government, to be set out to the uttermost, and that by divers and sundry writers; and the whole doings and government of the Britons, the first inhabitants of the land, who continued their rule longer than any other nation,[379] to be nothing spoken of nor regarded of any, especially sithence° the reign of Cadwaladr, having so many monuments of antiquity to declare and testify the same, if any would take the pains to open and discover them to the view of the world.

The second thing that moved me thereunto is the slanderous report of such writers as in their books do enforce everything that is done by the Welshmen to their discredit, leaving out all the causes and circumstances of the same; which do most commonly not only elevate or dissemble all the injuries and wrongs offered and done to the Welshmen, but also conceal or deface all the acts worthy of commendation achieved by them. Search the common chronicles touching the Welshmen, and commonly thou shalt find that the King sendeth some nobleman or other with an army to Wales, to withstand the rebellious attempts, the proud stomachs, the presumptuous pride, stir, trouble, and rebellion of the fierce, unquiet, craking,° fickle, and inconstant Welshmen, and no open fact laid down to charge them withal, why war should be levied

---

[379] **Marg.** 'Robertus Coenalis. li. 2, par. 2.'

against them, nor yet they swerving abroad out of their own country to trouble other men.

Now this history doth show the cause and circumstances of most of those wars, whereby the quality of the action may be judged. And certainly no man is an indifferent witness against him whom he counteth his enemy or adversary, for evil will never speaketh well. The Welshmen were by the Saxons and Normans counted enemies before the twelfth year of Edward I, while they had a governor among themselves; and afterward, when King Edward had brought the country to his subjection, he placed English officers to keep them under, to whom most commonly he gave the forfeits and possessions of such Welshmen as disobeyed his laws and refused to be ruled by the said officers. The like did the other kings that came after him. The said officers were thought oftentimes to be over-severe and rigorous for their own profit and commodity, which things caused the people often to disobey and many times like desperate men to seek revengement, having those for their judges which were made by their overthrow, and also wanting indifferency in their causes and matters of griefs. For the kings always countenanced and believed their own officers, by them preferred and put in trust, before their accusers whom they liked not of. Whereupon the inhabitants of England, favouring their countrymen and friends, reported not the best of the Welshmen. This hatred and disliking was so increased by the stir and rebellion of Owain Glyndŵr, that it brought forth such grievous laws as few Christian kings ever gave or published the like to their subjects.[380] These things being so, any man may easily perceive the very occasion of those parentheses and brief notes of rebellion and troubles objected to the Welshmen, without opening of cause or declaration of circumstances.

The Normans, having conquered England and gotten all the lands of the Saxon nobility, would fain have had the lands of the Welshmen also, whereupon divers of them entered Wales with an army, so that the Welshmen were driven for their own defence to put themselves in armour. For the which fact they are by some writers accused of rebellion, whereas by the law of nature it is

---

[380] The Penal Laws of 1402 barred Welshmen from holding public office, bearing arms, or owning property in towns; the laws, which extended to Englishmen married to Welsh women, were only fully repealed under Henry VIII.

lawful for all men to withstand force by force.[381] They were in their own country, the land was theirs by inheritance and lawful possession. Might they not therefore defend themselves from violence and wrong, if they could? What right or lawful title had the Earl of Chester to Rhufoniog and Tegeingl? Or the Earl of Salop to Dyfed, Cardigan, and Powys? Or Robert Fitzhammo to Glamorgan? Or Bernard Newmarch to Brecknock? Or Ralph Mortimer to Elfael? Or Hugh Lacy to the land of Ewias?[382] Or any other of them to any country in Wales? By what reason was it more lawful for those men to dispossess them of these countries with violence and wrong, than for them to defend and keep their own? Shall a man be charged with disobedience, because he seeketh to keep his purse from him that would rob him? I mean not by this to charge those noble men which won these countries by the sword. But I speak it to note the partial dealing of the writers and setters forth of those histories, that should have reported things indifferently, as they were done, and laid down the causes and circumstances of every action truly, who being altogether partial, favouring the one side and hating the other, do pronounce of the fact according to their private affections, condemning oftentimes the innocent, and justifying the wrongdoers.

 These considerations, I say, besides my bounden duty, caused me to venture to take this thing in hand. The translation of Humphrey Llwyd I have conferred with the British book, whereof I had two ancient copies, and corrected the same when there was cause so to do. And after that the most part of the book was printed, I received another larger copy of the same translation, being better corrected, at the hands of Robert Glover, Somerset herald,[383] a learned and studious gentleman in his profession, the which if I had had at the beginning, many things had come forth in better plight than they now be. Again, I got all the authors that I could come by, which have anything written of the affairs of Wales, as Gildas, Asser Menevensis, Galfrid, William of Newburgh, Matthew Paris, Matthew Westminster, Thomas Walsingham, Ponticus Virunius, Polydore Virgil, John Leland, John Bale, John Prise, Matthew

---

[381] **Marg.** '*Vim vi repellere licet.*' (It is permitted to resist force with force.)
[382] Earl of Chester to Rhufoniog [...] Hugh Lacy to the land of Ewias?] The series of rhetorical questions summarizes the initial Norman conquests in Wales in the period 1067-99.
[383] Robert Glover] Herald and genealogist (1544-88).

Parker, John Caius, William Lambarde, and all the English chronicles printed. In written hand I had Gildas Sapiens *alias* Nennius, Henry Huntingdon, William Malmesbury, Marianus Scotus, Ralph Coggeshall, John Eversden, Nicholas Trivet, Florentius Vigorniensis, Simeon of Durham, Roger Hoveden, and other which remain in the custody of John Stow,[384] citizen of London, who deserveth commendation for getting together the ancient writers of the histories of this land. I had also the British books of pedigrees, John Castoreus, and Sylvester Giraldus Cambrensis, which with divers other rare monuments of antiquity, I received at the hands of the Right Honourable the Lord Burghley, High Treasurer of England;[385] who also directed me by his letters to all the offices where the records of this realm are kept, out of the which I have gathered a great part of this history, and more would have done if the time had permitted. The copy I have conferred with the aforenamed authors, and where I found them to entreat of the matters therein contained, I have noted them in the margin, and in such authors as are printed I have most commonly directed thee, gentle reader, to the page or chapter of the book where thou shalt find the same history treated of. Again, where I found anything of Wales worthy the noting in the said authors being not contained in the copy, I have inserted the same in a smaller letter with this mark * before it, whereby it may be discerned from the copy itself. Further, such things as were briefly set down in the copy without signification of cause or declaration of circumstances, if I found the same in any of mine authors treated of and further opened, I have likewise inserted it in his due place. In the possession and succession of families, I have sought what I could for the time, and have laid down most of the noble families of England which had lands in Wales, or descended out of that country. I was greatly furthered in this work by the painful and studious travail of the right worshipful Sir Edward Stradling, Knight, Thomas Powell of Whittington Park, and Richard Broughton, Esquires.[386]

---

[384] John Stow] Chronicler (*c.* 1525-1605); his extensive manuscript collection was consulted by most of the leading antiquaries and topographers of the period.

[385] Lord Burghley, the High Treasurer of England] William Cecil, Lord Burghley (1521-1598) took an interest in British antiquities, and in particular in his own Welsh pedigree.

[386] Sir Edward Stradling (1529-1609) of St Donat's, distinguished as an antiquary and book-collector; Thomas Powell, gentleman of Oswestry, Shropshire; Richard Broughton, presumably a member of the Broughton family of Marchwiel,

In the *Description* I have taken the less pains, looking daily for the coming forth of the painful and studious travail of some other, who hath laboured in that behalf, and studied all the Roman and British histories concerning the ancient names of nations and places within this island, so that my labour were superfluous in that behalf.[387] Herein if happily° I have swerved or omitted anything which should have been laid down in this history, I neither did it wittingly nor willingly, and therefore being ready upon better information to amend that which shall be found to be amiss, if any so shall be, I am the rather to be borne withal, because I am the first setter out in print of this history. For things can never be so well done at the first, when there is but few that do travail therein, as they may in process of time, when every man putteth to his helping hand – which courtesy I am to desire of thee, gentle reader, for the perfecting of this work.

Concerning the alteration of the estate, there was never anything so beneficial to the common people of Wales as the uniting of that country to the crown and kingdom of England, whereby not only the malady and hurt of the dissension that often happened between the princes of the country, while they ruled, is now taken away, but also an uniformity of government established, whereby all controversies are examined, heard, and decided within the country.[388] So that now the country of Wales (I dare boldly affirm it) is in as good order for quietness and obedience as any country in Europe. For if the rulers and teachers be good and do their duties, the people are willing to learn, ready to obey, and loath to offend or displease. And if it please God once to send them the Bible in their own language according to the godly laws already established,[389] the country of Wales (I doubt not) will be comparable to any country in England.[390]

Denbighsire, not to be confused with the Catholic antiquary Richard Broughton of Huntingdonshire (d. 1635).

[387] Undoubtedly a reference to William Camden's eagerly-awaited *Britannia* (1586).

[388] within the country] The Council in the Marches of Wales, with its seat at Ludlow, Shropshire, had jurisdiction over Wales together with the four English counties of Gloucestershire, Herefordshire, Shropshire and Worcestershire. See the Introduction, pp. 19-20.

[389] according to the godly laws already established] In accordance with the Act of 1563, William Salesbury's translation of the New Testament had appeared in 1567; William Morgan's complete translation of the Bible would appear in 1588.

[390] country] county, or region.

II. Cadwaladr:
The Beginning of the Principality and Government of Wales.

Cadwaladr, the last king of the Britons[391] descending from the noble race of the Trojans, by extreme plagues of death and famine was driven to forsake this his realm and native country, and to sojourn with a great number of his nobles and subjects with his cousin Alan, King of Little Britain, which is called in the British tongue *Llydaw*.[392]

Cadwaladr, being in Britain,[393] was certified that a great number of strangers, as Saxons, Angles, and Jutes,[394] had arrived in Britain and, finding it desolate and without inhabitants (saving a few Saxons which had called them in, and certain poor Britons that lived by roots in rocks and woods), had overrun a great part thereof and, dividing it into divers territories and kingdoms, inhabited that part which was then and now at this day is called *Lloegr* in the British or Welsh tongue, and in English England; with all the cities, towns, castles, and villages which the Britons had builded, ruled, and inhabited by the space of 1827 years, under divers kings and princes of great renown, whereupon he purposed to return and by strength of British knights to recover his own land again.

After he had prepared and made ready his navy for the transporting of his own men, with such succours as he had found at Alan's hand, an angel appeared unto him in a vision[395] and declared that it was the will of God that he should not take his voyage towards Britain, but to Rome to Pope Sergius, where he should make an end of his life, and be afterwards numbered among the blessed. For God had appointed that the Britons should have no more the rule and governance of the whole isle, until the prophecy of Merlin Ambrose should be fulfilled. Which vision, after that Cadwaladr had declared to his friend Alan, he sent for all his books of prophecies, as the works of both Myrddins or Merlins (to wit, Ambrose and Sylvester, surnamed Myrddin Wyllt), and the words which the Eagle spake at the building of Caer Septon, now called

---

[391] **Marg**. '680'
[392] *Llydaw*] There follows a note on the history of Little Britain and the names of its kings, omitted here.
[393] Britain] Brittany
[394] **Marg**. 'Galfride. John Castoreus.'
[395] **Marg**. 'A fable confirmed with blind prophesies.'

Shaftesbury, and after long study found the time to be now come whereof they had prophesied.

*[396] Of this admonition given to Cadwaladr there be divers opinions. Some hold that this was signified to him in a dream, of the which mind is Polydore Virgil, and divers other. Some other do think that (if any such vision were) it was some illusion of a wicked spirit, or a fantastical conceit of Cadwaladr himself, being a man of a mild and quiet nature, and wearied with troubles and miseries. Other reject it altogether as a fable, not worthy to be recorded in books.[397] But howsoever it was, certain it is that after his going over to Alan, he never returned again to Britain.

Of these two Merlins thus writeth Giraldus Cambrensis *in suo Itinerario*:[398]

> Erant Merlini duo, unus qui & Ambrosius dictus est, quia binomius fuerat, & sub rege Vortigerno prophetavit, ab incubo genitus, & in urbe ab ipso denominata Caervyrdhin, urbs Merlini, inventus. Alter de Albania oriundus, qui Calidonius dictus est, à Calidonia sylva, in qua prophetavit: & Sylvester, quia cùm inter acies bellicas constitutus, horribile monstrum nimis in aera suspiciendo prospiceret, dementire caepit: & ad sylvam transfugiendo, sylvestrem usque ad obitum vitam perduxit. Hic autem Merlinus tempore Arthuri fuit, & longè pleniùs & apertiùs quàm alter prophetasse perhibetur.

Haec Cambrensis.[399] In English thus:

> There were two Merlins, the one named also Ambrose (for he had two names) begotten of a spirit, and found in the town of Carmarthen, which took the name of him and is therefore so called, who prophesied under King Vortigern. The other born in Albany or Scotland, surnamed Calidonius of the forest Calidon,

---

[396] The asterisk and the use of a smaller type face in the 1584 text indicate that the following material, down to 'esteem such things' is Powel's insertion.

[397] **Marg**. 'Holinshed, p. 183.' The cited passage in Holinshed's *Chronicles* (London: Henry Bynneman, 1577) reads: 'A long process is made by the British writers of this departure of Cadwaladr and of the Britons out of this land, and how Cadwaladr was about to have returned again, but that he was admonished by a dream to the contrary, the which because it seemeth but fabulous, we pass over.'

[398] *in suo Itinerario*] 'in his *Itinerary*'.

[399] *Haec Cambrensis*] 'Thus [says] Cambrensis'.

wherein he prophesied, and was called also Sylvestris, or of the wood, for that he beholding some monstrous shape in the air being in the battle fell mad and, flying to the wood, lived there the rest of his life. This Merlin was in the time of King Arthur, and prophesied fuller and plainer than the other.

270 Concerning the words of the Eagle at the building of Caer Septon in Mount Paladr in the time of Rudhudibras,[400] in the year after the creation of the world, 3048, some think that an eagle did then speak and prophesy. Other are of opinion that it was a Briton named Aquila[401] that prophesied of these things, and of the recovery of the whole isle again by the Britons, bringing with them the bones of Cadwaladr from Rome, as in the said prophecies is to be seen.

By these toys and fables, men may learn what folly and vanity the wit of man, being not stayed and directed by the word of God,
280 is prone and subject unto. And certain it is that the simple and ignorant have been in all ages deluded and brought to great errors and blindness by the practice of Satan, with these feigned revelations, false prophecies, and superstitious dreams of hypocrites and lewd persons, whereof (as it is manifest in histories) much bloodshed and mischief hath ensued, and many relying upon the same have been utterly overthrown and perished. Wise men therefore will never regard or esteem such things.

Alan therefore counselled Cadwaladr to fulfil the will of God, who did so, and taking his journey to Rome lived there eight years
290 in the service of God, and died in the year of Christ 688. So that the Britons ruled this isle, with the out-isles of Wight, Môn (in English called Anglesey), Manaw (in English Man), Orkney, and Uist, 1137 years before Christ until the year of his incarnation 688. And thus ended the rule of the Britons over the whole isle.

*[402] The Britons, being sore troubled with the Scots and Picts and denied of aid at the hands of the Romans, sent for the Saxons

---

[400] **Marg.** 'Galfride. Castoreus.' Geoffrey of Monmouth himself expressed scepticism about the prophecies supposedly spoken by an eagle at the building of Shaftesbury, and declined to record their content.

[401] Aquila] John Bale included 'Aquila Septonius' [Eagle of Septon] in his index of British authors, the *Scriptorum illustrium majoris Britanniae* [...] *catalogus* (1557-59).

[402] From the asterisk to the end of this section, the text is marked by Powel as his insertion.

to come to defend them against their enemies; who coming at the first as friends to the Britons, liked the country so well, that they became their mortal enemies and drove them out of the same.[403]

About the year of Christ 590, Gurmundus an arch-pirate and captain of the Norwegians, after that he had conquered Ireland,[404] being called by the Saxons to their aid against Careticus King of the Britons, overcame the same Careticus in battle, and compelled him and his Britons to flee beyond the rivers of Severn and Dee to Cambria, now called Wales, and to Cornwall, and some to Britain Armorick,° where they remain to this day, and gave Lloegria, now England, to the Saxons. And albeit that Cadfan, Cadwallon, and Cadwaladr were sithence entitled kings of all Britain, yet they could never recover again the quiet possession of the whole island afterwards.

After the departure of Cadwaladr out of the land, the Britons were governed within the country of Wales or Cambria by those men whereof this history following doth entreat, which were commonly called kings of such provinces and countries as they possessed, until the time of Owain Gwynedd,[405] who (being in the days of King Stephen and Henry II) was the first that named himself Prince of Wales, and so the rest after him kept that title and style. And yet nevertheless they are sometimes called 'princes' before him, and 'kings' after him, as I have observed by divers charters and old records which I have seen in the Tower of London and elsewhere. Howbeit, this author calleth the chiefest of them 'kings' till the time of the said Owain, and sithence 'princes'.

III. The Voyage of Madoc ap Owain Gwynedd

After the death of Owain[406] his sons fell at debate who should inherit after him, for the eldest son born in matrimony, Edward or Iorwerth Drwyndwn, was counted unmeet to govern because of the maim upon his face.[407] And Hywel who took upon him all the rule was a base son, begotten upon an Irishwoman. Therefore Dafydd

---

[403] **Marg.** '450'
[404] **Marg.** 'Galfride. Castoreus.'
[405] **Marg.** 'Humphrey Llwyd.'
[406] death of Owain] Owain Gwynedd, ruler of North Wales, died in 1170.
[407] Iorwerth Drwyndwn [...] maim upon his face] The nickname 'Drwyndwn' means 'broken-nosed'.

gathered all the power he could and came against Hywel, and fighting with him slew him, and afterward enjoyed quietly the whole land of North Wales, until his brother Iorwerth's son came to age, as shall hereafter appear.

Madoc, another of Owain Gwynedd his sons, left the land in contention betwixt his brethren, and prepared certain ships with men and munition, and sought adventures by seas, sailing west and leaving the coast of Ireland so far north that he came to a land unknown where he saw many strange things. This land must needs be some part of that country of which the Spaniards affirm themselves to be the first finders sith Hanno's time;[408] for by reason and order of cosmography this land to the which Madoc came must needs be some part of Nova Hispania[409] or Florida. Whereupon it is manifest that that country was long before by Britons discovered, afore either Columbus or Americus Vespucius led any Spaniards thither.

Of the voyage and return of this Madoc there be many fables feigned, as the common people do use in distance of place and length of time rather to augment than to diminish. But sure it is, that there he was. And after he had returned home and declared the pleasant and fruitful countries that he had seen without inhabitants – and upon the contrary part, for what barren and wild ground his brethren and nephews did murder one another – he prepared a number of ships, and got with him such men and women as were desirous to live in quietness, and taking leave of his friends took his journey thitherward again.

Therefore it is to be presupposed that he and his people inhabited part of those countries, for it appeareth by Francis Loves that in Acuzanus and other places, the people honoured the cross.[410] Whereby it may be gathered that Christians had been there before the coming of the Spaniards. But because this people were not many, they followed the manners of the land they came unto, and used the language they found there.

---

[408] **Marg**. 'Humphrey Llwyd.' Hanno the Navigator was a Carthaginian explorer who described a journey around the western coast of Africa (*c.* 500 BC).
[409] Nova Hispania] New Spain, i.e. Mexico.
[410] Francis Loves [...] honoured the cross] Francisco Lopez de Gomara, secretary to Hernan Cortes and author of the *Historia General de las Indias* (1554), described the natives of Acuzamil (Cozumel) as worshipping a great cross associated with a rain god.

*⁴¹¹ This Madoc arriving in that western country, unto the which he came in the year 1170, left most of his people there, and returning back for more of his own nation, acquaintance, and friends to inhabit that fair and large country, went thither again with ten sails, as I find noted by Gutun Owain.⁴¹² I am of opinion that the land whereunto he came was some part of Mexico. The causes which make me to think so be these:

1 The common report of the inhabitants of that country, which affirm that their rulers descended from a strange nation that came thither from a far country: which thing is confessed by Moctezuma, king of that country, in his oration made for quieting of his people, at his submission to the King of Castile, Hernando Cortes being then present, which is laid down in the Spanish chronicles of the conquest of the West Indies.

2 The British words and names of places, used in that country even to this day, do argue the same. As when they talk together, they use this word *gwrando*, which is 'hearken' or 'listen'.⁴¹³ Also, they have a certain bird with a white head which they call *pengwin*, that is, 'white head'.⁴¹⁴ But the island of Corroeso, the cape of Bryton, the river of Gwyndor, and the white rock of Pengwyn, which be all British or

---

⁴¹¹ From this point to the conclusion of the extract, the text is marked as Powel's insertion.
⁴¹² Gutun Owain] Welsh poet of the later fifteenth century; there is no mention of Madoc in his surviving work.
⁴¹³ **Marg.** 'David Ingram.' Ingram was an English sailor who claimed to have walked through much of the interior of North America, from Tampico, Mexico, to Nova Scotia. His account was published by Hakluyt in 1589.
⁴¹⁴ **Marg.** 'Sir Humphrey Gilbert, *Discovery.*' Powel cites George Peckham's account of Humphrey Gilbert's voyages, *A True Reporte of the late discoveries* [...] *of the Newfound Landes* (London: John Charlewood, 1583). As Peckham reports, 'Madoc ap Owain Gwynedd, departing from the coast of England, about the year of Our Lord God 1170, arrived and planted there himself and his colonies, and afterward returned himself into England, leaving certain of his people there, as appeareth in an ancient Welsh chronicle, where he then gave certain islands, beasts, and fowls, sundry Welsh names, as the Island of Penguin, which yet to this day beareth the same. There is likewise a fowl in the said countries, called by the same name at this day, and is as much to say in English, Whitehead, and in truth, the said fowls have white heads.' In fact, of course, the heads of penguins are largely or entirely black. Penguins do not dwell in Mexico.

Welsh words, do manifestly show that it was that country which Madoc and his people inhabited.

IV. Years of Conflict (1190s)

After that Llywelyn the son of Iorwerth had gotten the rule of North Wales to himself,[415] as right inheritor thereof, Roger Mortimer came with a great power to Maelienydd and built the castle of Cymaron, and so brought that country to his subjection, and chased away the two sons of Cadwallon ap Madoc, lords of the country. About the same time Rhys and Maredudd, the sons of Prince Rhys[416] (being two lusty gentlemen), gathered together a number of wild heads of the country and came to Dinefwr, and got the castle from their father's garrison, and afterward they went to Cantref Bychan, where the whole country received them gently and delivered the castle to their hands. Wherewith their father was sore displeased, and laid privy wait for them, and by treason of their own men (which were afraid any further to offend their lord and prince) they were taken and brought to their father, who kept them in safe prison.

The year ensuing there was a combat appointed betwixt the French king, with five knights with him, and King Richard with five other, which should end all controversies.[417] Of which fight King Richard was glad, but the French king like a snail drew in his horns and forsook the battle. And in Wales Prince Rhys gathered a great army and laid siege to the town and castle of Carmarthen, and in short time won them both, spoiling and destroying the same, and then returned with great booty. Then he led his said army to the Marches before the castle of Clun, which after a long siege and many a fierce assault he got and burned it. And from thence he went to the castle of Radnor, and likewise won it; to the defence whereof came Roger Mortimer and Hugh de Say, with a great army of Normans and Englishmen, well-armed and tried soldiers. Then Rhys, which had won the castle, determined not to keep his men

---

[415] Llywelyn ap Iorwerth Drwyndwn defeated his uncle Dafydd in battle in 1194, the date indicated here, though he did not consolidate his rule over Gwynedd until 1200.
[416] Prince Rhys] Rhys ap Gruffudd, ruler of South Wales, among the most powerful Welsh leaders of the post-Conquest period.
[417] **Marg.** 'Matthew Paris, p. 237; Matthew Westminster, p. 69.'

within the walls, but boldly like a worthy prince came into the plain besides the town and gave them battle – where his men, although for the most part unarmed and not accustomed to the battle, declared that they came of Britons' blood (whose title the noble Roman emperors did so much desire, as a token of manhood and worthiness), choosing rather to die with honour in the defence of their country than to live with shame, did so worthily behave themselves that their enemies forsook the field with great loss of their men, whom Rhys pursued till the benefit of the night shadowed them with her darkness. And forthwith he laid siege to the Castle of Pain[418] in Elfael, and got it. Thither came William de Braose the owner thereof, and made peace with Rhys, of whom he received the same castle again.[419] Not long after, the Archbishop of Canterbury, whom King Richard had substituted his lieutenant in England, came with a huge power towards Wales, and laid siege to the castle of Gwenwynwyn at the Pool.[420] But the garrison defended the hold so manfully that he lost many of his men, and could do no good. Therefore he sent for miners, and set them on work to undermine the walls; which thing when the garrison understood, and knowing that their enemies were three to one, they were content to yield up the castle, upon condition that they might depart with their armour freely. Which offer the Archbishop took, suffering them to pass quietly, and fortifying the castle again strongly to the King's use, and placing therein a garrison for the defence thereof, returned to England. But immediately Wenwynwyn or Gwenwynwyn laid siege to it again, and shortly after received it upon the same conditions that his men had given it up, and kept the same to his own use.

The next year after there was a great and a terrible plague through all the isle of Britain and France, of the which died a great number of nobles, beside the common people.[421] And the same year, the fourth day of May, Rhys the son of Gruffudd ap Rhys ap Tewdwr, Prince of South Wales, died – the only anchor, hope and stay of all that part of Wales, as he that brought them out of thraldom and bondage of strangers, and set them at liberty, and had

---

[418] Castle of Pain] Painscastle, founded in the early 1100s by Pain Fitzjohn.
[419] **Marg.** 'Ger. Dor.'
[420] **Marg.** 'Matthew Parker, p. 138.' Gwenwynwyn ap Owain Cyfeiliog (d. 1216), ruler of Powys.
[421] **Marg.** 'Holinshed, p. 534.'

defended them divers times in the field manfully, daunting the pride and courage of their cruel enemies, whom he did either chase out of the land, or compelled by force to live quietly at home.[422] Woe to that cruel destiny that spoiled the miserable land of her defence and shield, who as he descended of noble and princely blood, so he passed all other in commendable qualities and laudable virtues of the mind. He was the overthrower of the mighty and setter up of the weak, the overturner of the holds, the separator of troops, the scatterer of his foes, among whom he appeared as a wild boar among whelps, or a lion that for anger beateth his tail to the ground.[423]

*[424] In praise of this Prince there is a long discourse in the British book after the manner of the Welsh poets, whose worthy commendation is laid down at large by Ranulph monk of Chester in the seventh book of his history entitled *Policronicon*, the 31st chapter, and Grafton in the life of Richard I, page 92.

This Prince had many sons and daughters, as Gruffudd, who succeeded his father, Cadwallon, Maelgwn, Maredudd, and Rhys; and of the daughters one called Gwenllian was married to Ednyfed Fychan, who was ancestor to Owen Theodor or Tudor that married Queen Katherine the widow of King Henry V, and the rest were married to other lords in the country. After the death of Rhys, Gruffudd his son subdued all the country to himself, and enjoyed it in peace, until Maelgwn his brother (whom his father had disinherited) made a league with Gwenwynwyn the son of Owain Cyfeiliog, Lord of Powys, who both together levied a number of men and came suddenly upon Gruffudd at Aberystwyth, and slaying a great number of his men took him prisoner, and so recovered all the country of Cardigan, with the castle. Thus Maelgwn, having taken his brother, sent him to be imprisoned with Gwenwynwyn, who in despite° delivered him to the Englishmen. Then Gwenwynwyn, gathering a power, entered Arwystli and subdued the same to himself.

---

[422] **Marg.** '*Marwnad.*' (W. 'lament' or 'elegy'.)

[423] **Marg.** 'μμησις [mimesis, or imitation] *poetica*, Ranulphus Castrensis, lib. 7, cap. 31.' Powel's lament for Rhys is loosely modelled on the poem quoted in Higden's *Policronicon*, presumably a translation from the Welsh: 'O bliss of battle, child of chivalry, defence of country, worship of arms [...] The bliss of Wales passeth, Rhys is dead [...]': Ranulph Higden, *Policronicon*, trans. by John Trevisa (London: Wynkyn de Worde, 1495), fol. Cclxxxxix[r].

[424] This paragraph is marked as Powel's insertion.

Also about that time there was great war in North Wales, for Dafydd ap Owain, of late Prince, came with a great army as well Englishmen as Welshmen, purposing to recover the land again. But Llywelyn his nephew, who was the right inheritor of the same and then in possession thereof, came boldly and met him, and gave him battle, and putting his people to flight took him prisoner and kept him in safety, and afterward enjoyed the country quietly. Toward the end of this year Owain Cyfeiliog, Lord of the Higher Powys, died and left his land to Gwenwynwyn his son, after whom that part of Powys was called Powys Wenwynwyn, for a difference from the other called Powys Fadog (being the possession of the lords of Bromfield). At this time also died Owain the son of Gruffudd Maelor, Lord of Bromfield, and Brychtyr the son of Hywel ap Ieuaf, likewise Maelgwn the son of Cadwallon ap Madoc, Lord of Maelienydd. About the same time Trahaearn Fychan (a man of great power in the country of Brecknock), as he came to Llangors to speak with William Braose, lord thereof, was suddenly taken and (by the lord's commandment) tied to a horse's tail, and drawn through the town of Aberhodni or Brecknock to the gallows, and there beheaded, and his body hanged up by the feet three days. This cruelty, showed upon no just cause, made his brother, his wife, and his children to flee the land. The year ensuing Maelgwn the son of Prince Rhys, after he had imprisoned his elder brother, got his castles of Aberteifi and Ystradmeurig. Also, the youngest son of Prince Rhys won the castle of Dinefwr from the Normans.

The summer following[425] Gwenwynwyn, intending to extend the limits of Wales to their old metres,° gathered a great army, and laid siege first to the Castle of Pain in Elfael, which was of the possessions of William de Braose, making a proclamation that as soon as he had won the castle, he would burn all the whole country to Severn without mercy, in revenge of the murder of Trahaearn Fychan his cousin. But because he lacked engines and miners, he lay three weeks at that castle, and the murderers sent for succours to England; whereupon Geoffrey FitzPeter, Lord Chief Justice of England, gathered a great power, and joining with him all the Lords Marchers came to raise the siege.[426] And because the fortune of the battle is variable and uncertain, he sent first to Gwenwynwyn

---

[425] **Marg.** '1198'
[426] **Marg.** 'Holinshed, p. 537, Matthew Paris, p. 259'.

to have a treaty of peace concluded. But he and such as were with him would in no wise condescend to peace, whose answer was that they would at that journey revenge their old wrongs. Whereupon the English lords did first enlarge° Gruffudd the son of Prince Rhys of South Wales, whom they knew to be an enemy to Gwenwynwyn, which Gruffudd gathered a great power and joined with the English lords. And so they came towards the castle, against whom Gwenwynwyn came very stoutly, and there began a cruel battle with much slaughter on either part. But at the last the Englishmen got the victory, and Gwenwynwyn lost a great number of his men, among whom were Anarawd son to Eneon, Owen ap Cadwallon, Richard ap Iestyn, and Robert ap Hywel; also Maredudd ap Cynan was then taken prisoner with many mo. Matthew Paris sayeth that this battle was fought before Maud's Castle,[427] and that of the Welshmen there were slain 3700, and after this victory the English lords returned home with much honour.[428] And forthwith Gruffudd son to Prince Rhys recovered by force and good will of the people all his land, saving two castles Aberteifi and Ystradmeurig, which his brother Maelgwn by the aid of Gwenwynwyn had wrongfully taken from him. Then his brother Maelgwn (fearing his displeasure) took a solemn oath before noble and religious men, which were about to make peace betwixt them, that if his brother Gruffudd would give him pledges for the assurance of his own person, he would deliver him by a day the castle of Aberteifi. Whereupon Gruffudd did so. But as soon as Maelgwn got the pledges, he fortified the castle and manned it to his own use, and sent the pledges to Gwenwynwyn (who hated Gruffudd to the death), there to be kept in prison. But shortly after, by God's help, they brake the prison and escaped home.

    In the year 1199, Maelgwn son to Prince Rhys laid siege to the castle of Dineirth and, getting it, slew all the garrison which his brother Gruffudd had left to defend it. But at the same time Gruffudd won the castle of Cilgerran and fortified it.[429] This year, as King Richard did view the castle of Chalus in the country of Limousin,[430] he was stricken with a quarrel° and sore wounded,

---

[427] Maud's Castle] In 1198, Painscastle was successfully defended against Gwenwynwyn by Maud de Braose, wife of William de Braose; the castle was sometimes known locally as 'Matilda's Castle'.
[428] **Marg.** 'Humphrey Llwyd; Matthew Paris, p. 259.'
[429] **Marg.** 'Matthew Paris, p. 261; Matthew of Westminster, p. 75.'
[430] Limousin] conjectural; the text reads 'Lenuoyle'.

whereof he died the ninth of April, and left by his testament John his brother inheritor of all his lands, having no respect to his brother Geoffrey's son, Arthur, Duke of Britain,[431] who being the son of the elder brother was his right heir.[432] Then this John, surnamed Without-Land, was crowned King of England with great triumph. Wherefore the French king forthwith made war against him, to whom Arthur, Duke of Britain cleaved, thinking thereby to obtain the crown of England. Also the King of Scots by means of Hugh Bigod came to York, and openly swore fidelity to the King of England.

The year after, Gruffudd son to Cynan ap Owain Gwynedd, a nobleman, died and was buried in a monk's cowl at the Abbey of Conwy.[433] And so were all the nobles (for the most part) of that time buried, for they were made to believe by the monks and friars that that strange weed was a sure defence betwixt their souls and hell, howsoever they died. And all this baggage and superstition received they with monks and friars a few years before that out of England. For the first abbey or friar house that we read of in Wales, sith the destruction of the noble house of Bangor,[434] which savoured not of Romish dregs, was the Ty Gwyn,[435] built the year 1146, and after they swarmed like bees through all the country. For then the clergy had forgotten the lesson that they had received of the noble clerk Ambrosius Telesinus, who writing in the year 540, when the right Christian faith (which Joseph of Arimathea taught at the Isle of Avalon) reigned in this land, before the proud and bloodthirsty monk Augustine infected it with his Romish doctrine, in a certain ode hath these verses:[436]

---

[431] Britain] Brittany

[432] **Marg.** 'Matthew of Westminster, p. 92.'

[433] **Marg.** 'Humphrey Llwyd.'

[434] the destruction of the noble house of Bangor] The slaughter of the monks of Bangor at the instigation of Augustine of Canterbury is discussed in the *Breviary*, above, pp. 74, 118-19.

[435] *Ty Gwyn*] The White House, i.e. Whitland Abbey.

[436] **Marg.** 'Taliesin. In those days the Britons refused the doctrine of Augustine as erroneous and corrupt.' The second edition of Holinshed's *Chronicles* (1587) reprints these verses and adapts the passage with reference to the burial in a cowl of King John. Holinshed also heightens the anti-Romanism of the passage significantly, so that 'after they swarmed like bees' becomes 'Afterwards these vermin swarmed like bees, or rather crawled like lice over all the land, and drew in with them their lousy religion, tempered with I wot not how many millions of abominations' (1587, Vol. 6, p. 195).

>
> Gwae'r offeiriad byd
> Nys angreifftia gwyd
> Ac ny phregetha.
> Gwae ny cheidw ey gail
> Ac ef yn vigail,
> Ac nys areilia.
> Gwae ny theidw ey defaid
> Rhae bleidhie, Rhufeniaid
> 600   A'i ffon gnwppa.

Which may thus be Englished almost word for word:

> Woe be to that priest yborne,
> That will not cleanly weed his corn
> And preach his charge among.
> Woe be to that shepherd (I say)
> That will not watch his fold alway,
> As to his office doth belong.
> Woe be to him that doth not keep
> 610   From Romish wolves his sheep
> With staff and weapon strong.[437]

And because no man should doubt of them, I have set them here as they were written by him that made them. Whereby it may be proved that the Britons, the first inhabiters of this realm, did abhor the Romish doctrine taught in that time, which doctrine (I am sure) is little amended now in the church of Rome. And that may be to us a mirror to see our own folly, if we do degenerate from our forefathers the ancient Britons in the sincerity of true religion, as we do in other things.

---

[437] More literally, 'Woe to the worldly priest who neither chastises vice nor preaches; woe to him who neither guards his flock, being a shepherd, nor nurtures them; woe to him who does not keep his sheep from Roman wolves with his knobbed staff.'

V. Llywelyn ap Gruffudd

When all the lords and barons of Wales understood of the death of the Prince,[438] they came together and called for Llywelyn and Owain Goch, the sons of Gruffudd son to Prince Llywelyn, brother to Dafydd, as next inheritors (for they esteemed not Roger Mortimer son to Gwladus sister to Dafydd, and right inheritor by the order of law), and did them homage, who divided the principality betwixt them two. Then the King, hearing of the death of the Prince, sent one Nicholas de Myles as Justice of South Wales to Carmarthen, and with him in commission Maredudd ap Rhys Gryg and Maredudd ap Owain ap Gruffudd, to disinherit Maelgwn Vachan of all his lands. Wherefore the said Maelgwn fled to the princes to North Wales for succour, with Hywel ap Maredudd (whom the Earl of Clare had by force spoiled of all his lands in Glamorgan), against whom the King came with a great army, who, after he had remained a while in the country and could do no good, returned home again. This time died Ralph de Mortimer, who had married Gwladus Ddu, daughter to Prince Llywelyn and sister to Dafydd, whose inheritance descended to Sir Roger Mortimer his son who also should of right have been Prince of Wales.

*[439] The Prince of North Wales was the Superior Prince of all Wales, to whom the other princes of South Wales and Powys did pay a certain tribute yearly, as appeareth by the laws of Hywel Dda,[440] and in divers places of this history; and was the right heir of Cadwaladr, as is evident by all writers, whose line of the heir male from Rhodri Mawr endeth in this Dafydd the son of Llywelyn, the son of Iorwerth, the son of Owain Gwynedd, the son of Gruffudd, the son of Cynan, the son of Iago, the son of Edwal, the son of Meurig, the son of Edwal Voel, the son of Anarawd, the

---

[438] the death of the Prince] Dafydd ap Llywelyn Fawr, Prince of Gwynedd, died 1246 without leaving an heir. He was succeeded by sons of Dafydd's elder half-brother, Gruffudd ap Llywelyn, who had died in an apparent attempt to escape the Tower of London in 1244.

[439] The ensuing discussion of the descent of the title of Prince of Wales through the bloodline of Roger Mortimer, down to the phrase 'the right of the inheritance lieth', is marked as Powel's insertion.

[440] Hywel Dda] (Howell the Good), celebrated Welsh monarch of the tenth century; the laws of Wales were codified in his reign, remaining central to Welsh legal practice until the union with England in the 1530s.

son of Rhodri Mawr, the son of Esyllt, the daughter and sole heir of Cynan Tindaethwy, the son of Roderick Molwynog, the son of Idwal Iwrch, the son of Cadwaladr the last King of the Britons.

Llywelyn ap Iorwerth, Prince of North Wales, father to Dafydd, married two wives, whereof the first was Joan, the daughter of King John, by whom he had issue Dafydd and Gwladus. His second wife was Eva the daughter of Fulke de Breant, by whom he had no issue. Dafydd succeeded his father in the principality of Wales, and died without issue; after whose decease the right of the inheritance descended and fell to his sister of the whole blood Gwladus, the wife of Ralph, Lord Mortimer of Wigmore, who had issue Roger Mortimer, of whom mention is made in this place, Peter John, a friar preacher, and Hugh, Lord of Chelmarsh.

Roger Mortimer, Lord of Wigmore (and by right of inheritance Prince of Wales) married Mawd de Braose, daughter of William de Braose, Lord of Brecknock, by whom he had issue Edmund, Roger, Lord of Chirkland, William, and Geoffrey; and two daughters, Margaret, married to the son of the Earl of Oxford, and Isabel, married to John Fitzalan, Earl of Arundel. This Roger died *anno* 1282, and was buried in the Abbey of Wigmore.

Edmund Mortimer, Lord of Wigmore, married Margaret Fiennes, and had issue Roger, John (slain in a tourney at Worcester), Edmund, Hugh, and Walter; and two daughters, Maud, married to Theobald Lord Verdon, of whom the Earl of Shrewsbury and the Earl of Essex are descended, and Joan who died without issue. He lieth buried in the said abbey at Wigmore.

Roger Mortimer, Lord of Wigmore, married Joan, the daughter and heir of Sir Peter Geneville, and had issue Edmund Mortimer, Lord of Wigmore, Sir Roger Mortimer, and Geoffrey, Lord of Towyth, called in stories *Comes Jubinensis*; and seven daughters, Katherine, married to Thomas Beauchamp, Earl of Warwick, Joan, married to James Lord Audley, Agnes, Countess of Pembroke, Margaret, married to Thomas Lord Berkeley, Maud, married to John Charleton Lord Powys, Blanche, married to Sir Peter Graunson, knight, and Beatrice, married to Edward, son and heir of Thomas Brotherton, Earl Marshal, and after his death to Thomas de Braose. This Roger Mortimer escaped out of the Tower and fled into France, and afterward returned again with Queen Isabel the wife of King Edward II, and Edward the prince her son, by whom (after the putting down of the said King) he was created Earl of March, and was afterward attainted. Edmund Mortimer, Lord of

Wigmore, married Elianor,⁴⁴¹ late widow of William de Bohun, Earl of Northampton, one of the daughters and heirs of Bartholomew Badlesmere, Lord of Leeds in Kent, and by her had issue Roger, and John who died without issue. He died in the castle of Ludlow, and lieth buried in the said Abbey of Wigmore.

Roger Mortimer, Lord of Wigmore, was by King Edward III (*an. regni sui* 29)⁴⁴² restored to the Earldom of March, and all his grandfather's inheritance, honours, and possessions, the said attainder being repealed and made void. He had issue by Philippa his wife (the daughter of William Montague, Earl of Sarum), Edmund, Earl of March, and died at Roveray in Burgundy, the 26th of February *anno* 1359, whose bones were afterward translated to the Abbey of Wigmore.

Edmund Mortimer, Earl of March and Lord of Wigmore, married Philippa, the daughter and sole heir of Lionel, Duke of Clarence, in whose right he was Earl of Ulster. He had issue Roger, and Edmund that was taken by Owain Glyndŵr; and two daughters, Elizabeth married to Sir Henry Percy, knight, son and heir to Henry Percy, Earl of Northumberland;⁴⁴³ and Philippa married first to John Hastings, Earl of Pembroke, and after his death to Richard, Earl of Arundel, and last to John, Lord St John. He died in the city of Cork in Ireland *anno* 1381, and lieth buried in the said Abbey of Wigmore.

Roger Mortimer, Earl of March and Ulster, Lord of Wigmore, Trym, Clare, and Connaught, married Alianore, the eldest daughter and one of the heirs of Thomas Holland, Earl of Kent, by whom he had issue Roger and Edmund, who both died without issue; and two daughters, Anne, married to Richard Plantagenet, Earl of Cambridge, and Eleanor, Countess of Devon, who died without issue. The said Richard and Anne had issue Richard, Duke of York, and Isabel, married to Henry Bourchier, Earl of Essex, of whom the Earl of Essex now living is descended. Richard Plantagenet, Duke of York, married Cecily, the daughter of Ralph Neville, Earl of

---

⁴⁴¹ **Marg.** 'This Elianor had issue by the Earl Bohun, who inherited her part afterward'.

⁴⁴² *an. regni sui* 29] 'in the twenty-ninth year of his reign'.

⁴⁴³ This clutch of historical individuals – Edmund Mortimer, Owain Glyndŵr, Elizabeth Mortimer, Henry Percy, and his father the Earl of Northumberland – all figure prominently in Shakespeare's *Henry IV Part 1*. Shakespeare, however, follows Holinshed in conflating Edmund with his nephew of the same name, and changes Elizabeth's name to Kate.

Westmorland, and had issue Edward IV, King of England, Edmund, Earl of Rutland, George, Duke of Clarence, and Richard, Duke of Gloucester, afterward King of England by the name of Richard III; and three daughters, Margaret, married to Charles, Duke of Burgundy, Elizabeth, married to John de la Pole, Duke of Suffolk, and Anne, married to Henry Holland, Duke of Exeter, and after to Sir Thomas Saint Leger, knight.

Edward IV, King of England, married Elizabeth, the daughter and one of the heirs of Richard Woodville, Earl Rivers, and had issue King Edward V, who died without issue, and Elizabeth, married to King Henry VII, and mother to King Henry VIII of famous memory, father to the Queen's Majesty that now is: who by lineal descent is the right inheritrice of the Principality of Wales.

By these pedigrees it is evident that the title which Owain Glyndŵr pretended to the Principality of Wales was altogether frivolous, for he was not descended of the house of North Wales by his father, but of a younger brother of the house of Powys (whose portion by inheritance is laid down by me in the description of the Lordship of Powys before, which was but a very small thing).[444] There be divers gentlemen even at this date in Wales which are come of the house of North Wales lineally; but I know none which are lawfully descended of Llywelyn ap Iorwerth, called by Matthew Paris 'Leolinus Magnus', but such are come out of the house of Mortimer, in the which house by order of descent the right of the inheritance lieth.[445]

About this time Harold, King of Man, came to the court and did homage to King Henry, and he dubbed him knight.[446] The summer following, Rhys Fychan son to Rhys Mechyl got the castle of Carreg Cennen, which his mother of mere hatred conceived against him had delivered to the Englishmen. The abbots of Conwy and Stratflur made suit to the King for the body of Gruffudd ap Llywelyn, which he granted unto them, and they conveyed it to Conwy, where he was honourably buried. Then also William Ferrers, Earl of Derby, and his wife died, being either of them a

---

[444] The passage cited, not among the excerpts in this edition, states that Glyndŵr's inheritance was limited to the Lordship of Glyndyfrdwy in Powys Fadog.

[445] It is notable that Powel, in demonstrating Elizabeth I's right to the Principality of Wales, lays far greater emphasis on her Mortimer forebears than on the Tudor bloodline, celebrated by Welsh bards and by English poets including Spenser and Drayton.

[446] **Marg.** 'Matthew Paris, p. 938.'

hundred years of age.⁴⁴⁷ Not long after William de Longa Spata, Earl of Salisbury, was slain in the Holy Land, leaving one daughter behind him married to Henry Lacy, Earl of Lincoln. The same time likewise died Gwladus, daughter to Prince Llywelyn, and wife to Sir Ralph Mortimer, in the castle of Windsor. The year next following was so dry that there fell no rain from the eleventh day of March to the Assumption of our Lady. In the year 1254 there arose a great debate between the princes of Wales. For Owain could not be content with half the principality, but got his younger brother Dafydd to him, and they two levied a great power to disinherit Llywelyn, who with his men met with them in the field, and after a long fight gave them an overthrow, where he took them both prisoners and then seized all their lands into his own hands, enjoying alone the whole Principality of Wales.

The year ensuing, all the lords of Wales came to Prince Llywelyn and made their complaints to him with weeping eyes, how cruelly they were handled by Prince Edward and others of the nobles of England, their lands being taken from them by force; and if at any time they did offend they were punished with extremity, but where they were wronged they found no remedy. Therefore they protested before God and him that they would rather die in the field in defence of their right than to be made slaves to strangers, whereupon the Prince, pitying his estate and theirs, determined together with them utterly to refuse the rule of the Englishmen, and rather to die in liberty than to live in thraldom, shame, and opprobry. And gathering all his power, first recovered again all the inland country of North Wales, and afterward all Meirionnydd, and such lands as Edward had usurped in Cardigan, which he gave to Maredudd the son of Owain ap Gruffudd, and Builth he gave to Maredudd ap Rhys, chasing away Rhys Fychan out of the same, and so honourably divided all that he won amongst his barons that he kept nothing to himself but the perpetual fame of his liberality. Then also he recovered Gwrtheyrnion from Sir Roger Mortimer. The summer following Prince Llywelyn made war against Gruffudd ap Gwenwynwyn (who served the King) and won all Powys from him save the castle of Pool, and a little of Caereinion and the land by Severn side.

---

⁴⁴⁷ William Ferrers [...] a hundred years of age] William de Ferrers, 5th Earl of Derby (1193-1254) died in his early sixties. His wife survived him, dying in 1280, but is unlikely to have been a centenarian.

Rhys Fychan ap Rhys Mechyll, meaning to recover his lands again, obtained of the King a great army, whereof one Stephen Bacon was captain, and came to Carmarthen by sea, and marching from thence towards Dinefwr laid siege to the castle. But the Prince's power came with his cousins to raise the siege, where there was fought a bloody battle as ever was fought in Wales of so many men, and in the end the Englishmen were put to flight, and lost of their men above 2000 soldiers. From thence the Prince's army went to Dyfed and burned all the country, and destroyed the castles of Abercorran, Llanstephan, Maenclochog, and Arberth, and then returned home with much spoil.[448] And forthwith, not being able to abide the wrongs that Geoffrey Langley, Lieutenant to the Earl of Chester, did to them, the Prince entered the Earl's lands and destroyed all to the gates of Chester on either side the water.[449] Whereupon Edward the Earl fled to his uncle (who was then chosen King of Romans) for succour, and returning back with an army, durst not fight with the Prince, who had 10,000 armed men, every one sworn to die in the field if need required in the defence of their country. Yet Gruffudd ap Madoc Maelor, commonly surnamed Lord of Dinas Bran (which is a castle standing upon a very high mountain, of situation impregnable in the Lordship of Chirk), forsook the Prince and served the Earl with all his power – which Earl was counted a cruel and unjust man, having no regard to right, promise, or oath.

The next year Prince Llywelyn, seizing to his hands Cemeis, and making peace betwixt Rhys Gryg and Rhys Fychan his brother's son, got the castle of Trefdraeth or Newport, with all Roose saving Haverford. Then, destroying the country in his way towards Glamorgan, he razed the castle of Llangynwyd, and returning to North Wales met with Edward, Earl of Chester, by the way, whom he caused to retire back, and then destroyed the lands of the said Gruffudd, Lord of Bromfield. Therefore the Kings of England and Almain° wrote to him gently to depart home, which he refused to do, but dividing his army into two battles, in every of the which (as Matthew Paris sayeth) there were 1500 footmen, and 500 horsemen well appointed. Whereupon Edward sent to the Irishmen

---

[448] **Marg.** '1256'
[449] **Marg.** 'Matthew Paris, p. 1251; Thomas Walsingham, *Ypodigma*, p. 61.' Matthew Paris, Matthew of Westminster, and Thomas Walsingham are all cited frequently in the margins of this and the following six paragraphs.

to come to his succours, whereof the Prince being certified made ready his ships and, sending them to the sea with sufficient power to resist the coming of his enemies that way, prevented him; so that the Irishmen were overcome and sent home with great loss. Wherefore the King with his son (being in a great rage) gathered all the strength of England from St Michael's Mount to Tweed, and came to North Wales as far as Deganwy, but the Prince caused all the victuals to be removed over the river of Conwy, and kept all the straits and passages so narrowly that the King was compelled to retire to England with great loss.

Then Prince Llywelyn, calling to him all the power of South Wales, came to the Marches, where Gruffudd, Lord of Bromfield, yielded himself to him (because the King could not defend his lands), and seizing to his own hands all the lands in Powys, he banished the Lord Gruffudd ap Gwenwynwyn, and won the castles of Gilbert de Clare, Earl of Gloucester, where also he gave the Englishmen an overthrow, and slew a great number of the worthiest soldiers and such as the King loved well. Therefore the King called his strength to him and sent to Gascony and Ireland for succours, and then coming to Wales in harvest time destroyed all the corn that was in his way. Yet he went not far beyond Chester, but returned back without doing any notable act, for God (as Matthew Paris sayeth) defended the poor people that put their whole confidence in him. The Lord James Audley (whose daughter Gruffudd, Lord of Bromfield, had married) brought a great number of horsemen from Almain to serve against the Welshmen, who with their great horses and unaccustomed kind of fight overthrew the Welshmen at the first encounter. Wherefore the Welshmen shortly after, minding to revenge that displeasure, made road into the said Lord Audley's lands, where the Almains set upon them, pursuing hard such as fled to the straits, who (using that flight for a policy) returned again so suddenly and so fiercely upon the Almains that they, being not able to retire, upon the sudden were almost all slain. At this time there was great scarcity in England of beeves and horses, whereof they were wont to have many thousands yearly out of Wales, and all the Marches were made as a desolate and desert place.

The next spring all the nobles of Wales came together and swore to defend their country to the death and never to forsake one another, and that upon pain of cursing. But shortly after Maredudd ap Rhys of South Wales, not regarding his oath, served the King.

Then the King called a Parliament for a subsidy to conquer Wales,[450] when he had so many losses, and of late all the country of Pembroke burnt and spoiled, where the Welshmen had found salt plentifully which they lacked. In the which Parliament William de Valence accused the Earls of Leicester and Gloucester as the workers of all this mischief, whereupon the Parliament broke without the grant of any subsidy.

Again, shortly after, the same Parliament by prorogation was held at Oxford, where the King and Edward his son were sworn solemnly to obey the laws and statutes of the realm, but the King's brethren Guy and William, with Henry, son to the King of Almain, and John, Earl Warren, forsook the oath and departed away. And there the lords of Wales offered to be tried by the law for any offence they had committed against the King unjustly; but Edward would not hear of it, but sent one Patrick de Canton as Lieutenant for the King to Carmarthen,[451] and with him Maredudd ap Rhys, and this Patrick desired to speak (upon peace) with the Prince's council. Whereupon the Prince, meaning good faith, sent his brother Dafydd (whom he had set at liberty) with Maredudd ap Owain and Rhys ap Rhys to Emlyn to entreat with them of peace. But Patrick, meaning to entrap them, laid an ambushment of armed men by the way, and as they should have met these men fell upon the Welshmen and slew a great number of them; but the lords which escaped raised the country forthwith, and followed Patrick and slew him and the most part of all his men. And after this the Prince, desirous of peace and quietness, to redeem the same and to end all troubles, and to purchase the King's good will, offered the King 4000 marks, and to his son 300, and to the Queen 200 to have peace. But the King answered, 'What is this to our losses?', and refused it.

*[452] It appeareth by the records in the Tower that about this time (to wit, *anno 43* Henry III) there was a commission to William, Bishop of Worcester, John Mansel, Treasurer of York, the King's Chaplain, and Peter de Montfort, to conclude a peace with the Welshmen. But it is like that there was nothing done to any effect in that behalf, for the war continued still. Notwithstanding, I find

---

[450] **Marg.** '1258'
[451] **Marg.** 'Matthew Paris, p. 1301. To this Patrick the Lordship of Cydweli was given, if he could win the same and keep it. Matthew Paris, p. 1307.'
[452] This paragraph is marked as Powel's insertion.

by Matthew Westminster that there was a certain truce agreed upon between the King and the Welshmen for a year. I read also in the same author, that the Bishop of Bangor was this year about Michaelmas sent from Llywelyn the Prince, and all the barons of Wales, to the King to desire peace at his hands, and to offer unto him the sum of 16,000 pound for the same, so that he would grant the Welshmen to have all their matters heard and determined at Chester, as they were wont to have, and to suffer them to enjoy the laws and customs of their own country; but what answer the bishop brought again, the said author maketh no mention.

The year 1260, Prince Llywelyn destroyed the lands of Sir Roger Mortimer, because he contrary to his oath maintained the King's quarrel, and took from him all Builth saving the castle, which the Prince's men got by night without bloodshed, and therein much munition. And so after the Prince had passed through all South Wales, he returned to his house at Aber, betwixt Conwy and Bangor. The year following died Owain ap Maredudd, Lord of Cedewain. And this summer certain of the Prince's men took upon a sudden the castle of Sir Roger Mortimer in Maelienydd, and slew the garrison, taking Hywel ap Meurig the captain thereof with his wife and children, and the Prince's lieutenant came and destroyed it. Then Sir Roger Mortimer, hearing this, came with a great strength of lords and knights to Maelienydd, where the Prince came also, and Sir Roger kept himself within the walls of the broken castle, and sent to the Prince for licence to depart without hurt. Then the Prince, having his enemy within his danger, took compassion upon him because he was his cousin, and suffered him to depart with his people without hurt. From thence the Prince went to Brecknock at the request of the people of that country, which swore fidelity unto him, and so returned to North Wales.

Prince Llywelyn, being confederate with the barons against the King, destroyed the Earldom of Chester and razed two of Edward's castles, Deganwy and Dyserth, and thither came Edward and did nothing to speak of. This year John Strange the Younger, being Constable of Montgomery, came with a great number of Marchers by night through Ceri to Cedewain; which thing when the countrymen understood, they gathered themselves together, and slew 200 of his men, but he escaped with the rest back again. Shortly after, the Marchers and the Welshmen met besides Clun, where the Englishmen had the victory and slew a great number of Welshmen. At this time Dafydd the Prince's brother (whom he had set at liberty) forsook him and succoured his foes with all his power. Then Gruffudd ap Gwenwynwyn got the castle of Mold and razed it. At this time died Maredudd ap Owain the defender of South Wales. The year ensuing King Henry lead a great army towards Wales,[453] and by means of Ottobuono, the Pope's legate, there was a peace concluded betwixt the King and the Prince at the castle of Montgomery upon Calixtus's day, for which peace the Prince gave the King 30,000 marks, and the King granted the Prince a charter to receive from thenceforth homage and fealty of all the nobility and barons of Wales saving one; so that all the foresaid barons should ever after hold of the Prince as their liege lord, and he to be called and written from thenceforth Prince of Wales. And in witness of this, the King put his seal and hand to the said charter, which was likewise confirmed by the authority of the Pope. The year after this died Goronwy ap Ednyfed Fychan, a noble man and chief of the Prince's council. In the year 1270 died Gruffudd, Lord of Bromfield, and was buried at Valle Crucis.

Here endeth the British copy. That which followeth unto the death of this Prince was collected by Humphrey Llwyd, gentleman.

At this place leaveth the British book, and writeth no further of the end of this Prince, but leaveth him at the highest and most honourable stay that any Prince of Wales was in of many years before – the writer (peradventure) being abashed or rather ashamed to declare the utter fall and ruin of his countrymen, whereunto their own pride and discord did bring them, as it doth evidently appear to him that searcheth out their histories. But I, intending to finish the history during the government of the Britons, have sought out in other chronicles written in the Latin tongue, especially in the chronicle of Nicholas Trivet (who wrote from the beginning of the reign of King Stephen to the coronation of Edward II) and such other, as much as I could find touching this matter.

The year 1270, John Earl Warren slew Alan Le Zouche, Lord Chief Justice, in Westminster Hall. The year following Edward with his brother Edmund went to the Holy Land, where at Acre he was in danger to be slain by a villain (under the colour of delivering of a letter) who gave him five wounds with a knife. And the year 1272 died Henry, King of England; and Edward his son,

---

[453] **Marg.** '1268'

coming from the Holy Land two years after, was crowned at Westminster King of England, to which coronation the Prince of Wales refused to come,[454] although he was sent for, laying for his excuse that he had offended many noblemen of England, and therefore would not come in their danger without he had for pledges the King's brother, with the Earl of Gloucester, and Robert Burnell, Chief Justice of England, wherewith the King was sore offended, but he dissembled his displeasure for that time.

King Edward could never brook Prince Llywelyn, sithence the time that he was driven to slight by him, at their meeting in the Marches, whereof mention is made before. On the other side, Llywelyn liked no better of the King than the King did of him. Again those noblemen which for their disobedience were disinherited by Llywelyn were received and entertained of King Edward, which things caused the Prince to fear some evil practice by those and other such as hated him, if he should have been at the King's coronation to do his homage and fealty, according to the writ directed unto him in that behalf – as appeareth by an instrument sent by the said Prince to Robert Kilwarby, Archbishop of Canterbury, the Archbishop of York, and other bishops sitting then at their convocation in the New Temple at London, *anno* 1275, wherein the causes of this war are contained. Which instrument itself (as it was then sent) is extant at this day, written in parchment with the Prince's great seal thereunto appendent, which I have seen and copied out of the original verbatim, being then in the custody of Thomas Yale, Doctor of Law,[455] of late Dean of the Arches (a great searcher and preserver of the antiquities of Wales).[456]

When the Archbishop could not conclude a peace, he denounced the Prince and his complices accursed.[457] Then the King sent his army by sea to the Isle of Môn or Anglesey, which they won,[458] and slew such as resisted them, for the chiefest men served the King, as their oath was. So they came over against Bangor, where the arm of the sea called Menai (which divideth the isle from

---

[454] **Marg.** 'Thomas Walsingham'

[455] Thomas Yale] The same Thomas Yale (d. 1577) who had advised Thomas Twine on Welsh spelling; see p. 31.

[456] Several pages of documents relating to the failed negotiations of 1275-76 are here omitted.

[457] **Marg.** 'Nicholas Trivet.'

[458] **Marg.** 'Holinshed, p. 791.'

the mainland) is narrowest, and the place called Moel y Don, and there made a bridge of boats and planks over the water, where before Julius Agricola did the like when he subdued the isle to the Romans,[459] and not betwixt Man and Britain, as Polydore Virgil ignorantly affirmeth. This bridge accomplished so that threescore men might well pass over in a front, William Latimer with a great number of the best soldiers, and Lucas Thany, Steward of Gascony, with his Gascons and Spaniards (whereof a great number were to come to serve the King) passed over the bridge, and there saw no stir of enemies. But as soon as the sea began to flow, down came the Welshmen from the hills and set upon them fiercely, and either slew or chased them to the sea to drown themselves – for the water was so high that they could not attain the bridge, saving William Latimer alone, whose horse carried him to the bridge, and so he escaped.

*[460] There were slain and drowned at this time many worthy soldiers: and amongst other this famous knight Sir Lucas de Tany (here named), Robert Clifford, Sir William Lindsey, and two gentlemen of good account that were brethren to Robert Burnell, then Bishop of Bath. There perished in all thirteen knights, seventeen young gentlemen, and to the number of 200 footmen, which happened upon St Leonard's day. Thomas Walsingham writeth that the King lost in this voyage, a little before this, fourteen ensigns, at which time the Lord William de Audley, and the Lord Roger Clifford the younger, and many other were slain, and the King himself was driven to take the Castle of Hope[461] for his safeguard.

In the meantime was the Earl of Gloucester and Sir Edmund Mortimer with an army in South Wales, where were many that served the King, and there fought with the Prince's friends at Llandeilo Fawr, and gave them an overthrow, wherein on the King's side young William de Valence (his cousin-german) and

---

[459] **Marg.** 'Cornelius Tacitus in *Vita Agricolae*'; compare the account in the *Breviary*, p. 106.

[460] This paragraph is marked as Powel's insertion. The margin cites Holinshed, Walsingham, and the *Dunstable Chronicle* as sources for the names and numbers of the dead.

[461] Castle of Hope] not figurative. Caergwrle Castle in Flintshire, also known as 'Queen's Hope' was constructed by Llywelyn in 1277 and subsequently captured by Edward I, who granted it to his wife, Eleanor of Castile. The castle was destroyed in 1283.

four knights more were slain. And all this while the Prince destroyed the country of Cardigan and all the lands of Rees ap Maredudd, who served the King in all these wars. But afterward the Prince separated himself from his army with a few, and came to Builth, thinking to remain there quietly for a while, and by chance as he came by the water Wye there were Edmund Mortimer and John Gifford with a great number of soldiers, and either party were abashed of other.[462] Edmund Mortimer's men were of that country, for his father was lord thereof. Then the Prince departed from his men, and went to the valley with his esquire alone, to talk with certain lords of the country who had promised to meet him there.

Then some of his men, seeing their enemies come down from the hill, kept the bridge called Pont Orewin and defended the passage manfully, till one declared to the Englishmen where a ford was a little beneath, through the which they sent a number of their men with Helias Walwyn, who suddenly fell upon them that defended the bridge in their backs, and put them to flight. The Prince's esquire told the Prince (as he stood secretly abiding the coming of such as promised to meet him in a little grove) that he heard a great noise and cry at the bridge; and the Prince asked whether his men had taken the bridge, and he said, 'Yes'. 'Then', said the Prince, 'I pass not if all the power of England were upon the other side.' But suddenly behold the horsemen about the grove, and as he would have escaped to his men they pursued him so hard that one Adam Francton ran him thorough with a staff, being unarmed,[463] and knew him not, and his men being but a few stood and fought boldly, ever looking for their Prince, till the Englishmen by force of archers mixed with the horsemen won the hill and put them to flight. And as they returned, Francton went to spoil him whom he had slain, and when he saw his face he knew him very well, and struck off his head and sent it to the King at the Abbey of Conwy, who received it with great joy and caused it to be set upon one of the highest turrets of the Tower of London.

This was the end of Llywelyn, betrayed by the men of Builth, who was the last Prince of Britons' blood who bare dominion and rule in Wales. So that the rule and government of the Britons ever continued in some place of Britain, from the first coming of Brutus,

---

[462] **Marg.** 'Matthew of Westminster, p. 370; Nicholas Trivet; Thomas Walsingham, p. 10.'
[463] **Marg.** 'Prince Llywelyn slain.'

which was in the year before Christ's incarnation 1136, to the year after Christ 1282, by the space of 2418 years.

Shortly after that the King had brought all the country to his subjection, the countrymen themselves brought to him Dafydd, the Prince's brother, whom he kept in Rhuddlan Castle, and after put him to death at Shrewsbury.[464] Then the King builded two strongholds in North Wales, the one at Conwy, and the other at Caernarfon. When Rhys Fychan heard how all things went, he yielded himself to the Earl of Hereford, who at the King's commandment sent him to the Tower of London to be imprisoned there. And so the King passed through all Wales, and brought all the country in subjection to the crown of England to this day.

Thus endeth the History of the British Princes.

---

[464] **Marg.** 'Thomas Walsingham, p. 12.'

Glossary

actions	lawsuits
Alban / Albania	Welsh name for Scotland
Almain	German, Germany
animadversion	observation or consideration
antique	ancient
Armorica	Brittany
cantref	district containing one hundred settlements (*trefi*)
Cathanesia	Caithness
champion	level and open country
convent	assemblage of people
craking	bragging
Demetia	Dyfed, south-west Wales
depainted	depicted
despite	spite
Devanus	River Dee
divers	multiple, various
East Englishmen	inhabitants of East Anglia
eftsoons	soon afterward
eke	also
enlarge	set free
enstranged	made strange
erst	previously
experiment	experience
furniture	gifts, provision
hansel	good omen, augury
happily	by chance
improve	disprove
indite	compose, put into words
leese	lose
Lloegr / Lloegria	Welsh name for England
mainfully	forcefully, with all one's might
March	kingdom of Mercia
Menevia	St David's, Pembrokeshire
metres	measures, bounds
milk meats	dairy products
mo	more
natural	native

ne	nor
Orcades	Orkneys
Pool	Welshpool
propriety	correctness of diction
quarrel	crossbow bolt
radical	relating to the root of a word
recounted	considered
Redshanks	Picts
rite	custom
rout	group, category
severally	separately
sith	since
sithence	since
Solvathianus	Solway
sometime	once
stamp	form
stirp	stock, lineage
strange	foreign
Suevia	Sweden
Sueones	Swedes
supputation	computation
Wenta	Gwent, south-east Wales.

Authors whose Names and Works are Cited in this Book.[465]

Ammianus Marcellinus, Roman historian of the fourth century AD. His surviving work covers the years 353-378.

Annius of Viterbo, Dominican historian and fabricator, whose *Antiquities* (1498) include the works of pseudo-Berosus.

Antoninus. Authorship of the *Antonine Itinerary*, a survey of roads and stations throughout the Roman Empire, was traditionally ascribed to the Emperor Antoninus (reigned 138-61).

Appianus of Alexandria, Greek historian of the second century AD, author of the *Roman History*.

Aristotle (384-322 BC), Greek philosopher to whom the work *De mundo*, cited by Llwyd, was once attributed.

*Asser Menevensis (d. 908/9), Welsh cleric, biographer of King Alfred.

Athenaeus of Naucratis, Greek scholar of the late second century AD; his *Deipnosophistae* (Philosophers of the Banquet) includes extensive quotation from the works of Posidonius, an early authority on the Celts.

Aurelius Victor, Roman historian of the fourth century AD.

*Bale, John (1495-1563), Protestant historian and controversialist; Bale was a vehement critic of Polydore Vergil and a defender of the British History, including that recorded by pseudo-Berosus.

Beatus Rhenanus (1485-1547), classical scholar.

Bede, St (d. 735), Northumbrian historian, author of the *Historia ecclesiastica gentis Anglorum*. His sympathetic account of Augustine's mission to the English was sharply contested by Welsh scholars such as Llwyd.

Boethius, or Boece, Hector (1465-1536), Scottish historian, author of the *Historia Gentis Scotorum* (1527).

---

[465] This list is based on that compiled by T. (There is no equivalent list in L.) Additions to this list, marked with an asterisk, include those authors specified as sources for *The History of Cambria* on pp. 150-51.

Berosus. Chaldean priest of the third century BC. His writings are lost, but fragments attributed to him, covering world history from the Flood to the founding of Troy, and including details on the earliest rulers of Britain, were published by Annius of Viterbo in 1498. The author of these texts is now referred to as 'pseudo-Berosus'.

Caesar, Julius (100-44 BC), Roman general and dictator, whose *Commentarii de Bello Gallico* describes his invasion of Britain.

*Caius, John (1510-1573), English scholar, author of *Historia Cantabrigiensis Academiae*.

Capgrave, John (1393-1464), English chronicler and hagiographer.

Castoreus, John, also known as John Bever or John of London, early-fourteenth-century historian, credited with an abbreviation of Geoffrey of Monmouth.

Claudianus, Roman poet of the late fourth and early fifth centuries, author of panegyrics on the Emperor Honorius and his general Stilicho.

Coenalis, Robertus, or Robert Céneau (1483-1560), bishop and historian, author of *Historia Gallica* (1557).

Crantzius, or Krantz, Albert (d. 1517), German historian.

Diodorus Siculus, Greek historian of the first century BC, author of *Bibliotheca historica*, a universal history.

Dion. Cassius Dio, Roman historian (writing in Greek) of the early third century AD.

Elyot, Sir Thomas (d. 1546), author of *The Book Named the Governor* and *Bibliotheca Eliotae*, a Latin dictionary.

Eutropius, Flavius, Roman historian of the fourth century AD, author of *Breviarium historiae Romanae*.

*Eversden, John, monk active in the early fourteenth century, to whom parts of the *Bury Chronicle* were once attributed.

*Florentius Vigorniensis, or Florence of Worcester, twelfth-century historian, author of parts of the universal chronicle *Chronicon ex chronicis*.

Froissart, Jean, fourteenth-century French chronicler.

*Galfrid. See Geoffrey of Monmouth

*Geoffrey of Monmouth, twelfth-century historian, author of *Historia regum Britanniae* (*c.* 1136), the chief source for the legendary history of ancient Britain defended by Humphrey Llwyd among others.

Giambularius, ot Giambullari, Pier Francesco (1495-1550), Florentine writer, author of *Historia dell'Europa* (1566)

Gothus. Olaus Magnus, Swedish historian, author of *Historia de gentibus septentrionalibus* (1555).

Gildas, British priest and historian of the sixth century AD; his controversial remarks on the cowardice and treachery of the Britons were highlighted by Polydore Virgil.

Giraldus Cambrensis, or Gerald of Wales (d. *c.* 1223), Cambro-Norman cleric and scholar, author of two works of central importance on medieval Wales, *Itinerarium Cambriae* [The Journey through Wales] and *Descriptio Cambriae* [The Description of Wales].

Haymo Armenius. Probably Haymo of Halberstadt (d. 853), author of an *Epitome* of Eusebius's *Ecclesiastical History.*

Henry of Huntingdon, twelfth-century English chronicler, author of *Historia Anglorum*.

Juvenal, Roman poet of the late first and early second centuries AD, author of the *Satires*.

*Lambarde, William (1536-1601), legal historian and antiquary; known for his *Perambulation of Kent* (1570), he also composed (but did not complete or publish) an *Alphabetical Description of the Chief Places in England and Wales* (1730).

Lampridius, Aelius, possibly fictitious Roman biographer, contributor to the *Augustan History*.

Lazius, or Laz, Wolfgang (1514-1565), Austrian historian and cartographer.

Leland, John (d. 1552), English topographer and antiquary. His manuscript *Itineraries* were an indispensible source for all the major Elizabethan writers on British geography.

Lucanus, Marcus Annaeus (39-65 AD), Roman poet, author of the *Pharsalia*, on the civil wars between Caesar and Pompey.

Maior, a spurious Greek authority conjured into existence by Twyne's mistranslation of the phrase 'maioris nominis' (of greater name).

Mamertinus, Claudius, fourth-century Roman panegyrist, sometimes also credited with authorship of panegyrics written a century before his time.

Malmsburiensis. See William of Malmesbury.

*Matthew of Westminster, supposed author of the *Flores Historiarum*, in fact identical with Matthew Paris.

Marcellinus. See Ammianus Marcellinus.

Marianus Scotus, eleventh-century Irish chronicler, author of a *Chronicon*.

Marius Niger, Dominicus, or Domenico Mario Negri, late-fifteenth-century Venetian geographer, author of *Geographiae Commentariorum Libri XI*.

Matthew Paris, twelfth-century chronicler and illustrator, author of the *Chronica Majora* and *Historia Anglorum*; a manuscript in his hand was in the possession of the Earl of Arundel, and may well have been consulted by Llwyd.

Mela, Pomponius, Roman geographer of the first century AD, author of *De situ orbis*.

Meyerus, Jacobus (1492-1552), Flemish historian, author of *Annales rerum Flandricarum*.

*Nennius, ninth-century Welsh monk, traditionally the author of the *Historia Brittonum*.

Orosius, Paulus, Christian historian active in the late fourth and early fifth centuries, author of *Historiarum Adversum Paganos Libri VII*.

Panvinius, or Panvinio, Onofrio (1529-1568), Italian antiquary and historian of the papacy.

Parisiensis. See Matthew Paris.

*Parker, Matthew (1504-1575), Archbishop of Canterbury, noted for his scholarship and interest in early English church history.

Paulus Diaconus, or Paul the Deacon, eighth-century historian, author of the *Historia Langobardum*.

Pausanias, Greek geographer and travel-writer of the second century AD.

Plinius. Gaius Plinius Secundus, or Pliny the Elder (23-79 AD), author of the *Naturalis Historia*.

Plutarchus, Greek historian and biographer, active in the late first and early second centuries AD.

Polybius, Greek historian of the second century BC.

Polydorus Vergilius, or Polydore Vergil, Italian historian of England; his *Anglica Historia* outraged adherents of Geoffrey of Monmouth's British History through its pronounced skepticism regarding Brutus, King Arthur, and the valour of the ancient Britons.

Postellus. Guillaume Postel (1510-1581), French linguist and heretic, author of *Linguarum Duodecim Characteribus Differentium Alphabetum Introductio* (1538).

*Prise, John (d. 1555), Welsh reformer and historian, author of the first printed book in Welsh (*Yny Lhyvyr Hwnn*, 1546) and of an important defence of Geoffrey of Monmouth, *Historiae Brytannicae Defensio* (1573).

Ptolemaeus, or Claudius Ptolemy, Greek geographer and astronomer of the first century AD; a chief source of information on the population of Britain in the Roman era.

Ralph of Coggeshall, thirteenth-century chronicler, author of *Chronicon Anglicanum*.

Regino of Prüm (d. 915), abbot and historian, author of the *Chronicon*.

*Roger of Hoveden, twelfth-century chronicler, author of a general history of England, the *Chronica*.

Ruscellus, Hieronymus, or Girolamo Ruscelli, author of *La Geografia di Claudio Tolomeo Alessandrino* (1561).

Sextus Rufus, or Rufius Festus, fourth-century Roman historian; his *Breviarum* was published by Panvinius in 1558.

Sidonius Apollinaris (d. 489), Gallo-Roman panegyrist and letter-writer.

*Simeon of Durham, twelfth-century chronicler, concerned mainly with the north of England.

Spartianus, Aelius, possibly fictitious Roman biographer, contributor to the *Augustan History*.

Solinus, Gaius Julius, Roman writer of the third century AD, author of *Polyhistor*.

Suetonius, Roman historian of the early second century AD, author of the *Twelve Caesars*.

Sigebertus Gemblacensis, or Sigebert of Gembloux, twelfth-century historian, author of *Chronicon sive Chronographia*, a universal chronicle.

Tacitus, Roman historian of the first century AD; his *Agricola* recounts the military campaigns of his father-in-law, Gnaeus Julius Agricola, in Britain.

Trivet, or Trevet, Nicholas, early-fourteenth-century chronicler, author of *Annales sex regum Angliae*.

Virunius. Ponticus Virunius or Ludovico da Ponte (d. 1520), Italian humanist, author of an abridgement of Geoffrey of Monmouth, published by David Powel in 1585.

Volaterranus. Raffaello Maffei or Raphael of Volaterra (1451-1522), Italian humanist, author of an encyclopedia, *Commentariorum rerum urbanarum libri XXXVIII* (1506).

Vopiscus, Flavius, possibly fictitious Roman biographer, contributor to the *Augustan History*.

Walsingham, Thomas, English historian active in the late fourteenth and early fifteenth centuries; his *Historia Angliae brevis* was published by Matthew Parker in 1574.

William of Malmesbury, twelfth-century English chronicler, author of *Gesta regum Anglorum*.

William Parvus, or William of Newburgh, twelfth-century historian, author of *Historia rerum Anglicarum*, an early critic of Geoffrey of Monmouth.

BIBLIOGRAPHY

Armitage, David, *The Ideological Origins of the British Empire* (Cambridge: Cambridge University Press, 2000)

Boece, Hector, *Scotorum Historiae a Prima Gentis Origine* (Paris: Jodocus Badius, 1527)

—, *Chroniklis of Scotland*, trans. by John Bellenden (Edinburgh: Thomas Davidson, 1536)

Boorde, Andrew, *The Breviary of Health* (London: William Middleton, 1547)

Bowen, D. J., 'Gruffudd Hiraethog ac Argyfwng Cerdd Dafod', *Llen Cymru*, 2 (1952-53), 147-60

Brut y Tywysogion, or The Chronicle of the Princes, Peniarth Ms. 20 Version, ed. and trans. by Thomas Jones (Cardiff: University of Wales Press, 1952)

Buchanan, George, *Buchanan's History of Scotland* (London: J. Bettenham, 1733)

Camden, William, *Britannia* (London: George Bishop and John Norton, 1607)

—, *Britain*, trans. by Philemon Holland (London: George Bishop and John Norton, 1610)

Catullus, *The Poems of Catullus*, ed. by Guy Lee (Oxford: Clarendon Press, 1990)

Cawley, Robert, 'Drayton's Use of Welsh History', *Studies in Philology*, 22 (1925), 234-55

Claudian, [*Works*], trans. by Maurice Platnauer (London: William Heinemann, 1922)

Curran, John E., 'The History Never Written: Bards, Druids, and the Problem of Antiquarianism in *Poly-Olbion*', *Renaissance Quarterly*, 51 (1998), 498-526

Davies, Ceri, *Latin Writers of the Renaissance* (Cardiff: University of Wales Press, 1981)

Dee, John, *Monas Hieroglyphica* (Antwerp: William Sylvius, 1564)

—, *General and Rare Memorials Pertayning to the Perfect Arte of Navigation* (London: John Day, 1577)

Drayton, Michael, *Poly-Olbion*, in *The Works of Michael Drayton*, ed. J. W. Hebel, 4 vols (Oxford: Shakespeare Head Press, 1961), IV

Duncan-Jones, Katherine, *Sir Philip Sidney: Courtier Poet* (London: Hamish Hamilton, 1991)

Elyot, Thomas, *Bibliotheca Eliotae* (London: Thomas Berthelet, 1542)

Geoffrey of Monmouth, *History of the Kings of Britain: An Edition and Translation of De Gestis Britonum [Historia Regum Britanniae]*, ed. by Michael D. Reeve, trans. by Neil Wright (Woodbridge: Boydell, 2007)

George Peckham, *A True Reporte of the Late Discoveries [...] of the Newfound Landes* (London: John Charlewood, 1583)

Gerald of Wales, *The Journey through Wales and The Description of Wales*, trans. by Lewis Thorpe (Harmondsworth: Penguin, 1978)

Gottfried, Rudolf B., 'Spenser and *The Historie of Cambria*', *Modern Language Notes*, 72 (1957), 9-13

Gourvitch, I., 'The Welsh Element in *Poly-Olbion*: Drayton's Sources', *Review of English Studies*, 4 (1928), 69-77

Gruffydd, R. Geraint, 'Humphrey Llwyd of Denbigh: Some Documents and a Catalogue', *Transactions of the Denbighshire Historical Society*, 17 (1968), 54-107

—, 'The Renaissance and Welsh Literature', in *The Celts and the Renaissance: Tradition and Innovation*, ed. by Glanmor Williams and Robert Owen Jones (Cardiff: University of Wales Press, 1990), pp. 17-39

Hadfield, Andrew, 'Skeptical History and the Myth of the Historical Revolution', *Renaissance and Reformation / Renaissance et Réforme*, 29 (2005), 25-44

Harper, Carrie A., *Sources of the British Chronicle History in Spenser's Faerie Queene* (Philadelphia: J. C. Winston, 1910)

Henry, Bruce Ward, 'John Dee, Humphrey Llwyd, and the Name "British Empire"', *Huntington Library Quarterly*, 35 (1971-72), 189-90

Higden, Ranulph, *Policronicon*, trans. by John Trevisa (London: Wynkyn de Worde, 1495)

Highley, Christopher, *Shakespeare, Spenser, and the Crisis in Ireland* (Cambridge: Cambridge University Press, 1997)

Holinshed, Raphael, *The Chronicles of England, Scotlande and Irelande* (London: Henry Bynneman, 1577)

—, *The First and Second Volumes of Chronicles* (London: Henry Denham, 1587)

Horace, *Epistles*, ed. by Augustus S. Wilkins (London: Macmillan, 1965).

Jones, G. Penrhyn, 'Humphrey Lhuyd (1527-1568): A Sixteenth Century Welsh Physician', *Proceedings of the Royal Society of Medicine*, 49 (1956), 521–28

Koebner, Richard, '"The Imperial Crown of this Realm': Henry VIII, Constantine the Great, and Polydore Vergil', *Bulletin of the Institute of Historical Research*, 26 (1953), 29-52

Lambarde, William, *Alphabetical Description of the Chief Places in England and Wales* (London: Fletcher Gyles, 1730)

Leland, John, *Assertio inclytissimi Arturii Regis Britanniae* (London: R. Wolfe, 1544)

—, *The Assertion of King Arthure*, trans. by Ralph Robinson (London: John Wolfe, 1582)

Leland, John, and John Bale, *The Laboryouse Journey and Serche of Johan Leylande, for Englandes Antiquitees* (London: S. Mierdman, 1549)

Llwyd, Humphrey, *Cronica Walliae*, ed. by Ieuan M. Williams (Cardiff: University of Wales Press, 2002)

Maley, Willy, and Philip Schwyzer, eds, *Shakespeare and Wales: From the Marches to the Assembly* (Farnham: Ashgate, 2010)

Moore, G. C., *Gabriel Harvey's Marginalia* (Stratford-upon-Avon: Shakespeare Head Press, 1913)

Moore, William H., 'Sources of Drayton's Conception of Poly-Olbion', *Studies in Philology*, 65 (1968), 783-803

North, F. J., *Humphrey Lhuyd's Maps of England and of Wales* (Cardiff: National Museum of Wales, 1937)

Ocland, Christopher, *The Valiant Actes and Victorious Battailes of the English Nation*, trans. by John Sharrock (London: Robert Waldegrave, 1585)

Pears, Steuart A., *The Correspondence of Sir Philip Sidney and Hubert Languet* (London: Pickering, 1845)

Pocock, J. G. A., 'British History: A Plea for a New Subject', *Journal of Modern History*, 47 (1975), 601–24

Polydore Vergil, *Polydore Vergil's English History: From an Early Translation*, ed. by Henry Ellis (London: Camden Society, 1846)

Powel, David, *The Historie of Cambria, Now Called Wales* (London: Henry Denham and Ralph Newbury, 1584)

—, *Pontici Virunnii viri doctissimi Britannicae historiae libri sex* (London: Henry Denham and Ralph Newbury, 1585)

Salesbury, William, *A playne and a familiar introduction, teaching how to pronounce the letters in the Brytishe tongue, now commonly called Welshe* (London: Henry Denham, 1567)

Schwyzer, Philip, 'Purity and Danger on the West Bank of the Severn: The Cultural Geography of *A Masque Presented at Ludlow Castle, 1634*', *Representations*, 60 (1997), 22-48

—, 'A Map of Greater Cambria', in *Literature, Mapping and the Politics of Space in Early Modern Britain*, ed. by Andrew Gordon and Bernhard Klein (Cambridge: Cambridge University Press, 2001), pp. 35-44

—, *Literature, Nationalism and Memory in Early Modern England and Wales* (Cambridge: Cambridge University Press, 2004)

Slatyer, William, *The History of Great Britain [Palae-Albion]* (London: William Stansby, 1621)

Spenser, Edmund, *The Faerie Queene*, ed. by A. C. Hamilton, 2nd edn (London: Longman, 2006)

—, *A View of the State of Ireland*, ed. by Andrew Hadfield and Willy Maley (Oxford: Blackwell, 1997)

Stradling, John, *Divine Poemes* (London: William Stansby, 1625)

Tacitus, *Historiarum Libri*, ed. C. D. Fisher (Oxford: Clarendon Press, 1956)

Twyne, John, *De rebus Albionicis, Britanicis atque Anglicis* (London: Edmund Bollifant, 1590)

Virgil, *Opera*, ed. by R. A. B. Mynors (Oxford: Clarendon Press, 1969)

—, *The Whole XII Bookes of the Aeneidos of Virgill*, trans. by Thomas Phaer and Thomas Twyne (London: William How, 1573)

Williams, Glanmor, *Wales and the Reformation* (Cardiff: University of Wales Press, 1997)

Williams, Gwyn A., *Madoc: The Making of a Myth* (Oxford: Oxford University Press, 1987)

Williams, Penry, *The Council in the Marches of Wales Under Elizabeth I* (Cardiff: University of Wales Press, 1958)

INDEX: *THE BREVIARY OF BRITAIN*

A table containing the principal matters entreated of in this book, largely digested into the alphabetical order, as followeth:

Aaron, martyr, where buried 128
Aestiones 100
Albania, whence so called 98; described 95
Albion, why so termed 54
Anglesey in Wales 112
animosity of Britons 110; their ancient manners 109
Arfon 113
Attacotti, inhabiters of Albania, of Scottish original 93
Augustine the Monk 74; his intolerable arrogance 118

Bardi 56
Bath, how of old time termed 68
Bedfordshiremen 73
Bernard of Newmarch 130
Bernicia 62
Boadicia, or Bunduica, a valiant queen 132, 136
Bodotria 96
Boethius reproved 5, 56, 70-71, 77, 81, 86-92, 96, 97, 127
Boguelth, or Builth 130
Brecknock 106; by what Englishman first subdued 106
Brennus, whose son, and brother 101; why he slew himself 102; what language his soldiers used 102; his court or palace 119; was a perfect Briton 9-11, 101
Brenni, where they dwelt 103
Brigantes, were never in Scotland 78; their cities' names 78
Britain, why so named 57; how divided 59; the etymology thereof 57-58
Britain the less, or the Second 84
Britain the first, second, third, and fourth 84
Britons, how they celebrate Easter 115; their valiancy 130-39
British names corrupted by the Romans 55
Britons nigh France 59-60
Bristol 20, 68
Brustius's cruelty 129; his miserable death 129
Buckinghamshiremen 72

Cadevenna 120
Caesar, what he termeth a City 81
Caerbro castle in the Wight 66
Caer Andred, by whom overthrown 65
Caer Luel 95
Calais 64
Cambra 101
Cambria, why so called 98
Cambridge 72
Camudolanum 70
Camulodunum 70
Cangorum, where it standeth 114
Canterbury, why so called 65; metropolitan of England and Wales 65
Caradoc described 82
Caratacus, where he fought with Ostorius 82
Cardigan 122
Cartimandua's treason 82
castle of Clun 82
castle of Dover 64
castle of Emlyn 126
castle of Lion 118
Catguilia 126
Ceretica described 124, 128
Chepstow 128
Chester 75
Chichester 65
Cirencester 68
City of Legions 128
cities of Brigantes 78
Clun Castle 82
commendation of the baths at Bath 68
Conovia, by whom builded 114
Cornish, and Welshmen one nation 67
Cornwall 67
cruelty of Brustius 129
Cumberland, by whom in old time inhabited 79
Cymbri 99-101

Damnii 79

Danes came in 63
Danica Sylva [Forest of Dean] 121
David, how termed in British 123; translated the archbishopric to Menevia 124
death of Brennus 102
death of Brustius 129
Deheubarth 111, 122; why worse than Gwynedd 112, 122
Deira, in old time called Brigantia 77-78
Demetia 105, 111, 123-25
Denbigh 1-2; described 114-15
description of Albania 95
description of Cambria 98
description of Caradoc city 82
description of Ceretica 122, 126
description of Denbygh 114-15
description of Tegenia, or Igenia 116-17
description of Wales 98
Devani 75; how called of old by the Romans 81
divers kings possessed divers parts of Wales 111-12
division of Britain 59
division of England 62-63
division of Venodotia 112
division of Wales 98
divisions are dangerous 140 n. 364
Dorchester 73
Dorventani, why so called 76
Dover 64
Dover Castle, by whom builded 64
Druids 90
Dunetus, abbot 119
Dunwallo forsaketh his kingdom 116

Earls of Gloucester 106
Edinburgh, by whom builded 96
Edward I, entered Wales 106
Egbert, first monarch of Lloegr 62-63
Elbodius, archbishop of North Wales 115
Elfael 121
Elyot, Sir Thomas, Knight 55
Emlyn Castle 126
England, divided 62-63; by whom first so called 63

Englishmen, whence descended 63
etymology of Britain 57-58
etymology of Gaul 104
Euboniae 97
example of God's judgement 117
Exeter 67

family of Stuarts in Scotland 83
family of Greys in England 115
family of Fitzalans 119
Flavia 84
Flemings, driven out of their own country, what place they possessed 105
Flint town 117
Forest of Dean 121
France bounded 104
Franci, whence supposed to have sprung 101

Gadini 96
Gildas, reproved 140
Gildo 90
Gloucester, by whom builded 68
Golden Number, confuted and rejected 115-16
Grantchester 72
Guildford 65
Gwynedd 31, 106, 111-16; whence the kings thereof so called 112
Gillus, usurper 90

Hamo, with his twelve knights 126-27
Harold, last king of Danish blood 76
Hasting 140
Hebrides 94, 97
Hengistus, sent against the Scots and Redshanks 62
Henry II, vanquished 139
Henry IV [Holy Roman Emperor] 75-76
Henry IV [of England] 107
Henry VII 107
Henry VIII, 108
Henry, Earl of Lincoln, builded a castle 114
heralds, and heraldry, by Welshmen diligently retained 56-57
Hereford, where it lieth 117, 121

herring taking 113
Hibernenses, afterward called Scots 92
Holt 118
Hope 119
how many cities, so many kingdoms in Britain 81
Huntingdonshire 73

Iceni 70, 72, 87; what region they inhabited 72
idiom, or propriety of the British tongue 51-54
Ierne 54
Ilchester 68
Irishmen, called afterward Scots 85-86, 92
Ireland 6-7, 15, 17-18, 20, 29-30, 85-86, 90, 93-95, 97, 128; by whom first endued with Christianity 124
islands about Anglesey 112-13
islands nigh Wales 112-13
Isle of Anglesey 112
Isle of Thanet 64
Isle of Wight 66
Isle of Willows 72

Julius the martyr, where buried 128

Kennethus, King of Scots 86
Kent 62, 64-65
King of England's eldest son Prince of Wales 107
King Arthur 138
King of Powys, why swallowed into the earth 117
Kington 121

Lancashiremen, how termed of old 80
lasciviousness of the Scots 91
latitude of Wales 105
Laudonia 96; of the Redshanks how called 96
Lazius, Wolfgangus, reproved 62, 76
Legion City, site described 128
Leicestershiremen 74
Leominster 121
letters of the Britons, their order, form, and pronunciation 51
Leucopibia, how termed, and where it standeth 79, 95
Lincolnshiremen 74

Lichfield 74
Llandaff, where it standeth 127
Llanidloes 120
London, by whom builded, amplified, the names thereof 69; a colony of the Romans 70
longitude of Wales 105
Ludlow 121

Maeatae 96
Maelor, divided 118
Malmesbury 68
Malvern Hills 121
Manchester 81
Mandubracius, sent for Caesar into Britain 69
March, a kingdom of England 62, 70, 76, 80, 98
Maridunum 125
Marius stone, by whom and why created 79
Marlborough 66
Maxima Caesariensis 84
Maximus the Emperor, a Briton 137
Meridnia 113
Merlin, why so called, and where born 125
Meyerus, Jacobus, reproved 84
Mexicani 52

Neath 127
Newbury 66
Newport 66
Northamptonshiremen, whence so called 74
Northumberland, kingdom, how divided 62
Norwich 72

of communicating, a notable example 119
Orcades Islands, where they lie 97; by whom first found and subdued 71-72
order and signification of the British letters 51
Ostorius, where he fought with Caratacus 82
Oswestry 119
Owain Glyndŵr, rebelled 107
Oxford, described and commended 73
Oxfordshiremen 73

Parisi, to whom borderers 72
Patrick, where born 124
Pelagius, the arch-heretic, whence he came 117
Pembroke 125
Peterborough 72
Picts, by whom destroyed 86; by whom of the Romans first mentioned 92
place where the earth billowed under David's foot, and rose up in a hill 123
place where Ostorius fought with Caratacus 82
Polydorus Virgilius, reproved 4-6, 9, 12-13, 47, 55, 56, 58, 59, 67, 69-72, 81, 102, 127, 130-31, 136, 138, 140
Portchester 66
Portsmouth 66
Powys 75, 106, 112, 117-22; the prince's seat thereof 120
Powys, King, why swallowed into the earth 117
Presteigne 121
Prydain 56-58
Prytannia 55
Ptolomaeus 68, 78-82, 89, 95, 96, 113-14, 123-24, 126, 127; reproved 69, 70-71; excused 77

Quadi, now Bohemians 93, 97

Radnor 121, 130
Reading 66
Redshanks, where and by whom vanquished 79, 86; when they began to enter Scotland 93; how divided 93
rebellion, and treason, always by God punished 126
Rhys [ap Tewdwr Mawr], where slain 122
Rhythercus, where and by whom slain 85
Roderick the Great [Rhodri Mawr], monarch of Wales 111, 138
Rother 64
Ruscellus, Hieronymus, reproved 76
Rye 64
Richard de Clare, where and by whom slain 123

St Asaph 71, 115-16
Salisbury, how called in old time 67
Samson, Bishop of Menevia 124

Saxons called into Britain 60
Scotland 84; the kings thereof whence descended 83
Scots, when accustomed to eat man's flesh 91; what time they established their kingdom in Britain 95; how of old called 85
Scordisci, where they dwelt 103; why so called 103
Selgovii, and Otadeni 79
seventh kingdom of England, how called and divided 77
Severn 98, 119-20
Shaftesbury 67
Shrewsbury 75
Shrewsburymen, next unto whom, and which is their city 75; and from whence derived 75
Sicambri, whence supposed to come 101
signification and order of the Welsh or British letters 51
Siluri, where they lie 78, 82, 87, 127-28, 129
Sleidan, reproved 80
Southampton 66
Spaniards, retain their ancient tongue 104
Speenhamland, nigh Newbury 66 n. 118
Staffordshiremen 74
Stuarts, in Scotland, whence descended 83
Swansea 126

Tamesis 71; whereof that name proceeded 73
Tegenia, or Igenia, described 116-17
Tegid, Lake 113
Teifi, aboundeth with otters 123
Tenby 125
Thame, where it disburdeneth itself into Isis 73
Thule 93, 95
Trahernus, when he reigned in North Wales 83
treason, and rebellion, always by God punished 126
treason in a woman, being a queen 81, 82
trimarchisia 103
Trinobantes, inhabiters of Essex 69-70, 72
Trinovantum city, by whom builded, and how named 69

Valentia 84
Vanduara 79
Venodotia, or North Wales 112
Verulamium, why so called 72

Voadicia, Queen of the Iceni 87; *see* Boadicea

Wales, 1-32, 46, 50, 56, 60, 63, 73, 76, 80, 82, 83-84, 98-130, 138-39
Walden, what it signifieth 65
Wallingford 66
Warwickshiremen, where about they dwell, and their city, by whom founded 74
Watlingchester 72
Wenta, nigh what country, and how termed 127
Welshmen, why so called 104; lost their title of nobility 122
Westmorland 79
Whittington a town 119
Wigmore Castle 121
Winifred's Well 116-17
Worcestershiremen 75
Worcester 75
William Bastard, came in 63
Winchelsea 65
Winchester 66
Wroxeter, by whom destroyed 75

Yale 119
York 78
Ystrad Alyn 119

INDEX: *THE HISTORY OF CAMBRIA*

A table containing the principal matters, places, and persons in this book. The figures note the page:

Aberystwyth Castle, taken 161
Alan, King of Little Britain 153-55
Armorica 156
Augustine, monk, the Apostle of England 164

Britons, are spoiled of their country by the Saxons 155-56; they abhorred the Romish religion 165
Braose, William, traitorous fact 162

Cadwaladr goeth to Britain Armorick 153; admonished by an angel 153-54; goeth to Rome and dieth 155
Carmarthen taken 159
Caernarfon Castle, built 179
Cambria, Cymry, Cymraeg, they offer to be tried by the law 173; punished extremely, but when they complain they have no redress 170
Carreg Cennen Castle 169
Conwy Castle, built 179

Dafydd ap Owen Gwyneth 156; put out of the government of Wales 159 n. 415; taken prisoner by his nephew 162
Dafydd ap Gruffudd 166, 173, 174-75; forsaketh his brother 170; is taken and put to death 179
Deganwy 172

Ednyfed Fychan 161
Edward [I], Earl of Chester, retireth 171; goeth to the Holy Land, 175; crowned King of England 176; he brought all Wales to his subjection 179

Gwenwynwyn, lord of Powys 160; getteth again the castle of Pool 160; layeth siege to the Castle of Pain in Elfael 162; discomfited 163
Goronwy ap Ednyfed Fychan 175
Gruffudd ap Rhys, taken by his brother Maelgwn and sent to prison 161; set at liberty 163

Gruffudd ap Madoc Maelor, Lord of Dinas Bran 171
Gurmundus 156

Henry III, King of England, he and the Earl of Chester come to Wales 172; cometh to Montgomery and maketh peace with the Prince 175; he dieth 175

Iorwerth Drwyndwn 156

Langley, Geoffrey 171
Loegria, Lloegr 153
Llywelyn ap Iorwerth, taketh his uncle Dafydd prisoner 162
Llywelyn ap Gruffudd chosen Prince of Wales 166; divided the principality between him and his brother Owain 166; entered the Earl of Chester's land 170; causeth the Earl to retire 171; destroyeth the Earldom of Chester 174; maketh peace with the King 175; refuseth to come to King Edward's coronation 176; he is slain 178

Madoc ap Owain Gwynedd 156-59
Manaw 155
Merdhin or Merlin 153-55
monks and friars lately received in Wales 164
Mount Paladr 155
Mortimer, Roger, right heir to the Principality of Wales 166, 167

Owain ap Maredudd, Lord of Cedewain 174
Owain ap Gruffudd 166

Pool [Welshpool], taken by the Archbishop of Canterbury 160;
prophecies, causes of much hurt 155

Rhys ap Gruffudd, called the Lord Rhys, he taketh Carmarthen, Clun, Radnor, the Castle of Pain in Elfael 159-60; he dieth 160-61
Richard I, King of England, he dieth 163-64

Saxons, they spoil the Britons of their country 156
Sidney, Henry, Knight of the Order 15-23, 147-48

Taliesin 164-65

www.ingramcontent.com/pod-product-compliance
Lightning Source LLC
Chambersburg PA
CBHW061444300426
44114CB00014B/1836